Fun with the Family™ Vermont and New Hampshire

Praise for the *Fun with the Family*™ series

"Just in time to save the entire family from going stark-raving mad
during a too-quiet summer . . . this guide is chockfull of good stuff
for folks of all ages."
—*The Hartford Courant* (Conn.)

"Enables parents to turn family travel into an exploration."
—Alexandra Kennedy, Editor, *Family Fun*

"Bound to lead you and your kids to fun-filled days,
those times that help compose the
memories of childhood."
—Dorothy Jordon, *Family Travel Times*

Help Us Keep This Guide Up to Date

Every effort has been made by the authors and editors to make this guide as accurate and useful as possible. However, many changes can occur after a guide is published—establishments close, phone numbers change, hiking trails are rerouted, facilities come under new management, etc.

We would love to hear from you concerning your experiences with this guide and how you feel it could be improved and be kept up to date. While we may not be able to respond to all comments and suggestions, we'll take them to heart, and we'll make certain to share them with the authors. Please send your comments and suggestions to the following address:

The Globe Pequot Press
Reader Response/Editorial Department
P.O. Box 480
Guilford, CT 06437

Or you may e-mail us at: editorial@GlobePequot.com

Thanks for your input, and happy travels!

INSIDERS'GUIDE®

FUN WITH THE FAMILY™ SERIES

fun WITH the Family™

VERMONT and NEW HAMPSHIRE

HUNDREDS OF IDEAS FOR DAY TRIPS WITH THE KIDS

LURA ROGERS SEAVEY AND
BARBARA RADCLIFFE ROGERS

SECOND EDITION

INSIDERS'GUIDE®

GUILFORD, CONNECTICUT
AN IMPRINT OF THE GLOBE PEQUOT PRESS

Text design by Nancy Freeborn and Linda Loiewski
Maps by Rusty Nelson © The Globe Pequot Press
Spot photography throughout © Photodisc

ISSN 1547-6804
ISBN 0-7627-2604-0

Manufactured in the United States of America
Second Edition/Second Printing

For Mary, with whom we have both learned
new ways to have fun with our family.

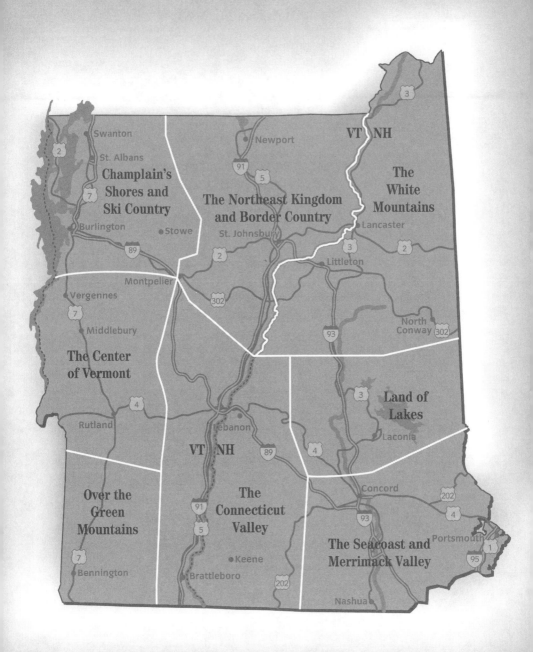

Swanton

Newport

VT NH

St. Albans

Champlain's
Shores and
Ski Country

The Northeast Kingdom
and Border Country

The
White
Mountains

Burlington

Stowe

St. Johnsbury

Lancaster

Montpelier

Littleton

Vergennes

North
Conway

Middlebury

The Center
of Vermont

Land of
Lakes

Rutland

Lebanon

Laconia

VT NH

Over the
Green
Mountains

The
Connecticut
Valley

Concord

Portsmouth

Keene

The Seacoast and
Merrimack Valley

Bennington

Brattleboro

Nashua

VERMONT AND NEW HAMPSHIRE

Contents

Introduction

Vermont and New Hampshire are called the twin states because of their similar shapes. (On a map these states look like upside down mirror images of each other.) In many ways, this nickname is appropriate as they have much in common. Vermont and New Hampshire share not only the blustery climate of the northeast but also a general atmosphere of friendliness and good old New England charm. They also share a lack of big cities; aside from Concord, you won't even find midsize ones once you go north of New Hampshire's two largest cities, Nashua and Manchester.

New Hampshire and Vermont have distinct seasons. This includes the severe winter cold that makes them a mecca for skiers and snow sports enthusiasts. It also includes midsummer temperatures that reach into the 90s. Happily, neither of these extremes ever lasts more than a few days. In the summer, temperatures are usually moderate, with daytime highs in the 70s and 80s. It almost always cools off in the evening, so be sure to bring sweaters or jackets for the whole family. Winter temperatures, however, will require well-insulated jackets or coats, along with waterproof boots for snow and slush. Sunglasses and sunscreen are a good idea in winter as well as summer, since the glare of the sun reflecting on snow can be twice as damaging as direct summer sun.

Nevertheless, as the old saying about New England goes, "If you don't like the weather, wait a minute." It is not unusual to have a day with temperatures in the 70s to be followed by a day in the 50s. When traveling in this region, and of course, depending on the season, you should bring a variety of clothing in order to adapt to sudden changes in the weather.

Barbara's Favorites

As a Child

- Camping at Sugarloaf Campground, Twin Mountain, N.H.
- Skiing at Gunstock, Gilford, N.H.
- The Woodman Institute, Dover, N.H.
- The Vermont Country Store, Weston, Vt.

As a Parent

- Ski weekends at Waterville Valley, N.H., and Smuggler's Notch, Vt.
- The Spa at the Equinox, Manchester, Vt.
- Fort No. 4, Charlestown, N.H.
- The Common Ground, Brattleboro, Vt.
- The Glen, Pittsburgh, N.H.
- Ice cream at The Piazza, Keene, N.H.

However much these two states may seem to be alike, their geography is quite different. New Hampshire has craggy, rocky hillsides and mountains, while Vermont has smoother, rounded landscapes. Both states do have notable mountain ranges. Vermont has the Green Mountains—the oldest mountain range in New England—while New Hampshire is noted for its White Mountains.

Despite their similarities and differences, what both of these states will offer you will be ample opportunity for family fun. Indoors or outdoors, quiet or noisy, passive or interactive, you'll be able to find many things for you and your family to enjoy.

New Englanders take their children with them when they travel, and they will be happy that you have brought yours.

Lura's Favorites

As a Child

- Echo Lake in North Conway, N.H.
- The Spa at The Equinox, Manchester, Vt.
- Loft rooms at The Snowy Owl, Waterville Valley, N.H.
- The Mount Washington Hotel, Bretton Woods, N.H.
- Heritage New Hampshire, Glen, N.H.
- Portsmouth Children's Museum, Portsmouth, N.H.
- Watching moose at Moose Alley, Pittsburgh, N.H.

As a Parent

- Story Land, Glen, N.H.
- Polar Caves, Rumney, N.H.
- Glacial Caves, Loon Mountain, N.H.
- Brattleboro Retreat Petting Farm, Brattleboro, Vt.
- Ice Cream at the Piazza, Keene, N.H.

Lodging and Restaurant Rates

In the "Where to Eat" and "Where to Stay" sections of this book, dollar signs indicate how much you should expect to pay for food and lodgings. We have tried to use the higher end of prices when we were given a range so that you will not get any unpleasant surprises. All room rates are for double occupancy unless otherwise specified. It is always a good idea to make reservations ahead of time, and when you do so, ask about any possible family rates or promotions with local attractions. Hours are given for restaurants when they are unusual; otherwise expect standard dinner hours.

Because admission fees change frequently, this book offers a general idea of the prices charged for the daily admission of a single visitor generally in a range from child to adult. Keep in mind that even though many museums and events offer free admission, a donation is often expected to help the facility with the costs of maintenance and keeping the attraction open to the public.

Rates for Lodging

$	up to $65
$$	$66 to $110
$$$	$111 and up

Rates for Restaurants

$	entrees under $10
$$	entrees $11 to $20
$$$	entrees $21 and up

Rates for Attractions

$	under $5
$$	$5 to $10
$$$	$11 to $20
$$$$	over $20
free	if there is no charge

Tourist Information

The New Hampshire Office of Travel and Tourism Development can be reached at (603) 271–2666 or Box 856, Concord, NH 03302-0856. Through this office you can get fall foliage reports, special events announcements, and ski and ice conditions. For a free pamphlet, call (800) FUN IN NH (386–4664).

To get a free copy of the *Vermont Traveler's Guidebook,* as well as a state highway map and answers to specific questions, contact the Vermont Department of Travel and Tourism, 134 State Street, Montpelier, VT 05602; (802) 828–3236. For winter travel information on Vermont, write or call for a free copy of *Vermont Winter Guide,* a full-color magazine-style publication with general information and a listing of lodgings throughout the state. Write to the Vermont Chamber of Commerce, P.O. Box 37, Montpelier, VT 05601-0037, or call (802) 223–3443 or fax (802) 223–4257.

To reserve campsites in Vermont state parks, you can call as early as the first week of January, weekdays 9:00 A.M. to 4:00 P.M., for minimum stays of two or four nights, depending on the park. For parks in the northwestern part of the state, call (800) 252–2363; the northeastern part, (800) 658–6934; the southeastern part, (800) 299–3071; and the southwestern part, (800) 658–1622. You can get general park information all year long at the state park Web site: www.vtstateparks.com.

Church and **Community** Suppers

Look in local newspapers, signs beside the road, and notices in general stores for community and church suppers. These are casual, inexpensive, fun, and a good alternative to restaurants for travelers with children. There will almost always be other children there to play with. The food will be plentiful and simple, with no surprises and no "funny flavors." Furthermore, this is a great way to meet local people and find out what's going on in the area. Seating is usually at long tables, and your neighbors will very likely engage you in conversation immediately. You'll soon forget everything you've heard about Yankee standoffishness.

Throughout the book, price ranges are given to help you plan your trip's budget. One exception, however, is ski areas. While we have given some rate information, prices vary so widely between weekends, weekdays, high and low season, and a wide variety of special packages, that it really is best to call and request rates for the dates you plan to travel. Be sure to ask about special lodging/lift packages, which can be a real bargain.

The prices, rates, and hours listed in this guidebook were confirmed at press time. We recommend, however, that you call establishments to obtain current information before traveling.

Attractions Key

The following is a key to the icons found throughout the text.

SWIMMING		**FOOD**	
BOATING/BOAT TOUR		**LODGING**	
HISTORIC SITE		**CAMPING**	
HIKING/WALKING		**MUSEUMS**	
FISHING		**PERFORMING ARTS**	
BIKING		**SPORTS/ATHLETICS**	
AMUSEMENT PARK		**PICNICKING**	
HORSEBACK RIDING		**PLAYGROUND**	
SKIING/WINTER SPORTS		**SHOPPING**	
PARK		**PLANTS/GARDENS/NATURE TRAILS**	
ANIMAL VIEWING		**FARMS**	

The Seacoast and Merrimack Valley

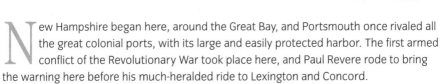

N ew Hampshire began here, around the Great Bay, and Portsmouth once rivaled all the great colonial ports, with its large and easily protected harbor. The first armed conflict of the Revolutionary War took place here, and Paul Revere rode to bring the warning here before his much-heralded ride to Lexington and Concord.

A later chapter in New England history was written along the Cocheco and Merrimack Rivers, whose falls in Dover, Manchester, and Nashua provided the power for huge mill complexes that made New Hampshire a major player in the industrialization of America.

Portsmouth and the Coast

History is all around you as you stroll the brick streets of Portsmouth, lined with stately Federal homes. But despite its air of being a colonial seaport, Portsmouth provides the modern traveler with amenities that make visiting a pleasure. Parking is ample and inexpensive in a well-placed downtown garage. A trolley circles the most popular sites, even going to the beaches in the summer. And Portsmouth is filled with restaurants of all stripes, most of them very good.

Isles of Shoals Steamship Company (ages 3 and up)
1/2 mile on left off I–95 exit 7, 315 Market Street, Portsmouth, N.H.; (603) 431–5500 or (800) 441–4620; www.islesofshoals.com.

The Isles of Shoals Steamship Company offers a wide variety of cruises through the historic and scenic Portsmouth Harbor on its two boats. Rates range from $14.00 to $29.00 for adults and from $9.00 to $19.00 for children. Passengers can choose between the MV *Thomas Laighton,* a 348-passenger replica of a Victorian steamship, and the modern 148-passenger *Oceanic.* Besides the sightseeing cruises that tour the islands, families

THE SEACOAST AND MERRIMACK VALLEY

with younger children might appreciate the shorter whale-watching tours, where they may see not only whales but also harbor seals, birds, and other spectacular ocean wildlife.

The crew is happy to work with children and eager to educate the entire family in the history of the area as well as marine biology. There are plenty of children's activities available on all cruises, and passengers can choose to bring lunch or take advantage of the snack bar on the all-day tours. Dinner cruises and theme cruises are also available; reservations are recommended.

Atlantic Queen II (ages 4 and up)

Rye Harbor State marina, off Route 1A, Rye Harbor, N.H.; (800) WHALE–NH or (603) 964–5220; www.atlanticwhalewatch.com. $$$–$$$$; children under 4 free.

The *Atlantic Queen II* offers both whale-watching tours and half- or full-day deep-sea fishing trips for the entire family. Sightings on all whale watches are guaranteed with rain checks. The *Atlantic Queen II* can reach high enough speeds to bring passengers to ideal sighting and fishing areas, with plenty of time to enjoy destinations such as Jeffrey's Ledge or the Stellwagen Bank National Marine Sanctuary. All sightseeing tours offer educational commentary, and the staff can answer questions concerning the wildlife, especially the mysterious world of whales. The boat offers an enclosed area for eating and has hot and cold food available. Bait and hooks are included in the price of fishing trips, although pole rental and filleting services are extra. Reservations recommended.

Island Cruises (all ages)

P.O. Box 66, Rye, NH 03870; tours from Rye Harbor State Marina, off Route 1A; (603) 964–6446; www.uncleoscar.com. Open July and August daily, June and September weekends only. Call ahead for schedules. Cruise rates: $$–$$$; children under 5 free.

You have your choice of two types of tours—the Isles of Shoals tour and a lobster tour. The Isles of Shoals cruise lasts for two hours, during which you will learn all about the history of the islands

On the **Water** Reminders

- Temperatures on the ocean are an average of ten to fifteen degrees cooler, so bring sweaters.

- Sunlight reflects off the water, so bring extra sunscreen and sunglasses or hats for everyone.

- The seacoast area is breathtaking when viewed from the sea, so bring your camera and plenty of film.

Thirteen Miles of **Coast,** Plenty of **Beaches**

There are lots of beaches to choose from on New Hampshire's coast, despite the short shoreline. To find a beach, just drive down Route 1A, which hugs the coast. (Be prepared for beach traffic on nice weekend days in the summer, though. To reach Hampton Beach from the junction of Routes 101 and 1A on a Saturday can take more than an hour. And it's only about a block away.)

Some of the following are state parks; others are private. Most charge a small fee for parking, and most have no telephone.

- **Wallis Sands State Beach,** Route 1A, Rye; (603) 436–9404. From here you can see the Isles of Shoals and sometimes even seals sunning themselves on cooler days. It is one of the larger beaches, 150 feet wide at low tide.

- **Rye North Beach,** Route 1A, Rye. This beach has a picnic area and great views of the busy little harbor.

- **Jenness State Beach,** Route 1A, Rye; (603) 436–9409. Jenness is our personal favorite and a little less crowded than others.

- **North Hampton Beach,** Route 1A, North Hampton; (603) 436–9404.

- **Hampton State Beach,** Route 1A, Hampton; (800) GET–A–TAN. Hampton Beach is the most crowded, but it also offers plenty of shops, arcades, live music, and other things to do during the day and evening. This is a great place to go if you have teenagers.

- **Seabrook Beach,** Route 1A, Seabrook.

and get a chance to see some of their wildlife. The lobster tour is only one hour long, but it's a really neat way for kids to learn everything they ever wanted to know about lobsters. You will see how they are caught and get to watch as a lobster trap is brought aboard with the day's catch.

Tuck Museum (ages 6 and up) 🏛 🎏 🏛

40 Park Avenue, on the Common, Hampton, N.H.; (603) 929–0781; www.hamptonhistorical society.org/tuck.htm. Open June through September, Sunday, Wednesday, and Friday 1:00 to 4:00 P.M., October through May Wednesday 9:00 A.M. to noon, Sunday 1:00 to 4:00 P.M.; **free.**

This small museum run by the Hampton Historical Society offers variety and a chance to get close to neat old things without having to view them behind glass. In addition to plenty of displays about the area's history, there is also Seacoast Fire Museum as well as a section dedicated to farming. One of the Tuck Museum's buildings is an old schoolhouse, and when the kids tire of exploring that, they can use the playground on the lawn while you check out the more "grown-up" stuff.

The Science and Nature Center at Seabrook Station

(ages 5 and up)

Seabrook Station, Route 1, Seabrook, N.H.; (603) 773–7219 or (800) 338–7482; www.seabrookstation.com. Open by appointment only; call weekdays from 8:30 A.M. to 4:00 P.M. Free.

Although it may seem strange to bring the kids to a nuclear power plant for a day of fun and education about nature, this really is a great place to go. The kids will learn, by using all sorts of interactive displays, all about energy sources, electricity and how it works, and how power generation affects the environment. In addition the Oascoag Nature Trail allows you to explore the salt marsh surrounding the plant. Here you will find plenty of informative signs, which tell all about the wildlife and ecology of this fragile and essential ecosystem.

Seacoast Trolley Company (all ages)

Market Square, Portsmouth, N.H.; (603) 431–6975 or (800) 828–3762; locallink.com/sea coasttrolley. Operates daily from mid-June through Labor Day, hourly from 10:00 A.M. to 5:00 P.M. (schedule of stops available on trolley or at tourist information booths). Fare: $; ticket good for reboarding all day.

This trolley is the perfect solution if you are nervous about getting lost or don't want to burn too much gas in beach traffic. The hour-long narrated tour will bring you to several out-of-town stops, including Rye Beach and Odiorne State Park. You can sit and enjoy the ride and hear all about the area, or get off wherever you want.

Water Country (ages 2 and up)

Route 1 (I–95 exit 5), Portsmouth, N.H.; (603) 436–3556; www.watercountry.com. Open daily June through Labor Day, 10:00 A.M. to 6:00 P.M., with extended hours during July and early August. Discounts are available when tickets are purchased on-line; reduced evening rates.

A day's pass to Water Country ($28 adults, $19 children under 4 feet tall, ages two and under free) includes unlimited use of all pools and slides. If you want to rent a tube or play laser tag, there is a small extra fee. Kids who are frustrated with the chilly waves of the Atlantic will love Water Country's giant wave pool, the largest of its kind in New England. They will also have a blast on one of the six water slide options or on Adventure River or the racing rapids. Lockers and plenty of changing rooms are available as well as places to eat.

Portsmouth Children's Museum (ages 2–14)

280 Marcy Street, Portsmouth, N.H.; (603) 436–3853; www.childrens-museum.org. Open Tuesday through Saturday 10:00 A.M. to 5:00 P.M., Sunday 1:00 to 5:00 P.M. Open Monday 10:00 A.M. to 5:00 P.M. during summer and school vacations. Admission: $, under age 1 **free.**

A successful children's museum offers all kinds of fun, cleverly disguising education as play. This one succeeds. There is a maritime theme in some parts of the museum, but it's also a great place for kids who are getting tired of fishy stuff. At the entrance you are greeted by the Yellow Submarine, and from there kids can travel to the different levels and rooms of the museum. Older children will enjoy many of the displays, and if they are over age nine, they are welcome to spend some time exploring without their parents. There is also a shop filled with toys, games, and science stuff.

Maritime Museum and Albacore Park (ages 4 and up)

Market Street Extension (Route 1 bypass), Portsmouth, N.H.; (603) 436–3680. Open every day 9:30 A.M. to 5:00 P.M.; Columbus Day through Memorial Day 9:30 A.M. to 4:00 P.M. Admission: $.

If you drive by the Maritime Museum property, once the kids see the enormous submarine

sitting off to the side you won't have to convince them to go. This attraction is fascinating for the entire family, and it's one of our favorites in the area. The museum itself is very small, only an introduction before you walk out along the little plank into a 1953 submarine, built nearby at the Portsmouth Naval Shipyard. The *Albacore* never actually participated in any wartime efforts, nor was she intended to. The vessel was designed as a model for a new breed of submarine, and at that time it was the fastest sub the world had seen. You will be able to explore it at leisure and learn about the technology introduced in this prototype. Kids will love being able to sit at the controls and flip switches or squeeze into the bunks. But best of all is the periscope, where children and adults will fight over who gets to look out next and peer at unsuspecting travelers on the nearby highway. Family admission is $10.

Fort Constitution (ages 4 and up)

Newcastle Harbor, N.H.; (603) 436–1552; www.geocities.com/Fort_Constitution/index.html. **Free.**

What kid can resist the chance to guard the ramparts of a fort? Certainly not ours, and especially not when the fort played such a key part in the beginning of the American Revolution. On December 14, 1774, colonists heard from Paul Revere that the British were planning to reinforce the poorly manned fort, so they raided it at night, carrying off its entire store of arms and ammunition by boat. They hid this in nearby Durham, from which it found its way south to be used against the British at the Battle of Bunker Hill.

Odiorne Point–Fort Dearborn (all ages)

Route 1A, Rye, N.H.; (603) 436–8043. Open daily 8:00 A.M. to 8:00 P.M. Admission: $; children under 12 and New Hampshire residents over 65 admitted free.

The role of Fort Dearborn, now known as Odiorne Point, was to protect the Portsmouth Naval Shipyard, where 22,000 workers in three shifts built submarines during World War II. Although the Germans did not have planes capable of crossing the Atlantic to bomb the base, they did have ships capable of destroying it from the sea. The location of Odiorne Point provided a clear view and direct aim at anything close enough to fire on the Navy Yard.

Reminders of the past are all around as you walk along the woodland and shore paths: stone walls, old apple trees, escaped garden flowers growing wild, foundations, a stone fountain, the line of an old road, a mound rising out of the forest, a "hill" with a huge door in it, granite fenceposts, and an occasional explanatory marker. But most of these relics have no sign, and you may come upon them unexpectedly beside a path.

It is almost impossible to get lost here. The trails and paths form a tangled web that can confuse you, but the area is bounded by water and a road, and you are never very far from either. Simply follow a trail until it meets one of these boundaries. You will see shore and marsh birds and an abundance of wildflowers here. Each season has its attractions. Spotting old foundations, stone walls, and cellar holes is easier in the winter or late fall, when leaves have gone; spring brings wildflowers and the bloom of the old-fashioned roses that have escaped from the cottage gardens. While the wind can be very chilly off the water in the winter, the sea breeze makes even the hottest summer day pleasant. (Yes, New Hampshire summers do have temperatures in the 90s.)

Where to Eat

BG's Restaurant, Newcastle Road, Portsmouth, N.H.; (603) 431–1074. Nice dining room that overlooks the water, offering lobster and plenty of other seafood at reasonable prices. Very inexpensive kids' menu. $–$$

Cafe Brioche, 14 Market Square; Portsmouth, N.H.; (603) 430–9225. Open 6:30 A.M. to 6:00 P.M. daily, until 11:00 P.M. on Saturday. This is a wonderful place to grab a bite and sit on the square at an outside table to people-watch. Serves fresh baked goods and light fare. $

Cafe Mediterraneo, 152 Fleet Street, Portsmouth, N.H.; (603) 427–5563. Local seafood prepared as though it were caught in the Mediterranean itself. Open for lunch and dinner daily. $–$$

The Ceres Bakery, 51 Penhallow Street, Portsmouth, N.H.; (603) 431–6518. Excellent baked goods and pastries for breakfast as early as 5:30 A.M., and also a great place for a light lunch of soup, salad, and quiche to go with their grainy breads. $

The Ice House, Newcastle Road, Rye, N.H.; (603) 431–3086. Inexpensive fried seafood with a nice outdoor picnic-like eating area and, of course, ice cream too! Watch out for golf balls from the course next door! $

Library Restaurant, 401 State Street, Portsmouth, N.H.; (603) 431–5202. Open for lunch and dinner, brunch on Sunday. A genteel setting in an old hotel. $$

New Asia, 99 River Road, just off Routes 4 and 16, Newington, N.H.; (603) 431–3121. Especially good Chinese food with very friendly service. Sunday buffet is an excellent value and doesn't skimp on the good stuff. $

Where to Stay

The Inn at Plaice Cove, 955 Ocean Boulevard, Hampton Beach, N.H.; (603) 926–1750. Offers modern amenities in a motel-like atmosphere. $$

Lamie's Inn, 490 Lafayette Road, Hampton, N.H.; (603) 926–0330. Classic New England inn, built in 1740, with its own well-regarded restaurant. $$

The Meadowbrook Inn, Interstate Highway Circle, exit 5 off I–95, Portsmouth, N.H.; (603) 436–2700 or (800) 370–2727. Offers budget and deluxe accommodations. $–$$

Sheraton Portsmouth, 250 Market Street, Portsmouth, N.H.; (603) 431–2300 or (800) 325–3535. Very modern and convenient with plenty of packages for vacationing families. $$–$$$

The Great Bay and Beyond

Several rivers flow into the Great Bay. Most of them were navigable in the colonial era, when they were lined with shipyards and docks for loading the giant white pines that the king commandeered for masts on his naval ships. Today these towns still have their historic homes, but most are visited less often than Portsmouth.

The Woodman Institute (all ages)
182 Central Avenue, Dover, N.H.; (603) 742–1038; www.seacoastnh.com/woodman. **Open Wednesday through Sunday 12:30 to 4:30 P.M. April through November, Saturday and Sunday in December and January; closed February and March. Admission: $, under age 14 free with paying adult.**

Samurai armor, polar bears, tropical birds, blue butterflies from Brazil, and South Sea island woodcarvings are just some of the things you will find in the showcases of the privately endowed Woodman Institute, housed in three buildings near Dover's Tuttle Square. Here polished wood-and-glass showcases full of exotic art, artifacts from primitive cultures, and natural history specimens have not given way to the newer concepts of interpretive displays. The old-style displays of Sioux beadwork, rows of gems, and butterfly collections, among others, will keep even young children riveted on the artifacts.
In a second brick building is one of New England's finest collections of the works of early furniture makers, plus well-lighted cases of nineteenth-century decorative arts and incidentals of daily living, from thimble cases to pocket watches and lace collars. The empha-

sis is on local life and history, but the building is a microcosm of life in Victoria's century and the one before it.

You should also take time to visit the Dam Garrison, the only surviving garrison house from the early days of the city. Dover once had several of these, protecting early settlers from the repeated Indian attacks that nearly destroyed the town several times. Inside the heavy log walls of the garrison, its small, dark rooms are furnished with the simple tables, chairs, and rope-sprung beds of the very early years along with personal items used by the first settlers. It evokes the harsh life faced by those who settled New Hampshire's coast, and children will be fascinated by this.

New Hampshire Farm Museum (ages 4 and up)

125 Plummer's Ridge, Route 16, P.O. Box 644, Milton, NH 03851-0644; (603) 652–7840; www.farmmuseum.org. Open Wednesday through Sunday from late June through October and weekends from Labor Day through the end of October, 10:00 A.M. to 4:00 P.M. Admission: $.

Living-history museums demonstrate what others merely explain. Set on an old farm, this one will show your family all about life in early, rural New England. The farm buildings, for example, are connected so that the farmer wasn't lost in a blizzard trying to do winter chores. You may tour the farm and listen to guides describe what life was like when the farm was in its early years of operation. On certain days you can also learn about specific farming skills, such as milking cows or tending the herb gardens.

Gilman Garrison House (ages 7 and up)

Corner of Water and Clifford Streets, Exeter, N.H.; (603) 436–3205. Open June through the end of September, Tuesday, Thursday, Saturday, and Sunday, noon to 5:00 P.M. Admission: $, under 6 free.

The Gilman Garrison House was built in the 1600s as a garrison and has been added onto several times since. It has always been a part of the area's history, from serving as a home for a royal governor to being the home of Daniel Webster when he attended Philips Exeter Academy.

Sandy Point Discovery Center (ages 3 and up)

Signposted from Route 33, Stratham, N.H. Take Depot Road, turning left at the T intersection; (603) 778–0015. Open Wednesday through Sunday, June through October, 10:00 A.M. to 4:00 P.M. Free.

Dedicated to bringing the busy role of the Great Bay into focus, this small science center has well-conceived displays, most of them interactive. These show the importance of tidal estuaries as a home for wildlife and demonstrate how they clean pollutants from the water. Tools from the bay's economic history bring fishing and salt-hay harvesting to life. Various ecosystems along the estuary are reached by trails from the center, and you can take nature guide leaflets to help you identify the wildlife—primarily birds— that you'll see.

Pawtuckaway State Park (all ages)

128 Mountain Road, Nottingham, N.H.; (603) 895–3301. Open 9:00 A.M. to 8:00 P.M. on week-ends from Memorial Day through the last week of June and on the two weekends after Labor Day. During the rest of the summer, open every day during the same hours. Admission: $; children under 12 and New Hampshire residents over 65 admitted free. You can still use the park after the season closes, but no facilities are available.

You can spend the afternoon here with a picnic or take a boat out on the lake, but we prefer going up the trail to the Pawtuckaway Boulders. These huge rocks were once part of nearby mountains, but they were broken off by glaciers and moved, then dropped where they sit today. Kids will love exploring the huge rocks, which can reach over 30 feet tall. You can also take trails to the top of one of the three mountains in the park area.

Where to Eat

Gregory's Grill, 780 Portsmouth Avenue (Route 33), Greenland, N.H.; (603) 431–0368. Open for lunch and dinner Tuesday through Sunday, early on Sunday for brunch buffet. Absolutely wonderful seafood as well as inland fare. Kids and parents will be at ease in the casual atmosphere, but there's nothing casual about the food. $–$$

Newick's, 431 Dover Point Road, Dover, N.H., (exit 6W from the Spaulding Turnpike); (603) 742–3205. Open daily 11:30 A.M. to 8:30 P.M., until 9:00 P.M. on Friday and Saturday. Classic shore-hall seafood restaurant. $–$$

Where to Stay

Ayers Homestead B&B, 47 Park Avenue, Greenland, N.H.; (603) 436–5992. Centrally located, absolutely beautiful rooms in a 1737 house. The best part is, families are very welcome, and there is even a large room with extra beds especially for families. Wonderful homemade breakfast in the rustic old kitchen. $–$$

Hickory Pond Inn and Golf Course, 1 Stagecoach Road, Durham, N.H.; (603) 659–2227 or (800) 658–0065. Continental breakfast, modern amenities, and very welcoming to families. The nine-hole golf course right on the property converts to cross-country ski terrain in the winter. $$

Highland Farm B&B, 148 County Farm Road (off Sixth Street), Dover, N.H.; (603) 743–3399. Convenient to Great Bay area and very scenic, with seventy-five acres to explore. Wonderful homemade breakfasts. $–$$, mid-week discounts.

Camping

Pawtuckaway State Park, Route 156, Nottingham, N.H.; (603) 895–3301. Attractive and well-spaced campsites, with swimming and hiking trails. $

Border Country

The towns and cities along New Hampshire's southern border seem to meld into Massachusetts as they approach the Merrimack River corridor. But on either side you will find quiet, attractive country villages, with white-spired churches and town commons. The built-up areas seem to cling largely to the former industrial centers along the river.

Kingston State Beach (all ages)

Off Route 125 in Kingston, N.H.; (603) 642–5741. Open daylight hours. Admission: $.

This is a public beach located on Great Pond for those who prefer freshwater swimming to the often-chilly ocean nearby. There are changing rooms available and a baseball field, as well as forty-four acres to explore. No boat launch, but canoes and kayaks are fine if you bring them down to the beach.

Sandown Depot Railroad Museum (ages 5 and up)

Route 121A, Sandown, N.H.; (603) 887–4621. Open June through October on weekends 1:00 to 5:00 P.M. Free.

This neat little museum is set up in an old train station that was once one of the busiest in southern New Hampshire. Here you can explore the restored station and telegraph office and learn how the railroads affected life in these small communities.

Canobie Lake Park (all ages)

Salem, N.H., off I–93 exit 2; (603) 893–3506; www.canobie.com. Open mid-April to May Saturday and Sunday noon to 6:00 P.M., Memorial Day to Labor Day daily noon to 10:00 P.M. Admission for an all-day pass for all rides and shows: $$$–$$$$.

After nearly a century, this amusement park for the family is still fun. It's filled with rides that include bumper cars, Ferris wheels, water slides, plus the Yankee Cannonball and the Canobie Corkscrew roller coasters. Canobie Lake Park has a back-in-time theme, complete with miniature old-fashioned cars, which kids can drive themselves, and an ornate carousel for the very young. One ride simulates the log flume of a century-old sawmill. Everyone enjoys the cruise on the steamship around Canobie Lake and the live entertainment throughout the park.

The Children's Metamorphosis (ages 1–8)

Abbot Court at Depot Square, Derry, N.H.; (603) 425–2560; www.childrens met.org. Open year-round, Tuesday through Saturday 9:30 A.M. to 5:00 P.M., Sunday 1:00 to 5:00 P.M., until 8:00 P.M. on Friday. Admission: $–$$, under age 1 free.

Kids won't mind the "E word" here because the exhibits are so much fun and the interactions so well done. Just about any subject may turn up in their changing and creative activities. The museum was recently moved and includes many new exhibits and theme rooms. Even your little ones will want to play in the Toddler Depot, and My House with dress-up toys and garden tea parties is sure to be a hit with young ladies. There's even a new climbing wall, safe for your extra-energetic ones to work it off. Plenty of restrooms and storage space for diaper bags and strollers.

Tee-Off at Mel's (ages 5 and up)

Route 3A, north of Litchfield Village, N.H.; (603) 424–2292. Open Sunday through Thursday 10:00 A.M. to 9:00 P.M., Friday and Saturday 10:00 A.M. to 10:00 P.M. Prices vary.

Everyone will find an amusement here, with choices such as batting cages, a driving range, go-karts, and a miniature golf course with a covered bridge and waterfalls, not to mention an ice-cream stand.

Nashua Historical Society (ages 7 and up)

5 Abbott Street, Nashua, N.H.; (603) 883–0015. Open March through November on Tuesday, Wednesday, Thursday, and Saturday. Free.

While you explore the interesting history of Nashua, the kids will be happily occupied by exhibits like the old schoolhouse. The museum specializes in exhibits and artifacts that relate to Nashua's role in the various wars and skirmishes of the state's early history. Exhibits change, so there's always something new.

Greenville Wildlife Park (ages 2 and up)

18 Blanch Farm Road (off Route 31), Greenville, N.H.; (603) 878–2255, www.greenville wildlifepark.com. Open April through November 1, Wednesday through Sunday 10:00 A.M. to 5:00 P.M. Admission: $$, under 3 free.

From baby sheep and goats that kids can hold and pet to alligators and lions, this low-key park has more than a hundred animals. One of only twenty-seven golden tabby tigers known to exist resides there, along with a spotted hyena, bears, and a Bactrian camel. Many other exotics have been rescued from life-threatening or substandard situations and given a safe home here as well. The emphasis is not just on looking at the animals, but understanding their habits too. Many are endangered species, and their fight for survival is brought home to children.

Silver Lake State Beach (all ages)

Route 122, Hollis, N.H.; (603) 465–2342. Open 9:00 A.M. to 8:00 P.M. Memorial Day through mid-September (staffed on weekends only early and late season). Admission: $; children under 12 and New Hampshire residents over 65 admitted free.

About 1,000 feet of beach extends around one side of Silver Lake, with a bathhouse, picnic grove, and playing fields. Yet this beautiful park is almost empty on weekdays. The beach extends for many yards of very shallow water, a comfort to parents watching small children.

Where to Eat

Black Forest Cafe, Route 101, Amherst, N.H.; (603) 672–0500. Bakery (with tables) open 8:00 A.M. to 6:30 P.M. (until 3:30 P.M. on Sunday). Dining room open 11:00 A.M. to 3:30 P.M. (Sunday 8:00 A.M. to 2:30 P.M.) The menu is filled with tasty, healthy choices and interesting sandwiches. $–$$

The Dog House, Route 101, Wilton, N.H. If it's sausage and tastes good, you'll find it at this tiny roadside stop. Hot dogs of all sizes and shapes, with accompaniments for all tastes. A good selection of ice cream tops it off; eat at the umbrella-covered picnic tables. $

Ya Mama's, 75 Daniel Webster Highway (Route 3), Merrimack, N.H.; (603) 883–2264. The informal trattoria atmosphere makes everyone at home instantly, and the food is just like you wish your Mama used to make. Desserts are splendidly rich. $$

Where to Stay

Nearly every hotel chain, in all price ranges, is represented in this area.

For More Information

Southern New Hampshire Convention and Visitor Bureau, Manchester, NH 03103; (603) 645–9889.

Manchester and Concord Region

The state's two most important cities—its capital and its largest city—are just a few miles apart, both on the Merrimack River. Concord has a benign and somewhat stately air, spreading outward from its capitol in the center of the city. Manchester's focal point is the sprawling redbrick mill complex, the remains of its once great manufacturing heritage. Today the mill buildings and the blocks of brick-company housing around them have been restored and recycled into offices, restaurants, and homes.

Lawrence L. Lee Scouting Museum and Max I. Silber Scouting Library (ages 5 to 15)

Bodwell Road, Manchester, N.H.; (603) 669–8919. Open July through August daily 10:00 A.M. to 4:00 P.M., and September through June Saturday only 10:00 A.M. to 4:00 P.M., or by appointment. **Free.**

This museum will interest any Boy Scout in the family, young or old. There are displays of various books, memorabilia, and other items, many of which are part of the collection of the founder of Boy Scouting, Lord Baden-Powell. There is plenty here to keep the boys interested, and the whole family may choose to camp or picnic on the grounds.

Amoskeag Falls (all ages)

Fletcher Street, at the Amoskeag Bridge, Manchester, N.H.; no phone. Observation deck open mid-April through October 31, 8:00 A.M. until 6:30 P.M. **Free.**

At any time of year, the observation deck on the east side of the river is a great place to view the Amoskeag Dam. Kids can see how a dam works, and the whole family can enjoy the city skyline. But the place becomes even more interesting in late May, when the salmon ladder is filled with fish making their way upstream to spawn. Before the dam, the salmon were able to jump the falls, but they had disappeared completely for many years. Now about 3,000 fish return to their spawning grounds each year. The fish ladder and exhibition area, which explains the life cycle and migration of the fish, are open April through June. Visit www.amoskeagfalls.com/history.htm for a full historical background of the site.

SEE Science Center (ages 2 and up)

324 Commercial Street, in the Amoskeag Mill Complex, Manchester, N.H.; (603) 669–0400; www.see-sciencecenter.org. Open Monday through Friday 10:00 A.M. to 3:00 P.M., weekends noon to 5:00 P.M. Admission: $, age 1 and under free.

More than sixty-five exhibits, nearly all of them hands-on, show the basic concepts of various fields of science. Everything from astronomy to the composition of atoms is covered, in terms kids will understand and with activities to bring the concepts to life.

Museum of New Hampshire History (ages 6 and up)

6 Eagle Square, Concord, N.H.; (603) 228–6688; www.nhhistory.org/museum.html. Open Monday through Saturday 9:30 A.M. to 5:00 P.M. (Thursday until 8:30 P.M.), and Sunday noon to 5:00 P.M. Closed Monday October through June. Admission: $$. Free to everyone Thursday evening.

This museum has a wide variety of displays that are suitable for the entire family. Many exhibits are interactive and really get kids involved in this richly historical state. This is a popular spot for schools to visit, so it is well equipped for children of all ages. The gift shop carries many traditional New Hampshire crafts, as well as old-fashioned toys and items designed for children.

Christa McAuliffe Planetarium (ages 3 and up)

Exit 15E from I–93, Concord, N.H.; (603) 271–STAR (7827); www.starhop.com. Open Tuesday through Sunday; call for reservations for shows, which are on a constantly changing schedule. Admission: $$.

For Concord residents and visitors alike, the Christa McAuliffe Planetarium is not just a great place to learn about the stars, but a place to pay homage to a Concord hero. The planetarium was named after the city's teacher and astronaut, who was to have been the first teacher in space until the space shuttle *Challenger* exploded, killing the entire crew. The shows are fun for the entire family, and this is a good place to sneak in education where the kids don't expect it. Reservations are highly recommended for the planetarium shows, and it is good to get there at least a half hour early. Because of the darkness, late admission and readmission are not allowed. Shows last approximately one hour.

Bear Brook State Park (all ages)

Route 28, Allenstown, N.H.; (603) 485–9874. Open 9:00 A.M. to 8:00 P.M. on weekends from Memorial Day through the last week of June and on the two weekends after Labor Day. During the rest of the summer, open every day during the same hours. Admission: $; children under 12 and New Hampshire residents over 65 admitted free. You can use the park after the season closes, but no facilities are available.

This rather large park offers hiking, ponds for swimming and fishing, tent camping, and cross-country skiing. This is also the site of the state's only public archery ranges, and there is even a wheelchair-accessible range. A nature center and canoe rentals add to its attractions, along with three unique museums that explore different topics: family camping, snowmobiling, and the Civilian Conservation Corps.

Kimball-Jenkins Estate (ages 6 and up)

266 North Main Street, Concord, N.H.; (603) 225–3932; www.kimballjenkins.com. Open June through Labor Day, Wednesday through Saturday 11:00 A.M. to 3:00 P.M. Admission and tours: $$.

Tours of this grand old Victorian home show the lovely estate as it was set up at the turn of the twentieth century. All tours are concluded with tea overlooking the perfectly landscaped gardens. There are also special family and children's events, such as a doll tea party and seasonal programs that teach children Victorian crafts and customs.

Silk Farm Wildlife Sanctuary (ages 6 and up)

3 Silk Farm Road (off Clinton Street, I–89 exit 2), Concord, N.H.; (603) 224–9909; www.nhaudubon.com. Open Monday through Saturday, 9:00 A.M. to 5:00 P.M. Free.

The Wildlife Sanctuary is operated by the New Hampshire Audubon Society, and this is also the society's headquarters. This is a great place to go for a hike—you can see all sorts of birds and small wildlife alongside Great Turkey Pond. There is also a good library for young naturalists to get lost in, and a shop with all sorts of great nature- and wildlife-themed trinkets and gifts.

Concord Community Music School (ages 1 and up)

23 Wall Street, Concord, N.H.; (603) 228–1196; www.ccmusicschool.org. Program dates, times, and admission vary.

The Community Music School is committed to providing entertainment and lessons to even very young children. Call or write to them for a schedule of the various classes, lectures, and concerts.

Clough State Park (all ages)

Off Route 114, Weare, N.H.; (603) 529–7112. Open daylight hours Memorial Day through mid-September. Admission: $; children under 12 and New Hampshire residents over 65 admitted free. You can use the park after the season closes, but no facilities are available.

This is a good park for an afternoon swim along the 900-foot river-beach. There are changing facilities, as well as picnic tables and a baseball field. You can bring your canoe or kayak, or rent a canoe or rowboat right at the park.

Mt. Kearsarge Indian Museum (ages 5 and up)

Mt. Kearsarge Road, Warner, N.H.; (603) 456–2600; www.indianmuseum.org. Open Monday through Saturday 10:00 A.M. to 5:00 P.M., Sunday noon to 5:00 P.M. May through October, weekends through mid-December. Admission: $$, age 5 and under free.

This museum is one of our personal favorites for several reasons, but most importantly for its philosophy. The collectors, Bud and Nancy Thompson, have felt very strongly about maintaining the true spirit of the Native people as they designed the museum, and they have avoided dry displays at all cost. The guides that accompany you through the museum are very well informed and will spend time on what interests you without bombarding you with a slew of meaningless facts. In the same spirit, there are only quotes accompanying each display instead of a list of dates and textbook information. (Should you want to learn more, your guide can explain anything in detail for you.)

A strong sense of the Native American reverence for nature and balance can be felt throughout the museum, and several of the exhibits are related to humans' relationship with nature as they saw it. In addition to these exhibits, there are plenty of artifacts to look at, such as embroidery made out of moose hair, decorative items made from porcupine quills, utensils and instruments made from carved bone, and even canoes. You may also tour the two acres surrounding the museum, which are filled with the various plants and herbs that were once used by the Native Americans for both food and medicine. The gift shop offers a chance to buy authentic crafts, including intricate beadwork and other handmade items like baskets and pottery. There are also plenty of good books available to give you a chance to take a piece of the day home with you.

Pat's Peak (ages 4 and up)

Route 114, Henniker, N.H.; (603) 428–3245 or (800) 258–3218; www.patspeak.com. Open for skiing from December through March, snow conditions permitting. Rates vary.

This is a good family ski area that is small enough that you don't have to worry about the kids getting lost. There are nineteen trails of varying difficulty, and lift lines aren't very long, as a result of limited ticket sales. The food at the lodge's restaurant surpasses that at most ski areas, since everything is home-cooked. Rentals are available for both skis and snowboards, and group or individual lessons are available, as well as a nursery for nonskiing toddlers.

Where to Eat

Alley Cat Pizzeria, 486 Chestnut Street, Manchester, N.H.; (603) 669–4533. Traditional Italian-style pizza cooked in their brick oven, featuring a 20-inch pizza. Free delivery to your hotel. $

Cafe Pavone, Arms Park Drive (off Commercial Street), Manchester, N.H.; (603) 622–5488. Open Monday through Friday for lunch and dinner, weekends for dinner only. Patio seating and great food make this a treat. $$–$$$

Charley Pepper's, 1181 Elm Street, Manchester, N.H.; (603) 668–3837. Open for lunch and dinner weekdays; weekends open at 4:00 P.M.; closed Monday. Offers standard pizza-and-burger fare with a great kids' menu and comfortable atmosphere. $

Fratello's Ristorante Italiano, 155 Dow Street (in the Amoskeag Mills Complex), Manchester, N.H.; (603) 624–2022. Open for lunch and dinner Monday through Friday, dinner only on weekends. Reasonable prices and a good selection for picky eaters make this a good place to bring the kids. $$

The Red Arrow, 61 Lowell Street, Manchester, N.H.; (603) 626–1118. Always open (except Christmas Day), the absolute classic diner, and a personal favorite. Smoke-free. $

Where to Stay

Highlander Inn, Route 3A South, near Manchester Airport, Manchester, N.H.; (603) 625–6426. Modern, spacious rooms, **free** movies and breakfast, and swimming pools make this more than just another airport hotel. $$

Holiday Inn, 71 Hall Street, Concord, N.H.; (603) 224–9534 or (800) 221–2222. A cut above the usual chains, in a modern building handy to I–93 and downtown Concord. $$

Camping

Bear Brook State Park, Route 28, Allenstown, N.H.; (603) 485–9874. Nearly a hundred tent sites with a beach just for campers; canoe and boat rentals; nature programs; and camp store. $

For More Information

Concord Area Chamber of Commerce, 40 Commercial Street, Concord, NH 03301; (603) 224–2508; www.concordnh chamber.com.

Annual Events

EARLY MAY

Spring Farming Day, Beaverbrook Farm, Hollis, N.H.; (603) 465–7787.

JUNE

Band Concerts, State House Plaza, Concord, N.H.; (603) 228–3901. Every Tuesday 7:30 P.M., mid-June to mid-August.

Market Square Day Weekend, Portsmouth, N.H.; (603) 431–5388. Clambake, historic tours, parade, concerts, street fair, and fireworks.

High Hopes Hot Air Balloon Festival, Old Wilton Road, Milford, N.H.; (603) 673–7005. Balloons, rides, crafts, and entertainment, with proceeds benefiting terminally ill New Hampshire children.

Prescott Arts Festival, 105 March Street, Portsmouth, N.H.; (603) 436–1034. Musicals, concerts, and dance continuously June through August.

DECEMBER

First Night, Portsmouth, N.H. New Year's Eve brings all types of entertainment for the family, beginning in the afternoon and lasting until the fireworks display at midnight.

The Connecticut Valley

The Connecticut River forms the border between Vermont and New Hampshire, although the river itself belongs to New Hampshire. The valley has been an artery for travelers since the earliest settlers arrived—and for the Abenaki even before that. One of the few covered bridges over this river connects Windsor, Vermont, to Cornish, New Hampshire.

Beside the river on the Vermont side is Route 5, a winding and often narrow road that weaves over and under I–91, through some fertile farmland, connecting towns from Brattleboro to the Canadian border. The views are best from the higher interstate, often sweeping across long valley and river vistas.

Across the river are the hills and mountains of New Hampshire, which you can see best from the Vermont shore. On the New Hampshire side are some of the valley's most interesting sights, such as a reconstructed fort from the French and Indian Wars at Charlestown. Routes 12 and 12A parallel the river in New Hampshire, and you can make a nice loop by going north on one side and south on the other.

The Monadnock Region

This region is named for its most obvious landmark, Mount Monadnock. Now the world's most often-climbed mountain, the peak offers incredible views and is breathtaking to gaze upon from afar. The land in this region is just as picturesque, and the well-kept roads and hilly landscape make even the major routes a beautiful place to go for an afternoon drive.

Ashuelot River Park (all ages)
West Street, Keene, N.H., across from intersection with Island Street. Daylight hours.
Free.

The Ashuelot River Park offers a wonderful place to picnic, walk, and relax in Keene. Beautifully landscaped picnic areas, stone walkways, and a gazebo overlook the Ashuelot River.

THE CONNECTICUT VALLEY

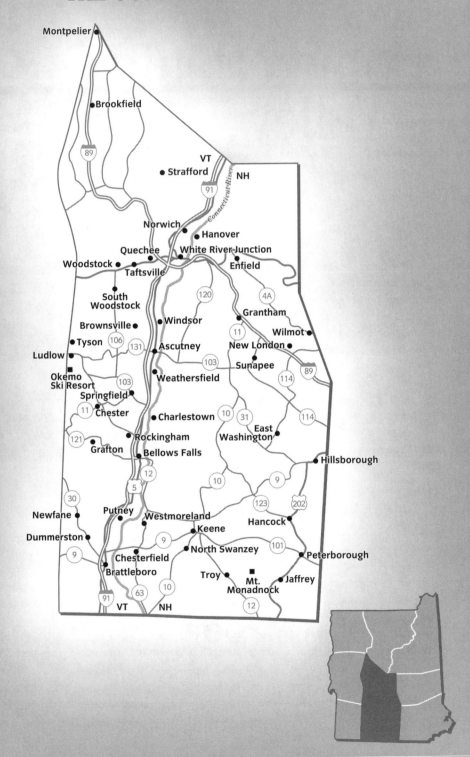

Spanning the river is a tiny suspension bridge donated by local companies. The park features a relaxing trail along the river, suitable for anyone. Often you will see canoes or kayaks floating along the peaceful waters. Dogs are welcome on leashes, and the parks department supplies **free** "doggie bags" to ensure that the grass stays sanitary for kids to play on.

Stonewall Farm (ages 3 and up)

242 Chesterfield Road, Keene, N.H. (take Route 9 west 3.2 miles from intersection with Routes 10 and 12; turn right onto Chesterfield Road and go 0.9 mile); (603) 357–7278; rubin@monad.net. Learning Center open Monday through Friday 8:30 A.M. to 4:30 P.M., Saturday 10:00 A.M. to 3:00 P.M. Free. Special events and classes individually priced. Call ahead for special events calendar and registration.

Stonewall Farm is a nonprofit working farm and educational center. The Learning Center offers exhibits (including a beehive you can watch), educational programs, special events, and presentations. The working farm covers more than 140 acres, encompassing farm fields, wetlands, and forest. The farm has a herd of Holsteins, which are milked each day in the dairy barn at 4:30 P.M. Belgian draft horses are another highlight of the farm, but don't forget the pigs, sheep, goats, and chickens, too! You can also visit the gardens or watch and learn about maple sugaring.

One of the highlights of the farm is its nature trails, which take you around not only the farm itself but the surrounding area as well. You can borrow a guide booklet to the "Natural History Trail," but we recommend going inside and paying the dollar for your own copy. This great guide to the land around the farm is much more than a sight-seeing map—it is a detailed tour of the entire farm. It includes information on stream ecology and insects, meadow regeneration, wetlands, and rare and common local plants and wildlife, plus plenty of tidbits of information and neat facts.

The Piazza (all ages)

149 Main Street, Keene, N.H.; (603) 352–5133. Open noon to 8:00 P.M. daily May through September.

We have chosen to include the Piazza in the attractions section because it is truly a landmark in Keene. No hot summer day should pass without their ice cream (and for some of us, no cold summer day, either!). What sets the Piazza apart from the average ice-cream place is its flavors and creative combinations. They offer 200 flavors of soft-serve, 200 flavors of frozen yogurt, and 200 flavors of sugar-free ice cream. That doesn't even include their regular ice cream, sundaes, and a plethora of add-ins. One warning: Allow plenty of time for the little ones (and yourselves) to make up their minds!

High Hopes Farm (ages 2 and up)

582 Glebe Road, Westmoreland, N.H. Take Route 9 for 4 miles west from intersection with Routes 10 and 12; turn right onto Glebe Road and go 2.7 miles; look for signs on your left; (603) 399–4305. Open July through December 24. Hours vary with season.

High Hopes is a favorite orchard of the area. Here the entire family can pick apples, blueberries, peaches, and other fruit and enjoy other farm activities as well. A tractor-pulled wagon brings pickers out to a choice spot in the orchard, and during pumpkin season, the "pumpkin-mobile" carries excited visitors. The farm also offers workshops and activities for children, including a make-your-own-scarecrow class and a train to Fantasy Farm. If you want a break from the abundant healthy fruit, stop to watch homemade doughnuts cook before your eyes. You can also watch apples turn into cider as they are pressed in front of you.

Chesterfield Gorge (ages 4 and up)

On Route 9, 6 miles west of intersection with Routes 10 and 12, Chesterfield, N.H. Daylight hours for hiking. Free.

Chesterfield Gorge is the perfect place for a short hike with beautiful views. Its 0.7-mile trail leads down and around the magnificent geological formation of the gorge, where rocks have been carved away by the water into a jagged and impressive chasm. The gorge has been lined with railings to help guide hikers away from the dangerous drop-offs, but we still recommend careful supervision of children while hiking here. At the visitor center, guests can pick up a very educational pamphlet on the gorge's geology and ecology as well as see several exhibits on local wildlife and culture. There is also a display of some of the state's first logging tools, which explains when and how they were used. This is a perfect hike for the family that does not consider itself "hikers"—it is short and not too challenging but very rewarding. Dogs are welcome on leashes; restrooms and ample parking available.

Pisgah State Park (all ages)

Route 63, Chesterfield, N.H.; daylight hours. Free.

This 13,000-acre park and hardwood forest offers several nice hiking trails and a chance to explore the wildlife of the area in depth. There are no facilities here, and camping is not allowed. This for the family that is already well acquainted with hiking.

Monadnock Berries (all ages)

545 West Hill Road, Troy, N.H.; (603) 242–6417; www.monadnockberries.com. Open mid-July through mid-September, 8:00 A.M. to 8:00 P.M. Free to visit.

This berry farm offers more than just its 7,000 pick-your-own bushes of high bush blueberries and raspberries. The family-owned and -operated farm is a fun place to go picnic and pet the farm animals, and it offers a play area for children and even a hand-weaving studio. If you don't feel like standing in the sun, their farm stand offers fresh-picked berries and plenty of other produce and gifts. The picking rows are wheelchair-accessible.

Stuart and John's Sugar House (all ages)

On Route 63 at Route 12 in Westmoreland, N.H.; (603) 399–4486. Open weekends early morning to 3:00 P.M. Free.

At the Sugar House, not only can you learn about the maple sugaring process, but your family can also enjoy hearty, homemade meals

drenched in as much pure, fresh maple syrup as you can imagine. The very casual atmosphere makes you feel at home immediately as you dig into piles of pancakes, a maple
sundae, or even maple baked goods like breads and pies.

Mount Monadnock (ages 5 and up)

**Main access from Dublin Road (Route 124 west of Jaffrey, N.H.); (603) 532–8862. Hiking day-
light hours. Daily use fee: $, children 11 and under free.**

Mount Monadnock is now thought to be the most-often-climbed mountain in the world,
and there's a good reason for that. It stands alone (the definition of monadnock) and its
bare granite summit has views that stretch from the White Mountains to Boston on clear
days. While the best climbing is in autumn, summer and spring (after mud and mosquito
season) are also good choices. The climb is steady but not brutally steep, and you'll meet
lots of other families with children scampering ahead of panting parents.

Eccardt Farm (all ages)

**2766 East Washington Road, East Washington, N.H.; (603) 495–3157. Afternoon and
evening milking time, 3:30 to 7:00 P.M. Free.**

Kids always love the chance to see and pet farm animals, and here they can see not only
sheep, goats, and bunnies but an aviary with exotic birds as well. You can watch the cows
being milked or, in the spring, see sap being turned into syrup. This is a real operating
dairy farm, where they can't seem to throw anything away, so the family might like to wander past the barns displaying the collection of old farm equipment, including tractors and
tools.

Harris Center (ages 4 and up)

**Off Route 123 (King's Highway) west of Hancock, N.H., about 2.5 miles, left at the signs;
(603) 525–3394. Open daylight hours. Free.**

Environmental and conservation issues are at the heart of the programs in the center's full
calendar of activities, field trips, outings, and workshops. Most are at the conservation
center, but some are at little-known places of natural interest nearby. Their 7,000 acres
cover two small mountains and are crossed by about 7 miles of trails to their summits
around wooded ponds and through jumbles of glacial boulders. The trails are open for
walking, skiing, or snowshoeing on your own or as part of their themed guided walks. One
nature trail has a descriptive booklet and is well suited to children's interests, and some of
the programs are especially designed for younger participants.

The Friendly Farm (ages 1 and up)

**Route 101, Dublin, N.H.; (603) 563–8444; www.friendlyfarm.com. Open daily mid-May
through Labor Day from 10:00 A.M. to 5:00 P.M., and the same hours on weekends through
mid-October. Admission: $–$$. Ask about the multiuse pass.**

This down-to earth farm keeps the low-key atmosphere intact while still exciting kids with the
outgoing animals. Almost all of the animals may be approached by kids—even young ones.
Staff members are attentive but nonintrusive and always have grain ready for the kids to feed

the geese. A special glass-topped incubator lets children watch chicks break out of their shells. After they are a few days old, visitors can hold them. Even the little rabbits are happy to see young children, letting them pet them. Bigger animals include the all-time favorite mud-covered pig, black sheep, a hill of goats, cows and calves, horses, and donkeys. An all-day affair can be made of this because the farm provides a lovely picnic area for visitors—and does not try to push vending services at you.

Where to Eat

High Tide, Route 9, just east of Hillsborough, N.H.; (603) 464–4202. Just east of town. Fast fried seafood, burgers, dogs, and ice cream, set in a shaded grove where you can eat at picnic tables while the kids take advantage of the well-equipped playground. $

Kimball Farm Ice Cream and Restaurant, Route 124, Jaffrey, N.H.; (603) 532–5765. Enjoy your giant cones (even the "small" size comes with a dish for the overflow) in their grove of hemlock and birch trees, where there are benches and picnic tables. Or order a meal from the full menu of carry-out favorites, eating outside or in their dining room. $

Lindy's Diner, 19 Gilbo Avenue, just off Main Street, Keene, N.H.; (603) 352–4273. This small family diner has for many years been a popular spot for politicians to stop and meet the people, and their placemats have the pictures to prove it. Offering traditional but not-too-greasy diner fare and breakfast all day (the eggs Benedict are excellent). $

Ocean Harvest, 433 Winchester Street, Keene, N.H.; (603)

357–3553. Open Tuesday through Saturday, usually from 11:00 A.M. to 8:00 P.M. (later if they're busy) and until 7:00 P.M. on Sunday. Drive right past the franchise eateries around the intersection of Route 10 (Winchester Street) and Route 101/9 to Keene's best fried clams and shrimp, broiled scallops, and fish sandwiches. $–$$

Sampan Restaurant, Main Street (Route 9), Hillsborough, N.H.; (603) 464–3663. Family-owned and family-friendly, this Chinese restaurant has specials almost nightly. Monday often brings two-for-one dinners; Tuesday is an all-you-can-eat buffet for $8.50 (half price for kids); Wednesday is "kids' night" with **free** gifts. The staff will spoil your kids rotten any night. $–$$

Thai Garden, 118 Main Street, Keene, NH; (603) 357–4567. Wonderful traditional Thai food, with excellent service that is more than welcoming to children. $–$$

Where to Stay

The Chesterfield Inn, Route 9, Chesterfield, N.H., 3 miles east of I–91 exit 3; (603) 256–3211 or (800) 365–5515. Cable TV, data ports, lounge, afternoon tea, baby-sitting available. Kids under 6 **free,** minimum stays may apply during special events and high season. $$$

The Currier's House, 5 Harkness Road, Jaffrey Center, N.H.; (603) 532–7670; www.the curriershouse.com. This charming 1810 home is located in a quiet village setting and welcomes children. $–$$

Green Meadow Nature Escape, Route 123, Acworth, N.H.; (603) 835–6580; www.tamarackfarm.com. This unusual bed-and-breakfast is on a 400-acre farm owned by the sixth generation of the same family. They welcome children, who are always fascinated by all the farm activities. You can watch or join in gathering maple sap in late winter or haying in the summer. You can also hike the many trails that lead from the farm. $

For More Information

Greater Peterborough Chamber of Commerce, Route 101 (P.O. Box 401), Peterborough, NH 03458; (603) 924–7234; www.roninhouse.com/gpcoc.

Brattleboro, Dummerston, Putney, Newfane

The back-to-the-land movement of the 1960s blends comfortably into the New Age in laid-back Brattleboro and Putney, Vermont. Main Street shops of both towns are rich in ethnic clothing, crafts, books, and natural foods, and an easy informality makes travel with children especially enjoyable here.

The Belle of Brattleboro (all ages)

Off Route 5 (Putney Road), just north of downtown Brattleboro, Vt., and 1.3 miles south of I-91 exit 3 traffic circle, next to the Marina Restaurant; (802) 254–1263; www.vermontmarina. com/Pages/cruiseboat.html. Wednesday through Sunday, cruises usually at noon and 4:00 P.M. Fare: $–$$, under age 4 free. Call for weekly schedule changes and reservations.

The *Belle* is a forty-nine-passenger wooden boat built in 1985 by Vermont craftsmen, highlighted by its mahogany tables and benches. This nonprofit, community-sponsored educational organization offers sightseeing cruises on the Connecticut River, narrated by Captain Aaron Betts. His knowledge of the area and of local wildlife adds a strong educational aspect to this relaxing ride, as well as making it interesting to all ages. You may pack your own picnic and eat at the tables or make prior arrangements to have food waiting for you. Snacks and nonalcoholic beverages are available on all cruises, and there is a waterfront restaurant next to the dock for those who want full service. Two-hour music cruises and sunset cruises are also available.

Vermont Canoe Touring Center, Inc. (ages 8 and up)

Located at the Veterans Memorial Bridge at West River, 1.3 miles south of I-91 exit 3 and just north of downtown Brattleboro, Vt.; (802) 257–5008. Open Memorial Day to Labor Day, seven days a week, 9:00 A.M. until dusk; Labor Day to Columbus Day open weekends (weather permitting); open also by appointment. Canoe and one- or two-person kayaks may be rented by the hour, day, or week with other combinations available. Life jackets, paddles, and parking are included.

The Vermont Canoe Touring Center offers families the chance to paddle peacefully along the Connecticut River, among the tall grasses in the oxbow, or up West River in either canoes or kayaks. With permission, rentals may be transported on your vehicle to your choice of locations to experience a wide variety of the area's scenic waterways. A shuttle service is offered to locations north and south on the Connecticut, as well as west to the Somerset and Harriman Reservoirs and east to Spofford Lake. While the Connecticut River is quite benign here in the summer, those who prefer no current at all might want to try the oxbow, a wide expanse of calm water that creates marshes and surrounds islands above the junction of the West River and the Connecticut River.

Bonnyvale Environmental Education Center (ages vary with program)

Off Route 5, Dummerston, Vt. (south of Brattleboro); (802) 257–5785. Most trips **free.**

The center has a busy schedule of outdoor activities, exploring local wildlife through hikes and walks accompanied by astronomers, geologists, zoologists, botanists, and other experts. A typical program might consider the world of raptors or examine an old-growth forest. Most of the trips are **free** but require advance registration. The Sunday morning "A.M. Ambles," also **free**, doesn't require registration: just show up at 8:30 A.M. on Sunday at the appointed place. Past ambles (about two hours long) have explored Putney Mountain, West River, and Hamilton Falls.

Brattleboro Retreat Petting Farm (all ages)

Route 30, ¼ mile past the Brattleboro Retreat entrance, on the left. Open 2:00 to 6:00 P.M. daily. Admission: $

The petting farm offers an opportunity for children to learn about and interact with all sorts of farm animals, some (such as the emus) quite exotic. Daily demonstrations show how cows are milked by hand and by machine, and visitors have the chance to feed Holstein calves and scratch the piglets' bellies. The relaxed family atmosphere encourages leisurely visits, and you are welcome to commune with the wide variety of animals for as long as you wish.

Brattleboro Museum and Art Center (ages vary with exhibits)

Union Station, left off I–91 exit 1, at the junction of Canal Street and Main Street, Brattleboro, Vt.; (802) 257–0124. Open mid-May through October, noon to 6:00 P.M. daily; closed Monday and holidays. **Free.**

This community museum, located in the handsome former railway station, may have special exhibits on nearly any subject, from Brattleboro's famous Estey organ factory to the farms along the Connecticut River. Performances and programs often add a greater dimension to the subject of the exhibit. Call ahead to find out if the current exhibit is one that will appeal to your family.

Brattleboro Farmers Market (all ages)

Route 9, just west of town, 1/2 mile from I–91 exit 2, May through October, Saturday 9:00 A.M. to 2:00 P.M. **Free.**

It's clear from the minute you enter the friendly circle of booths at this longtime Brattleboro favorite that children are welcome. A big sandbox beckons, and if you visit around

Local **Web Sites**

www.brattleboro.com

www.putney.net

www.reformer.com

www.southernvermont.com

lunchtime, there will be musicians performing, usually with a ring of children sitting on the grass at their feet. Local farmers and craftsmen bring their own children, so there will always be someone to play with. At lunchtime you'll find plenty of healthy foods from all cultures, but no hamburgers or hot dogs. Along with a few fine crafts, look for the products of local farms: dried flower wreaths, herb vinegars, fruit jams, pies, juicy berries, hard-to-find vegetables, apple cider, fresh-baked breads, cheese, maple syrup, and organic honey. Picnic tables invite you to spend a while over your lunch and enjoy the music. On Wednesday in the summer, you can stop for lunch at an abbreviated version of the Farmers Market on Main Street from 10:00 A.M. to 2:00 P.M.

The Robb Family Farm (all ages)

827 Ames Hill Road, West Brattleboro, Vt. (take Route 9 west to Christy's, then left onto Greenleaf Street, 1.5 miles to Ames Hill Road, and 1.5 miles to farm); (802) 257–0163 or (888) 318–9087; www.robbfamilyfarm.com. Open year-round from 6:00 A.M. to 6:00 P.M. Free to visit, rates vary for activities.

This family-owned and -operated dairy and maple farm is a great educational opportunity—not to mention great fun—for all ages. They offer horse-drawn hayrides for children and teach about the maple sugaring process and dairy farming.

Madame Cheri Forest (ages 3 and up)

From the Brattleboro traffic circle, go east 0.4 mile, over the Connecticut River bridge, and take a right onto Gulf Road. Take the first left, which will keep you on Gulf Road. Go 2.3 miles and the parking area will be on the right, across from the intersection with Egypt Road, Chesterfield, N.H. For more information, visit www.chesterfieldoutdoors.com.

The Madame Cheri Forest is a local favorite, and not just for its great hiking trails. The main attraction at Madame Cheri's is the ruins of her grand old home. Walking straight up the overgrown carriage path, visitors will be greeted by the stone foundation and impressive arched stairway that once led to a second floor sunning porch. In the 1930s and 1940s, Cheri was a mystery to conservative New Englanders, throwing lavish parties for her Zigfield Follies friends from New York City and otherwise shocking her staid New Hampshire neighbors. She was even rumored to have driven around Brattleboro in the heat of summer wearing nothing but her fur coat. The legacy of this flamboyant flapper and of her once-grand home has fascinated locals for a long time, but your kids will like it because it's the closest they'll get to a ruined castle in New England. Because of the tall, free-standing staircase, careful supervision of children is recommended.

For those who would like to explore the nearly 500-acre forest, there are trail maps at the parking area. Hikers can opt for a 0.4-mile easy walk along the shore of Beaver Pond or may choose to scale Mount Wantasiquet, which offers a breathtaking bird's-eye view of Brattleboro.

Putter's Paradise (ages 2 and up)

At Hidden Acres Camping Resort, Putney Road, 2.5 miles north of Brattleboro on Route 5, off I–91 exit 3; (802) 254–2098. Open from 9:00 A.M. to 8:00 P.M. daily, May 15 to October 15, weather permitting.

Putter's Paradise offers an eighteen-hole miniature golf course as well as a game room for the non-golfers of the family. There is also a snack bar with ice cream on site.

Putney Mountain (all ages)

West Mountain Road, Putney, Vt. Daylight hours. Free.

Although it's only 1,600 feet high, this mountain west of the village center has a 360-degree view of the river and valley and of all the surrounding hills and mountains. The easy trail begins near the Putney School, a private academy. From the top you can also watch hawks soaring on the thermals. In the center of Putney, in front of the town hall, look for a hawk count; there's often one posted.

Santa's Land (ages 12 and under)

Route 5, Putney, Vt.; (802) 387–5550 or (800) 726–8299; www.santasland.com. Open Memorial Day through December 24, seven days a week (weather permitting), 10:00 A.M. to 6:00 P.M. (gates close at 5:00 P.M.). Admission: $$–$$$, under 3 free.

Santa's Land is a traditional theme park for children, offering a Christmas village and visits with Santa. Children can play with the animals at the petting zoo or walk through the reindeer forest. There are also attractions such as a miniature train ride, a carousel, and a giant slide. You can also mingle with costumed characters throughout the park. Don't miss a stop at the Igloo Pancake House for a snack.

Ice-**Skating**

- **The Retreat Meadows,** Route 30, Brattleboro. During the winter, an area is cleared of snow for ice-skating. Please check the conditions before skating to be sure there are no thin ice patches. Ice fishing is popular at this spot as well.

- **Memorial Park,** take a left off Route 9 (at I–91 exit 2) over the covered bridge, then your first right; (802) 257–2311. The ice rink is lighted for evening skating, and you can rent skates there.

Jelly Mill Falls (ages 3 and up)

Route 30, Dummerston, Vt., northwest from Brattleboro about 3.5 miles. Just north of Stickney Brook Road, look for a small parking pull-out on the left. A very short trail leads to the falls. Daylight hours. Free.

Picture a wide stone staircase with a cool mountain brook splashing down its center, its edges shaded by overhanging trees. Put barefoot kids in the middle of the picture and a picnic basket on one side, and you have what summer is all about. What we like best about Jelly Mill Falls is that the steps are low and the flat parts long and barely sloping, so even small children can wade and splash there safely. On a hot day, it's a place for bathing suits; the rest of the time it's shallow enough for bare feet and rolled-up pant legs. The name comes from the old mill that once stood beside the falls, the stone foundations of which you can still see.

Newfane Flea Market (all ages)

Route 30, Newfane, Vt. Sunday from the beginning of June to the end of October. Free to browse.

This enormous flea market with more than 150 booths has become a local institution, nearing legend. The flea market has been here for more than a quarter of a century, and its unique mixture of professional dealers and one-time yard sale vendors gives everyone a chance to find a treasure or two—or that beloved junk they've always looked for. The trinkets and junk, as well as the toys that are always for sale, will keep the kids happy while you find your bargain antiques. There is plenty of food and parking on site.

Where to Eat

Anon's Thai Cuisine, 4 Fairground Road, Brattleboro VT; (802) 257-1376. The salad rolls are out of this world! $$

Brattleboro Food Co-op, Brookside Plaza, Main Street, Brattleboro, Vt.; (802) 257–0236. Deli within a market includes a salad bar and juice bar and specializes in organic choices. You can eat there or carry it out for a picnic. $

Chelsea Diner, Route 9, West Brattleboro, Vt., across from the state police barracks; (802) 254–8399. This diner is traditional in every way—from its classic boxcar exterior to the homemade fare on the menu. In addi-tion to the expected dishes, however, is a great selection of less typical choices, plus weekend Mexican food specials. For break-fast, try their French toast with pure Vermont maple syrup. Entrees are inexpensive, and there is always a children's menu available, with friendly waitstaff to accommodate the picky ones. $

Curtis' Barbecue, 40 Old Depot Road (Route 5 off I–91 exit 4), Putney, Vt.; (802) 387–5474. Open Tuesday through Sunday, 10:00 A.M. to dark. Curtis' is a local favorite, more for its atmosphere than for the finesse of its cuisine. Very laid-back, outdoor picnic table dining; offers barbecue chicken and ribs. $–$$

Dhaba, 1380 Putney Road, Brattleboro, Vt.; (802) 254–8702. Excellent authentic Indian food, unlike any other. Tandoori oven on site, and the waitstaff is great with kids. All ages love the mango lassi! $$

The Marina Restaurant, West River, Putney Road, Brattleboro, Vt.; (802) 257–7563. Overlooks the Retreat Meadows and West River, with beautiful sunsets and a view of Brattleboro's own sea serpent in the water. Burgers and seafood, served in front of a fireplace in the winter. $$

Panda North, Putney Road, Brattleboro, Vt.; (802) 257–4578. Impossible to miss with the huge TEA sign overhead, they serve both Chinese food and Sushi. $–$$

Putney Hearth Bakery and Coffee House, Putney Tavern Building, Route 5, Putney, Vt.; (802) 387–2100. Open Monday through Saturday 7:00 A.M. to 5:00 P.M. and Sunday 8:00 A.M. to 3:00 P.M. Coffee, fresh-baked pastries, and sandwiches are served in a relaxed cafe, with tables inside or on the long front porch of the historic building. The adjacent Heartstone Books has a welcoming reading nook surrounded by children's books, some new and some used. Browse or create your own impromptu story hour daily from 10:00 A.M. to 7:00 P.M. $

Vermont Country Deli and Cafe, Route 9 off I–91 exit 2, Brattleboro, Vt.; (802) 257–9254. Excellent deli food and pastries, perfect for packing a gourmet picnic. There is no dining area, but right down the street are picnic tables by the red covered bridge. $

Walker's Restaurant, 132 Main Street, Brattleboro, Vt.; (802) 254–6046. This downtown restaurant serves well-prepared steaks and seafood, along with sandwiches, burgers, and chili, in a relaxed, friendly environment. $–$$

Where to Stay

Brattleboro North KOA and Motel Cottages, Route 5, East Dummerston, Vt.; (802) 254–5908 or (800) 562–5909. Campground and motel cottages, with game room, laundry, and play areas. $

The Coach House Inn, River Bend Lodge and Restaurant, Route 30, Newfane, Vt.; (802) 365–7952. Friendly; offers kitchenette suites for families. $–$$

Dalem's Chalet, 78 South Street, West Brattleboro, Vt.; (802) 254–4323 or (800) 462–5009; www.dalemschalet.com. Set on a hillside of twenty-five acres, Dalem's has warm European atmosphere. Ponds and swans adorn the landscape. $–$$

The Putney Inn, Depot Road, I–91 exit 4, Putney, Vt.; (802) 387–5517 or (800) 653–5517; www.putneyinn.com. Large, modern rooms all have their own outside entrances. Breakfast is included; pets are welcome. The dining room has a friendly staff and serves favorite New England dishes made from fresh local ingredients. Children under 14 stay **free.** $$–$$$

For More Information

Brattleboro Chamber of Commerce, 182 Main Street, Brattleboro, VT 05301; (802) 254–4565; www.brattleboro.com.

Camping in Vermont

Camping in Vermont If your family likes to camp and you want to ensure a space during your vacation, call ahead and reserve one. Depending on the area and campground, there may be a minimum stay requirement for reservations, usually two to four nights. Reservations can be made during business hours, starting in January. Each of the four regions may be contacted, or you can visit the Vermont-wide Web site at www.vtstateparks.com.

For reservations:

> Northeast: (800) 658–6934
>
> Northwest: (800) 252–2363
>
> Southeast: (800) 299–3071
>
> Southwest: (800) 658–1622

Charlestown–Springfield Area

This strip of towns along the Connecticut River offers historical and educational sites of interest to children. Although the region straddles the river, it is brought together by one of the few toll bridges left between the two states (50 cents). It would be easy to spend at least a day or two checking out the activities around here.

The Fort at No. 4 (ages 3 and up)

Route 11, 1 mile north of village of Charlestown, N.H.; (603) 826–5700. Open 10:00 A.M. to 4:30 P.M., seven days a week, late May through October. Admission: $$, age 5 and under free.

This fort is a living-history museum, re-creating the 1744 settlement. Located on the Connecticut River, this town was prone to attacks during the French and Indian War, so the community fortified it. Today, the completely reconstructed fort is alive with costumed "residents" who show your family how they cooked, made clothes, lived, and defended their town. Every aspect of life has been re-created, down to the working blacksmith shop and farm animals. Visit the Great Hall, explore the defense towers along the river, or watch the musket-firing demonstrations.

Weekend activities begin with a Native American Planting Moon Festival in late May, celebrating the Abenaki's planting of their spring crops. Revolutionary War weekend in early June brings reenactors who portray British regulars and American militiamen in an encounter.

Springfield Art and Historical Society and Miller Art Center

(ages 7 and up) 🎨

9 Elm Street, Springfield, Vt.; (802) 885-2415. Open
mid-April to the end of October, Tuesday through Friday
10:00 A.M. to 4:00 P.M. and Saturday 2:00 to 5:00 P.M. **Free.**

Alongside a great variety of Springfield historical information,
this museum is a shrine of sorts to the country's first doll manufacturer, Joel Ellis. His vision was inspired by a discontent with the
world of stiff, unmovable dolls. Ellis designed the first dolls with
joints that enabled them to move and pose, bringing lifelike playmates
into children's playrooms everywhere. His idea was patented in the late
1800s and was the beginning of dolls as we know them.

How **Bogs** Are Formed

"A Spring-fed pond gathers no moss."

People have found bogs creepy and scary since they first began losing their
farm animals into them. While it is unlikely that a sheep would fall through
the small Springfield bog, other, larger bogs can be very dangerous—so dangerous, in fact, that they are the origin of our term boogie-man. But bogs are
actually just natural holes scooped out by glaciers, which then melted and
made small ponds called kettle ponds.

　　Over thousands of years, plant life (mainly sphagnum moss) begins to
grow around the edges and onto the surface of these ponds. Since these,
unlike most ponds, have no source of water (such as a spring or a brook
flowing in and out), the water is very acidic. Only a few plants can grow in
such an environment. But sphagnum moss thrives here. As it continues to
grow, the roots of previous years' moss grow thicker and thicker, eventually
forming a bed or mat right out over the top of the water. If this goes on long
enough, it can fill an entire pond, and the layers and layers of dead moss pack
down tightly to become a peat bog. In large bogs, you can still see the pond in
the middle, and there is open water underneath the mat. This makes them
very dangerous to walk on unless there is a boardwalk to support you. In the
Springfield bog, even though you probably won't fall through and drown, it is
still important to stay on the boardwalk to protect the fragile plants and to
keep your feet dry.

Springfield Bog (ages 4 and up)

Follow Route 11 west from Springfield, Vt. (River Street), take a right at Springfield Middle School, follow road 1.9 miles and park on left. The entrance to the trail is not obvious. Opposite the large pile of cement rubble, there is an earth barrier that closes off the old road. Climb over this, and follow the old road up to where you see signs for the bog on the right; (802) 885–2779. Daylight hours. Free.

The Springfield bog is more than 10,000 years old. As you enter the bog, be sure to pick up the orienteering sheet supplied by the town of Springfield and the Audubon Society, and make sure the kids have their compasses. Be sure to stay right on the boardwalk because the bog is fragile and you can fall through if you step off the walk. The "superdeck" walkway is specially designed to float on the bog and become part of it so the ecosystem isn't disturbed. It also allows you to feel like you are walking on the mosses yourself, as it moves up and down when you walk.

The plant life of the bog includes peat mosses, bog cranberries, and the fascinating carnivorous pitcher plant. The sour little cranberries can be picked and eaten when red. The pitcher plants, distinctly shaped as their name describes, collect water in their long, tubelike bodies. Insects land on the outer rim of the plant, and thanks to tiny little hairs, slide down into the pool of water, drowning. The plant then secretes its digestive juices in the water and "eats" the bug!

Udderly Delicious Ice Cream (all ages)

River Street, Springfield, Vt.

This mobile ice-cream stand is hard to miss: A truck painted to look like a giant cow is set off to the side of the road overlooking the Black River. As the story on the blackboard relates, Wendy's husband grew up on a dairy farm and wouldn't let her get a pet cow, so she painted her truck to look like one. And now the stand serves up fifty-four flavors of soft-serve, eighteen flavors of regular ice cream, special original sundaes, flurries, and even a great variety of "healthy" smoothies with plenty of add-ins to suit your tastes. Generous servings, reasonable prices.

The Eureka Schoolhouse (all ages)

Route 11, Springfield, Vt.; (802) 828–3051. Open late May through mid-October, 10:00 A.M. to 4:00 P.M., closed Tuesday. Free.

This fully restored 1785 schoolhouse was moved by concerned citizens in the 1950s to its present location. It is the oldest public school building still intact in Vermont, and one of the few public buildings from its time still standing. The school was originally constructed by a trapper and friend of the natives, William Bettergneau, who was supported in his efforts by a few families in the area. Bettergneau painted the schoolhouse yellow and gave it a blue roof. The school's first teacher was a Yale graduate named David Searle. According to legend, the school's name came from this enthusiastic young teacher's exclamation upon seeing his future school.

Unfortunately, the population of the area dwindled over the next century, and the school closed in 1900. After being recognized as an important site by area residents, the schoolhouse was gradually restored with the help of the Vermont Historic Sites Commission. The final touches were made for its historic reopening in 1968. The building is now furnished with antiques and actual items that were used at the school during its 115 years of operation and has many unique characteristics of buildings from its era, including twenty-four-pane windows. The friendly staff can also give you information about other historical sites in the area. The Springfield Area Chamber of Commerce operates the tours of the schoolhouse, and all maintenance is done by the Vermont Division for Historic Preservation.

The Green Mountain Flyer (all ages)

54 Depot Street, Bellows Falls, Vt.; (802) 707–3530 or (802) 463–3069; www.rails-vt.com. Morning and afternoon departures (call or visit the Web site for current schedule) June through October. Admission: $$–$$$, under age 3 free when held.

This old-fashioned train takes you on an ambling journey from Bellows Falls to the Chester depot, with a twenty-minute rest in the quaint little town before the return trip. The train, which was built in the 1930s, takes its time as it courses over the scenic rails of Vermont, so passengers have time to appreciate the views. Announcements tell you all about the interesting sights of the area as you pass the oldest covered bridge in the county, the Brockways Mill Gorge, and other points of interest. Windows open for comfort and good viewing and picture-taking, but do make sure everyone keeps his or her head inside. In Chester, be sure to stop by the Bay Window Caboose or the nearby country store and deli to grab a picnic lunch to eat at the tables or on the train. Beverages are available in the dining car.

Hugging Bear Inn and Shoppe (all ages)

244 Main Street, Chester, Vt.; (802) 875–2414, (800) 325–0519; www.huggingbear.com. Free to visit.

The Hugging Bear is not only an inn, but a marvelous 150-year-old Victorian house as well. After shopping in the creative gift shop, stop by and admire the 1905 carriage house. Constructed in the Colonial Revival style, it has a gambrel roof, a loft gable, and a cute cupola adorning the roof. Even if you are not staying at this great, family-oriented inn, you are welcome to visit.

Stellafane (all ages)

Breezy Hill, off Route 143, Springfield, Vt.; www.stellafane.com. After dark on a clear night. Free.

The name stellafane means "shrine to the stars," and that is the perfect description for this unique hilltop. Since 1926, astronomers have gathered on the top of Breezy Hill one weekend a summer to enjoy the spectacular views of the stars and meteor showers. The gathering is sponsored by Springfield Telescope Makers. Even if your trip doesn't coincide with the convention, bring a blanket and perch yourself on this hill on a summer night to experience the ultimate in stargazing, far from bothersome city lights. Mid- to late-August is the best time to see meteor showers, but anytime is good to explore the constellations at Stellafane.

Grafton Museum of Natural History (ages 6 and up)

Main Street, Grafton, Vt.; (802) 843–2111; www.sover.net/~gmnh/. Open 1:00 P.M. to 4:00 P.M. weekends and holidays from Memorial Day through Columbus Day and by appointment. Donation requested; children free.

This small community museum explains the natural environment of southern Vermont with live and interactive exhibits that encourage kids to watch bees make honey or learn why some rocks glow in the dark.

Grafton Blacksmith Shop (ages 6 and up)

School Street, Grafton, Vt. Open Thursday through Monday, June through October 10:00 A.M. to 3:00 P.M.; demonstrations 11:00 A.M. to noon and 1:00 P.M. to 4:00 P.M. Free.

Here kids can see the tools of ironworking and watch a blacksmith create nails, hinges, and other small items from red-hot metal. Follow the trail (used in winter by cross-country skiers) across sheep-filled meadows, past an exhibit on sheep and wool, and through the small covered bridge to Grafton's **Village Cheese Company,** on Townshend Road; (802) 843–2221 or (800) GRAFTON; open weekdays 8:00 A.M. to 4:00 P.M., weekends 10:00 A.M. to 4:00 P.M.

Grafton Swimming Pond (all ages)

West of the village on Route 121, after the paving ends. Daylight hours. Free.

Never crowded, this small beach has a roped-off area for youngsters, but you'll have to be the lifeguard, since it's unstaffed. But it's about as pleasant a little beach as you will find, and a real surprise in heavily touristed Grafton.

Watershed Center and Fish Ladder (all ages)

At the falls in the middle of Bellows Falls, Vt.; (802) 843–2111; www.nature-museum.org/river.htm. Open May 24 through August 31; Saturday 10:00 A.M. to 4:00 P.M., Sunday noon to 4:00 P.M. Ladder operates mid-June to early July, exhibits all year. Free.

The salmon migrating up the Connecticut River to lay their eggs were able to jump the falls before the dam was built, but they need some help now. The ladder provides them with a route around the falls and you can watch them migrating each year.

Where to Eat

Joy Wah, Route 5, Rockingham, Vt.; (802) 463–9761. Good Chinese food with a gorgeous view of the river. $

Oona's Restaurant, on the square in Bellows Falls, Vt.; (802) 463–9830. Great food, laid-back atmosphere. On Thursday nights, there is live music including country-western and blues, with a cover charge of $7.00 that is well worth it. $$

Penelope's, Main Street on the square, Springfield, Vt.; (802) 885–9186. A casual lunch spot in the center of town, Penelope's serves generous sandwiches, soups, and salads plus a long list of entrees. Although there's a lounge, they separate clienteles smoothly and it's very popular with families. The evening menu is standard American salads, burgers, and light fare. $

Where to Stay

Hartness House Inn, 30 Orchard Street, Springfield, Vt.; (802) 885–2115 or (800) 732–4789. Hartness House still seems like a gracious private mansion welcoming house-guests. The interior has been carefully restored and decorated with antiques and reproductions of turn-of-the-twentieth-century furnishings. Fireplaces add to its air of Victorian comfort. Every evening a volunteer guide takes guests to tour the historic observatory and see the antique telescope built by the original owner. "Weekend Getaway" packages make winter stays even more economical. Baby-sitting is available and children under 14 stay **free.** $$–$$$. Hartness House has a children's menu in its dining room, which serves lunch on weekdays only, dinner Monday through Saturday. Meals: $$

Hugging Bear Inn and Shoppe, 244 Main Street, Chester, Vt.; (802) 875–2414 or (800) 325–0519; www.huggingbear.com. Children

and families always welcome; hearty, plentiful breakfast included; living room, outdoor smoking porches. See the listing in the attractions section for more information. $–$$

The Old Tavern at Grafton, Main Street, off Route 35; (802) 843–2231 or (800) 843–1801. This historic inn prefers not to have children under 7, but the excellent dining room does have a children's menu. There is nowhere else in Grafton to stay, but Chester is close by. $$–$$$

For More Information

The Chester Area Chamber of Commerce, P.O. Box 623, Chester, VT 05143; (802) 875–2939.

Grafton Information Center, next to the Old Tavern, Grafton, Vt.; (802) 843–2255.

Windsor, Mount Ascutney, and Ludlow

This region of Vermont is best known for its incredible ski mountains. Because of the area's large resorts, there are many overpriced shops and restaurants, but there are still gems to be found among the hubbub. This is a great region to vacation in if you don't want to go too far. You'll have plenty of things to keep you occupied.

Okemo Mountain Resort (all ages)

312 Mountain Road, Ludlow, Vt.; (802) 228–6668 or (800) 78–OKEMO; www.okemo.com. Rates vary.

This is a large, full-scale resort. In the winter, Okemo is well known for excellent snowmaking and a great selection of intermediate trails, as well as beginner and expert trails. Private and group lessons are taught by an experienced staff. Many families take advantage of the slopeside condos, which provide that perfect central rendezvous place for parents and children. Teens will appreciate having their own club, Altitude After Dark, which offers a place for them to socialize in a safe environment, watch movies, play sports, dance to the DJ's music, or relax in the game room.

Summer brings plenty of great stuff too, like the Okemo Valley Golf Club, which offers pro lessons, an indoor practice area, virtual golf, and a fully stocked Pro Shop. Penguin Playground—a day camp for kids ages six to twelve—offers sports, field trips, fishing, hiking, swimming, and plenty of fun. Whatever your interests, there is more than enough to do at Okemo in the summer.

Okemo has ample ski and snowboard shops. In late September, it is home to the Fall Foliage Craft Fair, which has free admission and more than fifty artisans and craftspeople from the area. During this fair and on weekends during foliage season, the mountain's chairlift offers scenic rides to the top for spectacular foliage viewing.

Ascutney Mountain Resort (ages 3 and up)

Route 44, Brownsville, Vt.; (800) 243-0011; www.ascutney.com. Rates vary, but kids 6 and under always ski free. Specials for Vermont and New Hampshire residents and college students.

Ascutney stands alone, overlooking the Connecticut River at a height of 3,144 feet, one of the few of Vermont's ski areas that's not in the Green Mountains. Small and self-contained, it has always treasured its family clientele by offering many thoughtful extras. Sidewinders, a teen nightclub at the resort, is one.

Ski school includes both group and private lessons, and you can get group lesson packages with lift tickets. Full- and half-day children's programs are divided into age groups: age three to six (childcare is available with or without lessons), four to seven with instruction, and eight to twelve with instruction. The ten-acre self-contained Learn-To-Slide Park has its own lift, and the resort has a self-contained kids' learning area as well.

Ascutney also offers a good variety of summer activities for the entire family. A great opportunity for vacationers is the day camp for children, which enables them to have a fun, educational day while parents do all that "boring" stuff like museums and antiques shops. The camp offers nature hikes for a range of age groups; art programs; and plenty of other activities to keep youngsters happy. While your kids are at camp, you can swim in one of the pools, take tennis lessons with a pro player, or take your own relaxing hike through one of the many trails that garnish the mountain. Special packages and other group and family activities are offered as well, so be sure to call and see what's going on during your trip.

Wellwood Orchard (ages 3 and up)

529 Wellwood Orchard Road, Springfield, Vt. Take Valley Street from Springfield, about 3 miles, and look for signs; (802) 263-5200; www.sover.net/~wellwood/. Open mid-August to November 1. Free to visit.

Pick your own McIntosh, Cortland, Delicious, Northern Spies, and Heritage varieties of apples while you enjoy a view of Mount Ascutney. The farm also has a petting zoo, bunnies, and wagon rides through the orchards. Choose the perfect pumpkin from their patch while you're there.

Dorsey Park (all ages)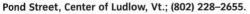
Pond Street, Center of Ludlow, Vt.; (802) 228–2655.

Ice-skating rink and tennis courts run by the Ludlow Recreation Department.

Where to Eat

Leslie's, Route 5, Rockingham, Vt., just off I–91 exit 6; (802) 463–4929. Fresh ingredients are important to the owners, who tend 250 tomato plants in a typical summer. Custom wooden furnishings are both stylish and casual; parents and children alike will be comfortable here. The chef prepares chicken and pasta dishes specially designed for children. $$

Windsor Station Restaurant, Depot Avenue, Windsor, Vt.; (802) 674–2052. Open Tuesday through Sunday 5:30 to 9:00 P.M. This former Boston & Maine Depot was built a hundred years ago, and after many years as a rail station, it has been restored as a family-run restaurant. Chicken Kiev, roast duckling, and Mama's pasta with seafood are the specialties. $$

Where to Stay

Ascutney Mountain Resort, Brownsville, Vt.; (802) 484–7711 or (800) 243–0011. Nearly 300 condo units right at the base of the mountain are convenient for skiing families in the winter and bargain priced in the summer. A restaurant, complete fitness center, indoor pool, and shops give it all the amenities, but without the pseudo-European glitz of some slopeside villages. This low-key place is great for families who don't need the packaged entertainment many resorts offer. $–$$ summer, $$–$$$ winter

Button Farm Lodge, Brownsville, Vt.; (802) 484–3300. This cozy B&B is very reasonably priced; a third night added onto a weekend is half price. On the property are Christmas trees, a good sledding hill, walking trails, a pond for skating, and trails for cross-country skiing and snowshoeing. $–$$

Echo Lake Inn, Route 100, Tyson, Vt.; (802) 228–8602 or (800) 356–6844. Rooms in the main building, with larger condo units in an adjacent building that was once a cheese factory. Suitable for children over 6; baby-sitting is available. $$–$$$

For More Information

Mount Ascutney Region Chamber of Commerce, P.O. Box 5, Windsor, VT 05089; (802) 674–5910.

Ludlow Area Chamber of Commerce, P.O. Box 333, Ludlow, VT 05149; (802) 228–5830.

Woodstock and Quechee

This lovely area is rich in nature and farming activities for the whole family. There are plenty of things going on at all times, and the region will give you a taste of true Vermont.

Quechee Gorge (ages 3 and up)

Take Route 4 west from White River Junction toward Woodstock, Vt. (you can't miss the gorge because the road goes right over the middle of it), park at either end of the bridge; (802) 295–2990. Open daylight hours. Free.

There is no denying that a big hole in the ground is cool. This one was carved by a river that rushed through more than 13,000 years ago as the glaciers began to melt and carry sand, gravel, and boulders in their waters. The glacier here ground a deeper and deeper channel through the solid rock, until it made this gorge, 160 feet deep and more than a half a mile long. The best place to see and appreciate the size of the gorge is from the highway bridge that crosses its center. Sidewalks create safe viewing points from both sides of the road, and an underpass at the east end (toward White River Junction) gets you safely from one side to the other.

To get "up-close and personal" with the gorge, follow the trail south from the east side, near the underpass. This takes you along the edge of the vertical walls in safety and wind its way down to the river level. About halfway down, there is a well-fenced overlook where you can see the river and the series of small falls that have created potholes in the riverbed. When you get to the bottom, although you will see people hopping across rocks in the river if the water is low, you should not follow them. Upstream is a dam from which water is sometimes released, and that causes the river to rise dramatically in a very short time. Ask for an informational booklet at the station at the end of the gorge near the underpass. It includes a trail map and good diagrams that explain how the gorge was formed.

Vermont Raptor Center, Vermont Institute of Natural Science

(ages 6 and up) 🚶 🐘 🍁

Churchill Road, Woodstock, Vt., which runs from the top of The Green in the center of Woodstock, just to the left of St. James Church. The Raptor Center is about 1.5 miles on your right; (802) 457–2779; www.vinsweb.org. Open daily May through October 10:00 A.M. to 4:00 P.M. and Monday through Saturday 10:00 A.M. to 4:00 P.M. the rest of the year. Admission: $–$$, age 4 and under free.

Injured birds of prey are brought to Woodstock from all over the state and treated here before being released back into the wild. Those raptors who are too badly injured to survive in the wild remain here in a homelike habitat where you can see them. There are usually more than forty birds, which may represent as many as twenty-six species. You may see bald eagles, peregrine falcons, and any number of owls. The institute has programs and guided tours Monday through Saturday from June through the end of October. The "Encounter with Birds of Prey" is held at 11:00 A.M.; a guided tour of the Raptor Center takes place at 12:30 P.M.; and a demonstration of raptors in flight is given at 2:30 P.M.

Other special programs take place during the year, including field trips specially designed for children. Next to the Raptor Center, two trails show how animals and plants depend on each other and on the earth. Stations along the way illustrate these relationships, which are explained in illustrated booklets for sale at the reception desk or for loan at the beginning of each trail. On the Communities Trail, one station has a special section where walkers are challenged to close their eyes and use their senses of touch, hearing, and smell as they follow a rope along the path through the woods.

Billings Farm Museum (all ages)

River Road, Woodstock, Vt., half a mile from The Green; (802) 457–2355; www.billingsfarm. org. Open daily May 1 through October 31, 10:00 A.M. to 5:00 P.M. and weekends in December same hours. Admission: $–$$, under age 3 **free.**

The Billings Farm is a step back in time to Vermont's rural roots. The working dairy farm has been operating since 1871, when it began as a "gentleman farm" where cattle imported from the Isle of Jersey were raised. (The term "gentleman farm" refers to one owned by a wealthy person, usually in the Victorian era, who did not depend upon the farm for his livelihood.) Today, it is a living farm. It features a horse barn, calf nursery, dairy barn, milk room, and other display areas that show the seasonal activities that once occupied the lives of Vermont farm families. The restored farmhouse includes the family's living quarters, the farm office, and the creamery, the house's most interesting feature for children. Here they can watch butter appear almost magically from cream as it is churned.

Begin your tour here by watching the film *A Place in the Land,* which describes not only the farm and it history, but also the adjacent parklands that extend up Mount Tom. Activities are interesting here every day, but special weekend programs throughout the season highlight certain features of farming and rural life. In May, a special Spring Farm Festival features sheep shearing and a number of craft demonstrations, and admission is only $1.00. July 4 brings a traditional family celebration with rousing music and ice-cream making. Later in the month, Cow Appreciation Day brings more ice cream and cow-related activities. Late in August, on Children's Day, anyone under twelve years old, accompanied by an adult, is admitted **free.** Wool spinning, farm animal programs, nineteenth-century games, and horse-drawn wagon rides are highlights of the day.

In mid-September, Wool Day features hand shearing and spinning, along with demonstrations of border collies' sheep-herding abilities. Visitors can make a felted ball of wool to take home. Later in the fall, apples, pumpkins, and other harvest activities all have days of their own, ending with a family Halloween, including pumpkin carving, mystery stories, a costume parade, and wagon rides. Children in costume accompanied by an adult are admitted **free.** Thanksgiving and Christmas also bring special events, and throughout the winter, special weekends are designated for horse-drawn sleigh rides and an exploration of the farm and its winter activities. Billings Farm has a small but excellent shop that features books for all ages on rural living and skills, as well as old-time craft kits suitable for children (corn-husk dolls, topsy-turvy dolls, clothespin dolls, and lavender ladies, among others).

Sugarbush Farm (ages 4 and up)

Hillside Road, Taftsville, Vt., 3 miles east of Woodstock off Route 4. Cross the red covered bridge on River Road, opposite the Taftsville Store, then drive to the top of the hill and turn left onto Hillside Road; (802) 457–1757. Open weekdays 7:30 A.M. to 4:40 P.M. year-round, weekends and holidays 9:30 A.M. to 4:30 P.M. Free.

This sugarhouse is set up year-round to show how maple sap is collected and made into syrup. The best time to visit, of course, is from late February through March, when the farm is a beehive of activity and the air is filled with sweet steam. There is always a **free** sampling table for syrup and for the cheeses and jams made at the farm. They have a maple trail, which follows the path that horses use to haul sap to the sugarhouse. In the summer, there will be a calf to pet, part of their dairy display.

Suicide Six (ages 3 and up)

Route 12, 3 miles north of Woodstock, Vt.; (802) 457–1666 or (800) 448–7900 for lodging.

Despite its mean-sounding name, Suicide Six is sure to be kid-friendly, with its diminutive 600-foot vertical drop. But its nineteen trails do offer challenges as well as gentle terrain for beginners. Good packages link lift tickets, lessons, and rentals to the Woodstock Inn; some weekday specials include **free** lifts. If you are tired of hearing your kids rave about snowboarding but thought it was just for kids, think again. The Adult Snowboarding Clinic is a weekend package with the Woodstock Inn that includes a full day of professional instruction: The program is designed just for adult learners. Several sessions are held each winter, with inn lodging and breakfasts included in the package.

The Woodstock Ski Touring Center (ages 5 and up)

The Woodstock Country Club on Route 106; (802) 457–6674.

The Ski Touring Center has more than 30 miles of trails and old carriage roads in the parklike setting of low Mount Tom and along a brook. A cabin

Ice-Skating and Sledding

- **Vail Field,** Route 106 just south of the village of Woodstock; (802) 457–1568. Nearby Woodstock Sports rents skates.

- **Lake Morey Inn,** just off Route 5 at the exit to I–91, Fairlee; (802) 333–4311. Offers skating on its outdoor rink, lighted every Saturday night. Rental skates are available here.

- **Mount Tom School,** Woodstock, a mile north of town on Route 12. Visiting children are welcome to join local kids on their favorite sledding hill.

along the trail has a fireplace to warm up in front of. Equipment rental is available and mid-week plans at the nearby Woodstock Inn include **free** trail passes.

Kedron Valley Stables (ages 8 and up)

Route 106, just north of the Kedron Valley Inn, South Woodstock, Vt.; (802) 457–1480 or (800) 225–6301; www.kedron.com. Open daily 10:00 A.M. to 5:00 P.M., with rides beginning hourly from 10:00 A.M. to 4:00 P.M., weather permitting. Reservations essential.

Trail rides and horse rentals are offered in the summer. There are also two work sleds with benches, several sleighs that hold between five and fourteen passengers, and a three-seater hotel sleigh. Rides last forty-five minutes to an hour.

Where to Eat

Bentleys, 3 Elm Street, in the center of Woodstock, Vt.; (802) 457–3232. The menu is interesting to adults (pan-seared trout, lamb medallions) but has plenty of favorites for less-sophisticated little palates, too. Burgers are sumptuous. The atmosphere is lively. $–$$

Mountain Creamery, 33 Central Street, Woodstock, Vt.; (802) 457–1715. Laid-back coffeehouse that serves great eggs, pastries, and inexpensive lunch-counter favorites. $

The Ott-Dog Snack Bar, Route 4, Quechee, Vt.; (802) 295–2075. Open daily mid-May through late October. This friendly family-run snack shop sells sandwiches and enormous ice-cream cones. $

Where to Stay

Kedron Valley Inn, Route 106, South Woodstock, Vt.; (802) 457–1473 or (800) 836–1193. Individually decorated rooms are comfortable and are adorned with items from the owner's collection of early needlework and patchwork quilts. Guest rooms are in three buildings, two of them historic land-marks as stops on the Underground Railroad. Your kids will especially like the room that was once a hiding place for runaway slaves.

Cribs are available and dogs are welcome, too. Horseback-riding is right next door. $$–$$$

The Lincoln Inn at the Covered Bridge, Route 4, West Woodstock, Vt. (3 miles from the center of Woodstock); (802) 457–3312; www.lincolninn.com. The Victorian farm-house has six homey, comfortable guest rooms and a dining room worth driving miles for. The owners are a cheery couple who make everyone feel instantly at home. $$–$$$

The Quechee Inn at Marshland Farm, Clubhouse Road, Quechee, Vt.; (802) 295–3133 or (800) 235–3133; www.quecheeinn.com. Baby-sitting available; 1793 manor house; beautiful rooms; no phones. Offers hiking trails on inn property, Nordic Ski School. Quechee Club privileges included. Fishing and canoeing equipment is available for rent. $$$

The Shire Motel, 46 Pleasant Street, Woodstock, Vt.; (802) 457–2211. Overlooks the Ottauquechee River. Second-floor decks have the best view; many rooms have good views as well. Children under 12 stay **free;** large rooms. $$–$$$

Woodstock Inn and Resort, On The Green, Woodstock, Vt.; (802) 457–1100 (for information) or (800) 448–7900 (for reservations); www.woodstockinn.com. Right in the center of town, this luxury inn is a full resort, with a sports center, tavern, cafe, and dining room. The Sports Center offers indoor tennis, squash and racquetball courts, a lap pool, whirlpool, Nautilus room, aerobics room, steam bath, saunas, and massage room. Their cross-country touring center rents snowshoes and skis. Inn guest packages can include ski rental and use of more than 30 miles of trails. You can walk to everything in Woodstock from here. Some rooms have VCRs; baby-sitting is available. Children under 14 stay **free.** $$$

For More Information

Woodstock Area Chamber of Commerce, 18 Central Street, P.O. Box 486, Woodstock, VT 05091; (802) 457–3555; www.woodstockvt.com.

White River Junction–Strafford Region

Engine 494 (ages 4 and up)
South Main Street, White River Junction, Vt. Free.

In the center of the town, which was built around its once-active rail station, stands Engine 494, a steam locomotive with its tender and caboose. At one time, as many as fifty trains a day hissed and chugged past the depot. This locomotive, Engine 494, was built in 1892 and once hauled coal to Marshfield Station, partway up New Hampshire's Mount Washington, to fuel the Cog Railway (see The White Mountains chapter). In 1939 Engine 494 represented the Boston & Maine Railroad at the New York World's Fair.

Montshire Museum of Science (ages 3 and up)
Montshire Road, Norwich, Vt. From Route 5 at the Ledyard Bridge from Hanover, N.H., follow signs to the museum. From I–91, take exit 13 and follow signs. The museum is close to the exit 13 intersection with Route 5; (802) 649–2200; www.montshire.net. Open all year, 10:00 A.M. to 5:00 P.M. daily. Admission: Adults $$, under age 3 free.

Hands-on is the operative phrase here, and the science in the Montshire Museum's hands is so much fun that kids won't even care that they're learning. All this active participation and observation is too much like playing. Although exhibits change frequently, you'll usually be able to watch ants work and boa constrictors sleep. Aquariums display ocean and freshwater life. The museum is full of buttons to push, and the occasional explanatory signs and labels aren't even required reading. Instead, ask the "explainers" who are always nearby. Even the building is constructed to teach, and you can see how it was built and is heated. More than a hundred acres along the river are part of the museum, too, with nature trails and picnic areas. Special events throughout the year explore some field of science or technology. Among the most popular events is igloo-building (see Annual Events).

COOL Facts

Samuel Morey from Orford, New Hampshire, tested the first steamboat on the Connecticut River in 1793. He fitted a steam engine to a tiny skiff for the first try, then continued to improve it in the waters of Lake Morey (later named for him). It is believed that the remains of the very first steamboat are still on the bottom of Lake Morey.

Justin Smith Morrill Homestead (ages 6 and up)

Justin Morrill Highway, 2 miles off Route 132, in Strafford village; (802) 828–3226. Open Memorial Day through Columbus Day 11:00 A.M. to 5:00 P.M. Wednesday through Sunday. Admission: $, under age 14 free.

This highly ornate Victorian home, its steep roof line decorated with "gingerbread" trim, is painted the color of peach ice cream (a popular house color in the mid-1800s). Its seventeen rooms, decorated in Gothic Revival style, are in all-original condition, complete with original furnishings. Gardens, barns, and outbuildings are original as well. Morrill, a congressman and senator from 1855 to 1898, is known as "the Father of the Agricultural Colleges" for creating the land-grant system that built them throughout the country. On weekends there is usually some interesting activity going on here, such as apple-pressing for cider or hay wagon rides around the pretty little village.

B.O.R. Rink (all ages)

Highland Avenue, White River Junction, Vt.; (802) 295–3236 or (802) 295–5036.

Offers ice-skating, with rentals.

Where to Eat

River City Cafe, 17 South Main Street, White River Junction, Vt.; (802) 296–7113. This cafe offers a great selection of sandwiches, teas, and coffees in a relaxed atmosphere. A local favorite. $

South Strafford Cafe, in the village center, South Strafford, Vt.; (802) 765–4671. Open year-round for lunch or afternoon tea or coffee. This bright, friendly cafe serves muffins, scones, soup, cheese plates, and good chili with cornbread at very low prices. $

Where to Stay

Birch Meadow B&B, 597 Birchmeadow Drive, Brookfield, Vt. (Route 14, north of Woodstock); (802) 276–3156. Luxury log cabins have woodburning stoves, lofts, and fully equipped kitchens. More than 200 acres of panoramic views, with hiking, cross-country skiing, and snowshoe trails, tobogganing in the winter, and hay rides in the summer. $$$

Comfort Inn, 8 Sykes Avenue, White River Junction, Vt. (I–91 exit 11); (802) 295–3051 or (800) 628–7727. Cable TV, data ports, nonsmoking rooms available. Children under 16 **free,** extra person $5.00. $–$$

Holiday Inn, Holiday Inn Drive, White River Junction, Vt.; (802) 295–3000 or (800) 648–6754. Lovely atrium, waterfall, nineteenth- century caboose on display, data ports, in-room safes, cable TV with movies, whirlpool, laundry room, game room. Children under 19 stay **free,** extra person $6.00. $$$

Hanover–Lake Sunapee Region, New Hampshire

This area is home to one of the country's most prestigious schools, Dartmouth College. Because of the infiltration of young, hip students, your teenagers might find this area particularly fun to explore. Of course, there are still plenty of things to do with the whole family and lots of nature sites to discover.

Hopkins Center (all ages)
Wheelock Street, Hanover, N.H.; (603) 646–2422. Hours and prices vary with performance.

The area's major performing arts venue, "The Hop" may have anything from classical music recitals to the circus going on in its several auditoriums. There's almost always something happening, and a good percentage of the offerings are designed for families or for children. If you're planning to be in the area, it's wise to call for a schedule.

Hood Museum of Art (ages 6 and up)
Wheelock Street, Hanover, N.H.; (603) 646–2426. Open year-round, Tuesday through Saturday, 10:00 A.M. to 5:00 P.M., Sunday noon to 5:00 P.M. **free.**

Although its collections are especially heavy in oceanic art and European prints, exhibits also include outstanding examples of Native American art, including beadwork, baskets, pottery, and masks. The kids probably will not be entranced by the complete suite of Picasso's Vollard etchings, but they should find the Native American collections more interesting. It's worth checking to see what's on display first, as not all collections are out all the time.

Muster Field Farm (ages 4 and up)
Harvey Road (off Route 114), North Sutton, N.H.; (603) 927–4276 or (603) 526–6643; www.musterfieldfarm.org. The farmstand is open noon to 5:00 P.M. in the summer, and the Matthew Harvey Homestead is open Sunday 1:00 to 4:00 P.M. during June, July, and August. Self-guided tours of the grounds are available year-round. **Free.**

The local militia—volunteer soldiers like the famous minutemen of Lexington and Concord—marched and fired their rifles as they trained for the Revolutionary and Civil Wars on the field beside the Matthew Harvey Homestead. These militia-practice days, known as musters, gave the farm its name. But unlike most of these old hill farms, this one is actually larger than it was when Matthew Harvey hosted the musters.

The last owner of the 250-acre property began collecting historic farm and rural buildings that were falling down or being torn down and brought them to his farm. When he died, he left it all as a working-museum farm, along with money so that the collection of buildings could continue to grow. You can see barns, two blacksmith shops, an ice house, an 1810 school house, even the octagonal ticket booth from the local fairgrounds. Barns are filled with old tools, wagons, and equipment.

You can tour the buildings and see the collections of old farm equipment **free** any day, or go on Sunday in July, August, and September, when the homestead is open from 1:00 to 4:00 P.M.—also **free.** Costumed people may be using the looms or spinning wheels and will show you how they work.

On special weekends demonstrations and activities fill the farm. In mid-July a Civil War encampment re-creates the daily life of the 5th Regiment New Hampshire Volunteers, with mess call, drills, and inspection of arms. Entire families dressed in costumes of that period pitch their white tents and camp on the farm, just as the militia families used to do.

Late August Farm Days also include an encampment and muster, as well as a chance for children—and adults—to try their hand at everything from making felt to walking on stilts. At Harvest Day in early October, you can carve pumpkins, join a parade, or discover how people used to preserve foods in preparation for winter (there's bean-threshing, corn-grinding, and open-hearth cooking). Admission to these special events is $4.00 for adults.

To get there, turn west from Route 114 in North Sutton—the road runs between Kezar Lake and the Follansbee Inn. This takes you right into the center of the farm.

Wadleigh State Beach (all ages)
Route 114, Sutton, N.H; (603) 927–4724. Daylight hours. Admission: $; children under 12 and New Hampshire residents over 65 admitted free.

Hardly anyone uses this beautiful pine-tree-shaded beach and picnic area on the shore of Kezar Lake. The picnic grove is especially nice, under tall red pines with a few white birches for contrast. Tables and fireplaces are nicely spaced, and all have a view of the water. It's easy to see why the native Penacook people favored this spot as their summer encampment. If you look along the shore of the lake, you can find the little freshwater mussels that brought them here to feast. From the park you can walk around the shore, a 3-mile walk along unpaved roads with nice views, including Mount Kearsarge.

Winslow State Park (ages 4 and up)
Kearsarge Mountain Road, off Kearsarge Valley Road, south from Route 11, Wilmot Flat, N.H. Daylight hours. Free.

After following the signs onto Kearsarge Mountain Road, you can drive up and up, saving much of the climb up Mount Kearsarge. The picnic area on a shoulder of the mountain offers sweeping 180-degree views of valley, lakes, and mountains. Barlow Trail leads in a 1.7-mile loop, and Winslow Trail is 1.1 miles along the upper slopes of Mount Kearsarge, an easy way to climb a mountain. Everyone still gets the sense of achievement—and the views—without the aching calf muscles.

Mount Sunapee II (ages 3 and up)

Sunapee Harbor, N.H. (off Route 11); (603) 763–4030. Cruises Saturday and Sunday, mid-May to mid-June at 2:30 P.M., daily mid-June through August at 10:00 A.M. and 2:30 P.M., Saturday and Sunday, September through mid-October at 2:30 P.M. Prices vary with season and length of cruise.

The ninety-minute trip is kept lively, even for children, by the captain's narration. Weekly substance- and smoke-free dance parties on board the boat are open to those under twenty-one.

Mount Sunapee State Beach (all ages)

Route 103B, Sunapee, N.H.; (603) 763–5561. Daylight hours. Admission: $, age 11 and under free.

A beautiful, long beach with lifeguards, bath houses, picnic tables, and concession stands. It is crowded in the summer on weekends, but not nearly as much as beaches in the Lake Winnipesaukee region.

Royal Arch Hill Cave (ages 4 and up)

Georges Mills, north of New London, N.H. To find the trailhead from Georges Mills, follow the road that leads from Route 11 to exit 12A off I–89. It goes under I–89, then to a T inter-section. Go right (south) toward New London, taking your first left at the top of a short hill. Park before you reach the PRIVATE PROPERTY sign and look for the small sign on an old woods road to the left. Daylight hours. Free.

Royal Arch Hill is not a true cave, such as those found in limestone. But this deeply under-cut granite cliff forms its own kind of cave. The trail is marked from the woods road, going through the woods and a rocky area before it begins to climb steeply up Royal Arch Hill to the cave. From above the cave, which is large enough to shelter a family, the view stretches from Georges Mills to Little Sunapee Lake, in New London.

Dartmouth Skiway (ages 3 and up)

Off Route 10, in Lyme, north of Hanover, N.H.; (603) 795–2143.

Dartmouth's racers practice for the Olympics and other competitions on these steep slopes, but it's also a good area for families, with friendly staff that seem to look out for them on the lifts and trails.

Norsk Cross-Country Ski Center (ages 4 and up)

Lake Sunapee Country Club, Route 11, New London, N.H.; (603) 526–4685 or (800) 426–6775; www.skinorsk.com. Weekends: $$–$$$, under 6 free. Weekdays slightly less. Rentals and lessons are available for both snowshoeing and skiing.

About 50 miles of cross-country trails are tracked and groomed at this popular area, along with snowshoe trails. A warming hut provides hot food and drinks. Pull sleds are available for children too small to ski.

Eastman Cross-Country Ski Center (pages 4 and up)

Close to exit 13 off I–89 in Grantham, N.H.; (603) 863–4500; www.eastman nh.com. Trail fees: $$.

This place is designed for families, with a delightful Troll House along the trail where children can win prizes. The warming huts serve "Troll House cookies," and pull sleds are available for tots. Lessons, ski patrol, and a shop for supplies and equipment round out the package. Eight trails cover about 16 miles. There's also a skating rink and snowshoe trail, with rental equipment for both. The center is also open the rest of the year for golfing, boating, and lodging.

Where to Eat

Molly's, 43 South Main Street, Hanover, N.H.; (603) 643–6645. Crowded at lunchtime and the after-work hour, Molly's makes up for the slow service with good food and a wide variety of choices. Kids are sure to find something they like here, including pizza. $–$$

Peter Christian's Tavern, 39 South Main Street, Hanover, N.H.; (603) 643–2345. A lively favorite for students, families, and everyone else, Peter Christian's serves giant sandwiches and hearty main dishes such as beef stew or lasagna. $–$$

Where to Stay

Follansbee Inn, Route 114, North Sutton, N.H.; (603) 927–4221 or (800) 626–4221; www.follansbeeinn.com. A comfortable, old-fashioned inn that has catered to families for generations. The inn has its own beachfront on the lake, and canoes and rowboats are reserved for guests. Full breakfasts begin each day, and you can choose what you like in the kitchen. Walking and ski trails connect it to Wadleigh State Park, across Kezar Lake, which has an island perfect for picnics. $$

Lamplighter Motor Inn, Newport Road, at exit 12 from I–89, New London, N.H.; (603) 526–6484; www.lamplightermotorinn.com. Some rooms have kitchenettes; all are spacious and include cross-country ski passes in the winter. $–$$

Maple Hill Farm Country Inn, 200 Newport Road, New London, N.H.; (800) 231–8637; www.maplehillfarm.com. Fireplaces and warm hospitality, plus **free** cross-country skiing at Eastman in their winter packages. Hearty farm breakfasts begin each day. $$

Mount Sunapee Motel, at Mount Sunapee State Park entrance, Sunapee, N.H.; (603) 763–5592. Nothing fancy, but clean and comfortable, with good-size rooms and budget-friendly rates. $–$$

The Shaker Inn, 447 Route 4A, Enfield, N.H.; (603) 632–7810 or (888) 707–4257; www.theshakerinn.com. Although there is probably not much to fire the imagination of children at the adjacent Enfield Shaker Museum, the inn that was once its Dwelling House is a wonderful place to stay. Rooms are spacious, furnished in reproduction Shaker pieces. The Shakers' built-in cabinetry remains in most rooms. It is the largest Shaker Dwelling House in existence, four-and-a-half stories tall, built of granite blocks. It's like living in a piece of New England history. The genial innkeeper, if he has time, has been known to take well-behaved children and their parents on a tour to the tower, high atop the building, and let them ring its giant bell. $$–$$$$

The dining room, where the brothers and sisters once supped in silence, is now in the hands of an excellent chef. There's a kids' menu of five favorites, including chicken wings, cheese pizza, and spaghetti. Meanwhile, adults can enjoy the likes of salmon encrusted with horseradish, pan-seared duck breast with rhubarb ginger sauce, or rack of lamb. $$

For More Information

Hanover Area Chamber of Commerce, Main Street, Hanover, NH 03755; (603) 643–3115; www.hanoverchamber.org.

New London Area Chamber of Commerce, Main Street (P.O. Box 532), New London, NH 03257; (603) 526–6575; www.newlondonareanh.com.

Annual Events

JANUARY

Ascutney's Winter Carnival, Brownsville, Vt., (802) 484–7711, late January. Includes events for both skiers and nonskiers, such as hot air balloons and fireworks displays.

The Brookfield Ice Harvest, at the Floating Bridge on Sunset Pond in Brookfield, Vt., just off I–89 north of Woodstock, (802) 276–3959, late January. Here is a rare chance for kids to see how ice used to be harvested before the days of refrigerators. Using historic tools and methods, everyone—visitors

included—joins in cutting, hauling, and storing blocks of ice that will last all summer. Sleigh rides, an ice sculpture demonstration, and other winter activities make it a full day.

FEBRUARY

Brattleboro Winter Carnival, Brattleboro, Vt., call (802) 254–4565 for dates and times. More than fifty family-friendly events, which include a parade, sleigh rides, sugar-on-snow parties, and music.

Fred Harris Memorial Tournament and Pepsi Challenge, (802) 254–4565. Ski-jumping tournament at Harris Hill, Brattleboro, Vt. Call for details.

President's Week Celebration, Ascutney and Brownsville, Vt., (802) 484–7711, mid-February. Features family activities, ice-skating, and a torchlight parade.

Sugar-on-Snow Celebration, Okemo and Ludlow, Vt., (802) 228–4041. This is a good chance to sample the sticky confection made from maple syrup.

The Great Igloo Build, Montshire Museum, Norwich, Vt., (802) 649–2200, late February. This event gives kids a chance to learn how to build a traditional Arctic shelter. Everyone has a chance to cut snow blocks, then to carry and stack them. By the end of the day, there's a small village of igloos.

Dartmouth Winter Carnival, Hanover, N.H., (603) 795–2143. Well worth visiting for its snow sculptures. Giant figures decorate the Dartmouth Green and the snow-covered lawns of the fraternity houses. It's fun to watch them being built, too.

MARCH

Sugar-on-Snow Supper, Cavendish, Vt., (802) 226–7885, mid-March. This has been an annual event for forty years, held at the Baptist Church.

Special weekend events at Billings Farm Museum, Woodstock, Vt., (802) 457–2355, spring through fall. A variety of special programs geared to children's interests.

APRIL

Special weekend events at Billings Farm Museum, Woodstock, Vt., (802) 457–2355, spring through fall. A variety of special programs geared to children's interests.

MAY

Special weekend events at Billings Farm Museum, Woodstock, Vt., (802) 457–2355, spring through fall. A variety of special programs geared to children's interests.

Brattleboro Spring Fusion, Brattleboro, Vt., mid-May. Downtown festival with food, music, and performers.

JUNE

Special weekend events at Billings Farm Museum, Woodstock, Vt., (802) 457–2355, spring through fall. A variety of special programs geared to children's interests.

JULY

President Calvin Coolidge Birthday Parade, Plymouth, Vt., (802) 672–3773, July 4. Held at the President Coolidge State Historic Site.

Cheshire County Outdoors, County Farm, River Road, Westmoreland, N.H., invites the public to tour the county's farm, pet farm animals, tour the dairy barns, go for wagon rides, and eat **free** ice cream; (603) 352–4550.

Village Days Festival, Brattleboro, Vt., (802) 254–4565, late July. Includes a craft fair, sidewalk sales, Riff Raft Regatta.

Windsor County Agricultural Fair, Barlow's Field in Springfield, Vt., (802) 886–8470, late July.

Old Vermont Fourth at the Billings Farm, Woodstock, Vt., (802) 457–2355, July 4.

Norwich Annual Fair, Vt., (802) 649–1614; early July. Features contests, midway, and fireworks.

Cow Appreciation Day, Billings Farm Museum, Woodstock, Vt., (802) 457–2355, mid-July. You can try your hand at milking and sample freshly churned butter and hand-cranked ice cream.

AUGUST

Cheshire Fair, Route 12, North Swanzey, N.H. (south of Keene), (603) 357–4740, early August.

Zucchini Festival, Ludlow, Vt., contact Ludlow Chamber of Commerce at (802) 228–5830, late August. The Zucchini Festival has become a New England tradition in recent years; don't miss the creative fun.

Special weekend events at Billings Farm Museum, Woodstock, Vt., (802) 457–2355, spring through fall. A variety of special programs geared to children's interests.

Annual Quechee Scottish Festival, at the Polo Field, Quechee, Vt., (802) 295–5351, late August. Includes pipers, sheep dog demonstrations, and athletic events.

SEPTEMBER

Apple Days Festival, Brattleboro, Vt., last weekend of the month. Craft fair, children's activities, apple pie contest.

Special weekend events at Billings Farm Museum, Woodstock, Vt., (802) 457–2355, spring through fall. A variety of special programs geared to children's interests.

OCTOBER

Newfane Heritage Festival, Newfane, Vt., (802) 365–7689, early October.

Townshend Pumpkin Festival, Townshend, Vt., mid-October. Costumes, pumpkin carving and contests, costume parade.

The Vermont Apple Festival, Springfield, (802) 885–2779, mid-October. This festival entertains children with a petting zoo, wagon rides, and music.

The Pumpkin Festival, downtown Keene, N.H., late October. This festival is spectacular by any measure. The Guinness Book of World Records measures it in terms of how many lighted jack-o'-lanterns are on display here each year, and it tops 20,000, handily making it the largest festival of its kind anywhere. But numbers alone don't describe the scene,

with the entire square and wide main street lined by glowing jack-o'-lanterns. All day Saturday you can see the collection grow while you feast on harvest goodies, including cider and homemade pumpkin pie and cookies.

Winchester Pickle Festival, center of Winchester, N.H., late October. This is clearly a tongue-in-cheek production, and everyone has a good time as more than 4,000 pickles are eaten in one day. Festivities begin with a parade and continue with sports competitions, an antique car show, a field full of scarecrows, barbecues, and other excuses to eat pickles.

The Horribles Parade, Brattleboro, Vt., October 31. Costumed children parade through downtown.

Grafton Fall Foliage Firemen's Festival, Grafton, Vt., (802) 843–2499, late October. Features **free** wagon rides, a flea market, and more; at the Fire Station.

Special weekend events at Billings Farm Museum, Woodstock, Vt., (802) 457–2355, spring through fall. A variety of special programs geared to children's interests.

Harvest Celebration, Billings Farm Museum, Woodstock, Vt., (802) 452–2355, mid-October. The fall activities of a nineteenth-century farm are demonstrated here: cider pressing, the pumpkin harvest, a husking bee, preserving, and more.

NOVEMBER

Special weekend events at Billings Farm Museum, Woodstock, Vt., (802) 457–2355, spring through fall. A variety of special programs geared to children's interests.

DECEMBER

Holly Days/Holly Nights, downtown Brattleboro, Vt., (802) 254–4565. Caroling, Santa visits, music, roasted chestnuts, street sales.

Prelude to Christmas, Chester, Vt., (802) 875–2444, early December. Chester's village green is lined by decorated trees. The Clauses light the trees at 4:00 P.M., and villagers join a candlelight procession, singing carols as they go from church to church. Afterward, everyone gathers for a caroling concert. Many people wear Victorian dress for the evening.

Christmas Fest, Walker's Tree Farm in Brownington, Vt., (802) 754–8487, early December. This is the time to choose and cut the perfect Christmas tree. Refreshments and sleigh rides available.

Torchlight parade and fireworks display, Okemo Mountain Resort, Vt., (802) 228–4041. One evening between Christmas and New Year's. Employees ski down the winding mountain trails carrying lighted torches.

Woodstock Wassail Celebration, Woodstock, Vt., second weekend. Call (802) 457–3555 for Wassail Celebration schedules. For parade information, call the Green Mountain Horse Association at (802) 457–1509. The town is filled with old-fashioned Christmas spirit. There's caroling, a carriage and wagon parade, a handbell concert, a Messiah sing-along, lighted trees and windows, and shops decorated for the holidays. Bring an offering for the Goodwill Wagon, which is filled by townspeople and visitors with gifts of clothing and food for families who would not have a Christmas without it.

Over the Green Mountains

I f you looked at a map of Vermont, you might be surprised to see that almost the entire area covered in this chapter—the whole southwest corner of the state—is surrounded by a pale green line, showing that it is part of the Green Mountain National Forest. This tract covers all but a few tiny corners of Bennington County and lops over into neighboring Windham County as well. Its western and southern boundaries are the state lines of New York and Massachusetts, respectively.

As a practical matter, you would hardly know that the lands around you are any different from the rest of the state. Roads pass through towns and villages, state parks are superimposed on the federal lands, and everything looks pretty much as usual. The vast area of wilderness in the high elevations do, however, show more Forest Service presence, with well-kept campgrounds, trails, and other low-key services for those who love and value the out-of-doors that the Forest Service is known for.

Mount Snow Valley (Wilmington and West Dover)

Depending on your point of view, Vermont's Green Mountains either begin or end in this region, as they drift off into Massachusetts. But even at the edges they are still formidable, as you will learn when driving over their spine on Route 9, which is the only year-round road traversing the region east to west.

OVER THE GREEN MOUNTAINS

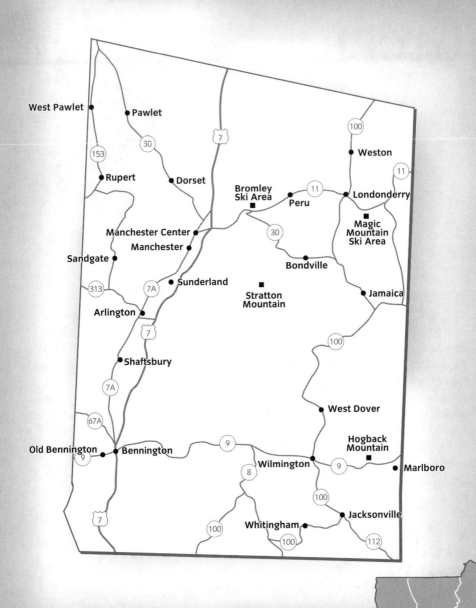

Adams Farm (all ages)

15 Higley Hill Road, off Route 100 north, Wilmington, Vt.; (802) 464–3762; www.adamsfamily farm.com. Open year-round, hours vary with season and activity. Admission varies with the farm activities.

Six generations of the same family have worked this farm, and they invite you to join them in many of the family activities there. In the winter, their sleigh rides are legendary in the Mount Snow valley, on three double traverse sleds pulled by Belgian draft horses. The ninety-minute rides are highlighted by a stop at a cabin in the middle of the woods, where hot cocoa is served in front of the old woodstove and music issues from a player piano.

You can go on an animal-tracking hike to learn how early farmers hunted in the cold months. As the snow begins to melt, it is time for maple syrup and time to visit the sugar-house to watch the whole process. Summer farm activities are hands-on and include milking a goat, feeding farm animals, going on evening hayrides, and taking a tractor ride to explore caves where bears once made their home. Weekly story hours in the Barn Theater feature storytellers, "moo-sic," and audience participation. In the fall, everyone enjoys choosing a pumpkin from the farm's patch or going on a haunted hayride on a Friday or Saturday evening in October. All year-round, the farm store sells what's in season from the gardens, as well as hand-spun woolens and maple syrup and candy. Also in the farm store are handmade children's clothes, quilts, and quality toys.

Living History Museum (ages 6 and up)

At the top of Hogback Mountain, Route 9, Wilmington, Vt.; (802) 464–5569. Call ahead for dates of historical reenactments. Open from May through October, Thursday through Monday 10:00 A.M. to 4:00 P.M. Admission: $, age 10 and under free.

On weekends when there's good weather, the fields around this museum are a great place to see re-creations of events and times from the Middle Ages up to World War II. Often you will find plenty of costumed and serious participants who are camping in Civil War–era tents or medieval pavilions, just as people would have done during the time they are depicting. You might even get to see a mock battle with smoke rising from the fields or a swordfight in traditional style.

The museum displays a musket used by soldier Abraham Boyd, who was born in Wilmington. He used this firearm in both the famous Battle of Bunker Hill in 1775 and the Battle of Bennington in 1777. The museum building is also home to an example of the cannon

DVTA **MOOver**

The MOOver is a public bus system run by the Deerfield Valley Transit Association. It's hard to miss the black-and-white cow-painted bus that brings people from Wilmington to West Dover at no charge. There are a number of stops for the bus in both Wilmington and West Dover, or you can flag it down anywhere on its route. For details, call (802) 464–8487, or visit www.moover.com.

that was most commonly used by both sides in the Civil War. Exhibits include many other wartime artifacts of the region as well and focus on several lesser-known battles that occurred in the area.

Hogback Mountain (all ages)
Route 9, Wilmington, Vt. Daylight hours; free.

You can't miss the top of the mountain if you go over it in the daytime—on a clear day, the view is 100 miles. Even if you're not stopping at the natural history museum, the gift shop, or the restaurant, the view is definitely worth getting the kids out of the car (and yes, there are restrooms inside the shop). Coin-operated binoculars and laminated maps of the mountains show you what you are looking at as you gaze across the valleys and mountains of Vermont, New Hampshire, and Massachusetts.

Southern Vermont Natural History Museum (ages 5 and up)
Hogback Mountain, Route 9, Marlboro, Vt.; (802) 464–0048. Open 10:00 A.M. to 5:00 P.M., Memorial Day through late October; in winter open most weekends 10:00 A.M. to 4:00 P.M. Admission: $.

This little museum just keeps growing. It began with a collection of several hundred mounted bird specimens and, with a new building, has grown to include a small raptor center where you can see live owls and hawks. The latest addition is a weather station with working meteorologists—appropriate for its mountaintop location.

Harriman Dam (all ages)
1/2 mile south of Whitingham Village, Vt., off Route 100; www.wilmingtonvermont.com. Open daylight hours. Free.

The Harriman Dam is not only quite a sight to see, it also has an incredible tale to tell. Built in the 1920s, its purpose was to block the Deerfield River and provide a source of electrical power. When the dam blocked the river, water filled in behind it for an area of 28 miles, drowning the town of Mountain Mills. Still sitting under the waters are fifteen farms and the village as it was left nearly a century ago. The new lake that it created, Lake Whitingham, also forced the engineers to move the entire railroad line. The new railroad was transportation for a lively tourist industry until a 1927 flood took out the trestle that spanned part of the lake. Today, the dam is 1,200 feet across and 200 feet high. Its "Glory Hole" is the enormous spillway, which sometimes collects the water in its gurgling mouth. A picnic area overlooks the dam.

Public **Swimming**

- **Wards Cove.** Route 100 south of Route 9 from Wilmington Center; after about 1 mile, turn right at the sign for Flame Stables. This road will bring you right to the water.

- **Medburyville.** From Wilmington Center on Route 9, go about 2.7 miles and take the bridge on the left. Take your first left after the bridge, and you will end up at the picnic area.

- **Somerset Reservoir.** Go 5 miles west from Wilmington on Route 9, then take Somerset Road. The reservoir, which is 9 miles long, is 10 miles down the road. There is a picnic area that is maintained by the New England Power Company.

- **Woodford State Park.** Route 9, Woodford (west of Wilmington); (802) 447–7169. Swimming beach with boat rentals, playground, and picnic tables.

Scenic Drive

Follow Route 9 from Bennington over the Green Mountains and scenic Hogback Mountain to Brattleboro. This winding road spends much of its time going up or down, often for long stretches at a time, but the surface is good. It literally goes right over the tops of two mountain ranges, with the best views from Hogback. **Free.**

Mt. Mills Cruise Boat (ages 5 and up)

Route 9, Wilmington, Vt.; (802) 464–2975; www.dvalnews.com/gmfc.html. Operates May through October, several trips a day. Reservations are important, because the boat is often filled by tour groups, especially in the fall. Call for rates.

Several ninety-minute cruises tour the Harriman Reservoir each day, with lively narration describing the geology and history of the impoundment lake and the town that lies submerged beneath its waters. Few can resist the fascination of a sunken ghost town. Operated by the Green Mountain Flagship Company, canoe, sailboat, and kayak rentals are also available for use on the Harriman Reservoir.

Mount Snow Resort (all ages)

Route 100, West Dover, Vt.; (800) 245–7669; www.mountsnow.com. Varied activities and prices.

Because of its location in the southern part of the state, Mount Snow gets a lot of skiers. It is, in fact, the southernmost of the major New England ski areas, so it's closer to the big population centers than any other. But it's big enough to handle the crowds, which soon disperse over its 130 trails, plus the 44 trails of the formerly separate Haystack Mountain and 137 acres of tree-terrain skiing.

Intermediate ski levels are well served here, and the area puts major emphasis on its facilities and instruction for beginning skiers as well. **Un Blanco Gulch** was the first snowboard park in the east, and it is a mecca for teens.

Along with the on-slope action, there are a lot of activities aimed at kids and families. The Ski Baba Trail, near the Carinthia Base area, is lighted until 9:00 P.M. each evening for sledding. (They do not rent sleds, so you will need to bring one or buy one there.)

On Saturday, teens ages 15 through 19 can dance the night away from 8:00 P.M. to midnight at their own dance club, **Planet 9 After Dark.** Its music and activities are open only to that age group. Kids ages 10 through 14 have **The Cave Club** in the main base lodge for dancing, games, and snacks, also only on Saturday, from 7:00 to 10:00 P.M.

Summer events at Mount Snow Resort have been expanding in recent years to take advantage of the beautiful landscape all year-round. Mount Snow has several great summer programs for children. One of our favorites is the week-long day camp, **Outdoor Adventure Camp,** for children ages 7 to 12. Three programs are offered: computers, filmmaking, and photography. These are available during the month of July. In all these programs, children get to experience hiking, mountain biking, archery, golf, and plenty of other fun outdoor activities.

For the younger children, ages 6 weeks to 6 years, the resort offers **Mount Snow's Mini Camp,** a licensed childcare provider. Divided by age and the individual child's abilities and interests, this program gives kids a chance to do arts and crafts, games, and hiking and to learn how to tend a garden, among other activities. For reservations in one of these special programs, call (802) 464-4152.

Water sports for small children are centered at Fountain Mountain, a special pool for kids only. The resort was rated one of the top ten U.S. family resorts by *Family Fun* magazine.

While the kids are off playing at camp or becoming the next George Lucas, there is plenty for the adults to do. The **Mount Snow Golf Club** has an eighteen-hole championship course and offers classes taught by pros at The Original Golf School. The school offers a wide variety of classes and programs for players of varying abilities.

If you like mountain biking or want to learn, rentals and instruction are available. The **Grand Summit Resort Hotel** will help you wind down after a long day of hiking or fun on the climbing wall; it offers a wide variety of spa services. Or you can start your day with a fitness class and then relax as you ride up the mountain on a scenic chairlift ride. When the kids get back from camp, if they aren't tired yet, you all can play a game of volleyball on the sand court or take a paddleboat ride around the lake. Like other New England resorts, Mount Snow is quickly changing the image of ski areas as winter-only vacation spots.

Mount Olga (ages 4 and up)
Trailhead at Molly Stark State Park, Route 9, Wilmington, Vt. Free.

Here is a mountain for the whole family, an easy trail with a gentle grade. It's a little more than 1.5 miles to the summit of this 2,415-foot elevation, and there is a tower to climb for views once you get there.

Ice-Skating and Cross-Country Skiing

- There is a rink at the Carinthia Base Lodge at Mount Snow (802–464–3333 or 800–245–SNOW) and another at Beaver Brook Park in Wilmington (802–464–8092).

- Timber Creek Cross-Country Ski Center is directly opposite Mount Snow (802–464–0999).

Sprague's Sugarhouse (ages 5 and up)
Jacksonville, Vt.; (802) 368–2776. Jacksonville is on Route 100, south of Wilmington. Open Saturday and Sunday, 10:00 A.M. to 4:00 P.M. There is a charge for sugar-on-snow candy, but admission to the sugarhouse is free.

Watch the sap boil into syrup in the old-fashioned wood-fired evaporator, look at displays of antique equipment, and try traditional sugar-on-snow candy (it's served with dill pickles to cut the sweetness). Along with the traditional methods is a full demonstration of modern techniques for maple syrup production.
Sprague's also operates a pancake house and restaurant, as well as facilitating special events.

Where to Eat

Holiday season note: During busy seasons, we highly recommend that you call ahead to make reservations—and to get an idea of the waiting time if there is one. It will save a lot of time and frustration.

Alonzo's Pasta & Grille, Crafts Inn, West Main Street (Route 9 west), Wilmington, Vt.; (802) 464–2355. Great children's menu, homemade pasta, steaks, seafood, relaxed atmosphere. Open every night of the week. $

Cafe Tannery, Route 100, West Dover, Vt.; (802) 464–2078; www.twotannery.com. Their claim of a "contemporary menu at yesterday's prices" is pretty accurate. Serves lunch and dinner; menu includes wraps, sandwiches, burgers, pasta, ribs, and burritos. Takeout available. $

Dot's Restaurant, two locations: downtown Wilmington, Vt. (802–464–7284), and Mountain Park Plaza in West Dover, Vt. (802–464–6476). Dot's opens bright and shiny at 5:30 A.M. and serves breakfast, lunch, and dinner until 8:00 P.M. on weekdays, 9:00 P.M. on weekends. This is a favorite for both visitors and locals, specializing in homemade danishes and muffins and award-winning "jailhouse chili." All menu items are also available for takeout. $

Dover Forge Restaurant, Route 100, West Dover, Vt., at the Andirons Lodge; (802) 464–2114. Specializes in homemade pasta and fresh fish; dinners include soup or salad. All children's entrees are half-price. $–$$

Poncho's Wreck Restaurant, Route 100, downtown Wilmington, Vt., south of the traffic light; (802) 464–9320. The kids will love the nautical theme of this restaurant, which was "shipwrecked 1972." There is a children's menu, along with great selections for the whole family, including Mexican fare like fajitas, lobster, steaks, and early-bird dinner specials from 4:00 to 6:00 P.M. $–$$

The Silo Family Restaurant and Fink's Pub, Route 100, West Dover, Vt., ¼ mile south of Mount Snow Resort; (802) 464–2553; www.silorestaurant.com. Open for lunch and dinner, the restaurant serves full and light entrees and has a complete children's menu. There's a summer patio and an entertainment and game room. $–$$

Skyline Restaurant, Route 9, between Wilmington and Brattleboro, Vt.; (802) 464–5535. Open for lunch and dinner daily, dinner Wednesday through Sunday during the winter. Sitting atop Hogback, the state's only mountain with a major road running right over its summit, Skyline has one of the best views in the state, but the food is good, too. They are particularly known for their waffles and omelets at breakfast. $–$$

Where to Stay

Horizon Inn, Route 9, Wilmington, Vt.; (802) 464–2131 or (800) 336–5513; www.horizoninn.com. Very friendly hosts invite you to spend your vacation in their mini-resort hotel. They offer, in addition to pleasant rooms, a heated indoor pool, sauna, and whirlpool, as well as a game room and color cable TV in all rooms. The location is high in the mountains but right on Route 9 between Mount Snow/Wilmington and Bennington. $$

The Inn at Quail Run, 106 Smith Road, Wilmington, Vt.; (802) 464–3362 or (800) 34–ESCAPE; www.theinnatquailrun.com. Children and nice pets are welcome, breakfast is included, and the color cable TV includes HBO. The inn also offers a heated swimming pool, sauna, and Jacuzzi. $$

The Lodge at Mt. Snow, Route 100, West Dover, Vt.; (802) 464–5112 or (800) 451–4289. The location doesn't get much handier for skiers, who can stay 300 yards from the base of Mount Snow. This lodge offers two double beds in each room, some with an additional pull-out sofa for the kids. Outdoor heated pool, games, lounge, and great views of the mountain. $$–$$$

Mount Snow Condominiums, Mount Snow, Vt.; (800) 664–6535; www.mtsnow.com. You may choose a condo in the base area of the ski resort or a mountainside hut. Units with up to three bedrooms are available, with fully equipped kitchens and cable TV. Enjoy the resort's perks, like fitness facilities, pools, saunas, and more. Packages are available that include skiing or other activities. $$$

Nutmeg Inn, Route 9 just west of Wilmington, Vt.; (802) 464–7400 or (800) 277–5402; www.nutmeginn.com. In a classic red Cape Cod cottage, this inn looks like a postcard picture of a New England home. Inside are wood-burning fireplaces, king- and queen-size beds, and a full country breakfast every morning. $$–$$$

Red Cricket Inn, Route 100, West Dover, Vt.; (800) 859–2585. The inn offers two family rooms and color cable TV. Shuttle service to the slopes is included, so you don't have to look for a parking space. $$–$$$

Timber Creek Rentals, Route 100, West Dover, Vt.; (802) 464–1222 or (800) 982–8922; www.timbercreek-vt.com. Both short- and long-term rentals of townhouses with two to six bedrooms, fully equipped kitchens, and varied amenities. Features cross-country skiing, health club, indoor pool, and shuttle service to the slopes. $$$

Viking Motel, 88 East Main Street, Wilmington, Vt.; (802) 464–5608 or (800) 722–4427;

www.vikingmotel.net. Two-bedroom family suites are available, and all rooms have color cable TV. Within walking distance to downtown Wilmington and shuttle service, live entertainment on weekends, families very welcome. $$–$$$

The Vintage Motel, Route 9, 1 mile west of the center of Wilmington, Vt.; (802) 464–8842. An outdoor heated pool, continental breakfast, and a fireplace lounge are among this motel's facilities. Barbecues, hiking trails, and a driving range are on the premises, and ski or snowmobile packages are available. $$

The White House, Route 9, just east of Wilmington, Vt.; (800) 541–2135 or (802) 464–2135; www.whitehouseinn.com. Suitable for children over the age of 10. This big, white, 1912 mansion on a hilltop is a landmark. Tracks of sleds radiate down its front lawn in the winter on a hill that looks like it was made just for sliding. An indoor pool beckons the kids; a whirlpool and sauna await their parents. In the winter, these are especially welcome after a day on the inn's own cross-country and snowshoe trails. They have a complete ski-touring center, with rentals available. The rooms are furnished with antiques. $$$

Yankee Doodle Lodge, 344 Route 100, West Dover, Vt.; (802) 464–5591 or (800) 388–5591. Family rooms and family rates are available and breakfast is served at this lodge, ¼ mile from Mount Snow. Heated outdoor pool, whirlpool, fireplace lounges, card room, game room. $$

Camping

Greenwood Lodge and Campsites, Route 9, Woodford, Vt. (west of Wilmington); (802) 442–2547. Surrounding the Youth Hostel are more than a hundred campsites, both open and wooded. Wheelchair-accessible campsites.

Molly Stark State Park, Route 9, Wilmington, Vt.; (802) 464–5460. A small campground with few frills and a quiet, bosky setting.

Woodford State Park, Route 9, Woodford, Vt. (west of Wilmington); (802) 447–7169. The park's 104 campsites include lean-tos. The swimming beach has canoe and rowboat rentals and a playground.

For More Information

Mount Snow Valley Chamber of Commerce, P.O. Box 3, Page House, Main Street, Wilmington, VT 05363; (802) 464–8092; www.visitvermont.com.

The Ski Triangle: Stratton, Bromley, and Magic Mountain

Although this region's three major ski areas make it synonymous with winter sports, there's plenty to do the rest of the year, too, as two of those mountains become summer playgrounds. Bromley's Alpine slide and its related activities have made it a major attraction quite apart from its winter fame as one of New England's first ski mountains.

COOL Facts

It Happened First at Bromley Mountain

- First to change the shape of the terrain by contouring the slopes.
- First in Vermont to roll snow to pack it down for skiers.
- One of the first to use snow-making machines.

Bromley Mountain Alpine Slide and Chairlift (ages 4 and up)

Route 11, 6 miles east of Manchester, Vt.; (802) 824–5522; www.bromley.com. Open weather permitting late May through mid-June weekends only, mid-June through Labor Day daily, September through mid-October weekends, Sunday through Friday 10:00 A.M. to 5:00 P.M., Saturday 10:00 A.M. to 6:00 P.M. Admission: $$, under age 6 free with adult.

America's longest alpine slide is a full ⅔ mile of fast fun, aboard a bobsled that rides without snow. But it is not the only kid-friendly activity at Bromley's Mountain Thrill Zone. The chairlift that takes skiers up the mountain in the winter becomes a scenic ride in the summer. Gravity-fueled DevalKarts are low-slung, four-wheeled carts suitable for those who are ten years old and up and meet the height requirements. Other attractions include a trampoline, miniature golf, and a fun park for children under age six, with bumper boats and an inflatable play space.

Bromley Mountain (ages 3 and up)

Bromley Mountain, Route 11, a few miles east of Manchester Center, Vt.; (802) 824–5522 (information), (800) 865–4786 (lodging); www.bromley.com. Ski area open from late November through March, snow permitting. Rates vary.

Being family-friendly has been the key to Bromley's year-round success. This ski area has an especially gentle slope for learners and small children and good packages that include lodging and lifts. Learner's packages add lessons at their well-regarded ski school, and some include a learn-to-ski guarantee. Views of Mount Equinox and the valley aren't the only bonus of its south-facing trails. This southern exposure makes it warmer in the iciest part of the season and shelters it from some of the worst winds.

Stratton Mountain (all ages)

Route 30, about 10 miles south of Manchester Center, Vt.; (802) 297–2200 (information), (800) 843–6867 (lodging); www.stratton.com. Skiing from late November through April, snow permitting. Gondola rides Sunday through Friday 10:00 A.M. to 5:00 P.M. and Saturday and holidays 10:00 A.M. to 7:00 P.M., late June through early October. Gondola fare: $$–$$$, age 6 and under free.

In the European ski village tradition, Stratton is a self-contained resort with slopeside condos, modern base facilities, and its own village of shops with Tyrolean architecture. Lifts, snow-making, trails, and the physical plant are all first class. Midweek specials include **free** lodging with the purchase of a three-day ski lift pass. College students and military personnel ski at half-price midweek.

Slopes and lifts for young skiers cover forty-five acres of gentle terrain, with three chairlifts and two surface lifts. These are like rolling rugs that carry youngsters safely to the top. This area is separated from mountain trails used by other skiers, so there's no pass-through by fast skiers.

Stratton is where Jake Burton Carpenter tested his first snowboard prototypes and where snowboarding began its meteoric rise. It's still one of the best places for boarders, with a snowboard school, frequent events, and quality facilities. Along with its championship halfpipe, the 3,000-foot boarding park has tabletops, quarterpipes, and spines. The half-pipe is lighted for night boarding.

Stratton has a cross-country ski center (802–297–1880), a ten-passenger sled for thirty- to forty-five-minute rides on weekends and holidays by reservation, and a lighted outdoor skating rink with rentals and skating parties (802–297–2200). They also have a snowshoeing program, with tours, rentals, and instruction.

Kidskamp programs include a wide range of ages, beginning with the Kidskare child-care facility (ages six weeks to five years). Young skiers can begin at age four with full- or half-day Kidskamp that mixes ski lessons with snowplay, or they can begin at age three with private lessons. Parents are welcome to accompany young skiers in private lessons (a great help when you are skiing with them later, since you will know what they have been shown in the lesson).

Junior skiers ages seven and up can choose beginning lessons on skis and snow-boards or junior group lessons. The beginning lessons include all-day lift tickets and equipment. The junior group lessons are graded so that youngsters learn with people of their own skill level. A Kidskamp for ages seven through twelve includes some challenges to help skiers develop skills and push themselves to new levels of confidence. The cost of these programs ranges from $25 for a junior group lesson to $79 for all-day childcare or Kidskamp.

Like other ski areas, Stratton Mountain is lively year-round, with sports and activities and a village filled with shops and restaurants. The gondola takes passengers to the top of the mountain for views in good weather in summer and fall (Stratton is southern Vermont's tallest mountain), and the resort offers golf, tennis, mountain biking, and hiking within easy reach. Kidskamp programs in the summer include hiking, swimming, crafts, golf, gondola rides, kite-flying, nature walks, and games. Prices range from $45 to $59, depending on the child's age and the program.

Sun Bowl Ranch (ages 2 and up)

Stratton Mountain, Vt.; (802) 297–9210 on weekends or (800) STRATTON on weekdays; www.stratton.com. Trail rides and hayrides mid-June to mid-October 9:00 A.M. to 5:00 P.M. Rates are $$–$$$ for hayrides. Donkey rides are $$.

In addition to trail rides on horseback, Sun Bowl Ranch offers rides in its farm wagon, which is pulled by two huge Belgian draft horses. Sleigh rides begin with the first snow cover (on weekends only). For an extra fee they will pack a picnic lunch for you to eat on the trail. Trail rides cost $25 to $50.

Stratton Mountain Skate Park (ages 12 and up)

Stratton Mountain, Vt.; (800) STRATTON; www.stratton.com. Open late June through early October, Sunday through Friday 10:00 A.M. to 5:00 P.M., Saturday and holidays 10:00 A.M. to 7:00 P.M. Daily fee: $$.

This state-of-the-art course has an interconnected halfpipe and street course, with full equipment rentals. Full day with crash pack is $25, which includes the skating fee.

Magic Mountain (ages 4 and up)

Route 11, Londonderry, Vt.; (802) 824–5645 or (888) MSTRMAG; www.magicmtn.com. Skiing from late November through mid-April, snow permitting. Rates vary.

We like Magic's casual atmosphere and friendly staff, as well as its complete lack of glitz. We also like the family crowd of serious skiers and the fact that each trail gives skiers a little challenge. A beginner's trail will have a short stretch that borders on intermediate, while intermediate trails will stretch a skier's talents just a bit beyond—but only for a short distance. A nice lodge, short lines, low lift prices, lots of variety, and trails for all levels make it a welcome alternative to the more resortlike areas. Magic Mountain has a tube park with plenty of lanes, an all-terrain park, and a half-tube for boarders.

Sleigh Rides and Cross-Country Skiing

- **Taylor Farm,** Route 11, West Londonderry, Vt.; (802) 824–5690. Sleigh rides are Friday through Sunday, noon to 8:00 P.M. Picnics around a campfire are $5.00 extra. You will need a reservation for both rides and picnics.

- **Karl Pfister Sleigh Rides,** Landgrove, Vt. (south of Bromley); (802) 824–6320. A four-passenger sled and two twelve-passenger traverse sleds with bench seats take guests for forty-five-minute rides across scenic pastures, days or evenings. Reservations are required.

- **Wild Wings Ski Touring Center,** Peru, Vt.; (802) 824–6793. Not far from Bromley, this family-oriented facility has miles of well-kept cross-country trails.

Public **Swimming**

- **Hapgood Pond Recreation Area,** off Route 11, Peru, Vt.; (802) 362–2307. Along with the beach at this Forest Service area, you will find campsites and walking trails. $4.00 per car.
- **Jamaica State Park,** off Route 30, Jamaica, Vt.; (802) 874–4600. Campground, picnic area, and walking trails suitable for strollers too.

Taylor Farm (ages 5 and up)

825 Route 11, Londonderry, Vt.; (802) 824–5690; www.vtcheese.com. Free.

Just south of Bromley Mountain Ski Area, this farm has a herd of about 125 Holsteins, whose milk the Taylors make into Gouda cheese. Visitors can learn about cheese making and, if they call ahead to check the times, even watch the process. One day each month in the summer the Taylors hold a Farm Day, with tours, wagon rides, and food samples. On winter weekends and during holiday weeks, Taylor Farm offers horse-drawn sleigh rides by reservation.

The Vermont Country Store (ages 5 and up)

Center of Weston, Vt.; (802) 824–3184; www.vermontcountrystore.com. Open 9:00 A.M. to 5:00 P.M. Monday through Saturday, year-round; July through October open until 6:00 P.M. Free.

Although it's a place to shop, this restored store is also a good place just to get the feeling of a general store of a century ago. Mixed in with the modern merchandise for sale now are its original wooden display cases and old high-button shoes hanging from the rafters. The store is the real thing, updated with good, reliable things you thought no one made anymore, like root beer candy and apple butter, dishcloths, and popcorn poppers that don't plug into an outlet. The building is original, too, with rambling ells added recently. The penny candy counter is phenomenal—rows of jars filled with temptation. Next door, their catalog outlet store sells first-quality overstocks and out-of-season goods at real bargain prices.

Where to Eat

Dostal's Lodge, Magic Mountain Access Road, Londonderry, Vt.; (802) 824–6700 or (800) 255–5373; fax (802) 824–6701; www.dostals.com. The dining room serves Wiener schnitzel and other international favorites. $–$$

Mulligan's, Stratton Mountain, Vt.; (802) 297–9293. A busy publike atmosphere, with hearty fare that runs from juicy, big burgers to Maine lobster. The food is dependably good, and children's meals are an excellent value, starting at $1.50. $

Village Sandwich Shop, in the Weston Village Store, Weston, Vt.; (802) 824–5477. Open daily 10:00 A.M. to 5:30 P.M. Sandwiches made on wholesome, hearty bread from Baba Louis Bakery are big enough to feed two when paired with a bowl of chili. You can eat on the covered porch or at picnic tables on the lawn. $

Where to Stay

Colonial House Inn and Motel, Route 100, Weston, Vt.; (802) 824–6286 or (800) 639–5033. A friendly cross between a home-style B&B and a motel, the inn serves home-cooked meals and has a bakery known for its fruit and berry pies and its coffee cakes. That should tell you what to expect at breakfast. $–$$

Dostal's Lodge, Magic Mountain Access Road, Londonderry, Vt.; (802) 824–6700 or (800) 255–5373; fax (802) 824–6701; www.dostals.com. An Austrian lodge with spotless motel-style rooms that are well furnished and roomy. For summer they have a large outdoor pool. Package plans come with or without meals (see the section "Where to Eat"). It's within skiing distance of the base of Magic Mountain, and most skiers are happy to opt for the good variety of menu choices and not have to drive somewhere for dinner. Summer visitors may want more flexibility. $–$$

Magic View Motel, 3806 Route 11, Londonderry, Vt.; (802) 824–3793. Close to both Magic Mountain and Bromley, with beautiful views. A refrigerator in each room. Family rooms sleep three to five people. Game room. $–$$

Trailside Condominiums, Magic Mountain, Vt.; (802) 824–5620; www.magicmountainlodging.com. Year-round lodging is available at the foot of the mountain, in fully equipped condos with kitchens. $$

White Pine Lodge, Route 11, Londonderry, Vt.; (802) 824–3909; www.thewhitepinelodge.com. Fully furnished suites have fireplaces and kitchens; pets are welcome. $–$$

Camping

Hapgood Pond Recreation Area, off Route 11, Peru, Vt.; (802) 362–2307. At this Forest Service area, you will find a swimming beach, campsites, and walking trails. (Follow the unpaved, scenic road from here to the village of Weston.) $

Jamaica State Park, off Route 30, Jamaica, Vt.; (802) 874–4600. A large campground, with lean-tos, tent and trailer sites, a picnic area, and walking trails. $

Bennington and Arlington

Okay, so the Battle of Bennington wasn't fought in Bennington. It was fought in nearby New York, but that was a geographical accident. Bennington was the supply base and the Continental army encampment. In case you've forgotten your history, Bennington was important because this was where George Washington's ragged army beat the well-trained and well-supplied British army and, in doing so, stopped their plan to encircle and cut off the Continental army. General John Burgoyne and his troops had to retreat, which led to the British surrendering altogether at Yorktown, Virginia. It was, quite literally, the turning point of the war for independence.

COOL Facts

The American flag was first carried into battle during the Revolutionary War, at the Battle of Bennington.

Bennington Battle Monument (ages 3 and up)

Monument Circle, Old Bennington, Vt.; (802) 447–0550. From the intersection of Route 9 and Route 7 in Bennington, follow Route 9 west to the village of West Bennington. Turn right at the green, where you will see the monument ahead of you. Open daily mid-April through October, 9:00 A.M. to 5:00 P.M. Admission: $

The momentous battle is commemorated by a stone monument 306 feet tall, the tallest structure in Vermont. You can take an elevator to the top. From this lookout you can see Vermont, Massachusetts, and New York. A diorama depicts the battle and the monument itself, and you learn interesting facts about the Revolution, the Green Mountain Boys (a famous Vermont fighting unit led by Ethan Allen), and early Vermont. An annual battle reenactment takes place here in August.

Bennington Museum (ages 8 and up)

West Main Street (Route 9), Bennington, Vt.; (802) 447–1571; www.benningtonmuseum. com. Open daily year-round, 9:00 A.M. to 6:00 P.M. June through October and 9:00 A.M. to 5:00 P.M. November through May. Admission: $$, under age 12 free.

The Bennington Museum explores regional art and history, with significant collections of American glassware and quilts. The museum has an old schoolhouse and features the largest public exhibit of Grandma Moses paintings in the world. Shown here, too, is the first American flag brought into battle (at the Battle of Bennington). While many of these treasures will not excite most children, the kids will be interested in the good exhibits of early toys and dolls.

Park McCullough House (ages 7 and up)

Corner of Park and West Streets, North Bennington, Vt.; (802) 442–5441; www.park mccullough.org. Follow Route 67A north from Bennington. In the village of North Bennington, follow the sign 1 block west. Guided tours begin on the hour, Thursday through Monday 10:00 A.M. to 4:00 P.M. May through October. Admission: $$, under age 12 free.

Tours of this elegant Victorian mansion take about an hour, which includes time to wander through the carriage barns and gardens. Kids will especially like the collection of carriages and sleighs and the playhouse on the front lawn. The playhouse is a miniature of the mansion, just big enough for one small room. Now fully wheelchair-accessible, the large mansion was the home of two former governors. Period clothing from the families who lived here is displayed, along with original furnishings and decorative arts.

Public **Beach**

Lake Paran, off Route 67A, North Bennington. Go north on Main Street, then turn right onto Houghton Street; follow small green-and-white sign after railroad tracks. This **free** public beach is not a huge attraction, but it's a nice side trip on a hot day.

Vermont State Fish Culture Station (ages 5 and up)

South Stream Road, Bennington, Vt.; (802) 447–2844. From Route 9 on the east side of town, turn south onto South Stream Road. Open daily 8:00 A.M. to 3:30 P.M. **Free.**

Kids are fascinated at the sight of thousands of trout swimming in the tanks. Anglers can't help but wonder which streams they will be released into—and when.

Sunset Playland (ages 4 and up)

Historic Route 7A, Bennington, Vt.; (802) 442–3555. Open April through September. In summer, open Monday through Friday noon to 9:00 P.M., Saturday and Sunday 11:00 A.M. to 9:00 P.M., but hours vary with the season and are shorter in the spring and fall. Prices: $.

A pleasant amusement park with miniature golf, batting practice, go-carts, and a snack bar.

Deer Park (all ages)

Veterans Memorial Drive, Bennington, Vt., behind the Chamber of Commerce visitor center; (802) 447–3311. **Free.**

This grassy park is a good place for kids to run and to watch the herd of deer who live in its central enclosure. The miniature covered bridge is a popular place to take pictures.

The Apple Barn (ages 5 and up)

Route 7, south of Bennington, Vt.; (802) 447–7780; www.theapplebarn.com. Open daily April 1 through January 5, 8:30 A.M. to 6:00 P.M. **Free.**

Primarily an apple orchard stand with a bake shop, the attraction here for children is the cornfield maze. English country houses with their trimmed hedge mazes have nothing on this one; you can get lost here just as easily.

Lake Shaftsbury State Park (all ages)

Historic Route 7A, Shaftsbury, Vt.; (802) 375–9978. Admission: $.

The 101 acres of this well-maintained park are for day use only. At its pond, held by a small dam, you will find a playground and rowboats,

COOL Facts

Eskers are long mounds of sand and gravel left behind by rivers that tunneled under glaciers as the glaciers began to melt. These rivers carried so much sand and gravel along with them that it settled and began to build up along the streambeds. By the time the glaciers had melted, these eskers had become long snakes of earth, much higher than the surrounding land, and the streams found lower paths to follow. Today, many sandpits, where sand and gravel are taken for construction and for sanding highways, are old eskers. Look for these by the roadside as you travel, and try to see the path the esker takes across the landscape.

paddleboats, and canoes for rent in the summer. The picnic area overlooks the pond, and a nature trail invites you to amble around its perimeter. The walk takes about half an hour. Kids who have studied about the glaciers that covered New England during the last Ice Age will want to follow the trail to the opposite side of the lake. There they can walk along the top of the esker, one of the best and most visible we've seen.

Bennington Community Built Park (all ages)

Kocher Drive (exit 1 off Route 7), Bennington, Vt.; (802) 442–1053 or (802) 442–2401. **Free.**

Everybody will be happy at this park, which offers full facilities including bathrooms, a picnic area, and barbecue grills. Little ones can play on one of two age-appropriate playgrounds, and the older kids can use the basketball courts, skateboard park, or even the BMX park, while the grown-ups enjoy the sculptures.

Candle Mill Village (ages 8 and up)

Old Mill Road, East Arlington, Vt.; (802) 375–6068 or (800) 772–3759; www.candlemillvillage. com. Open daily, year-round, 10:00 A.M. to 5:00 P.M. **Free** (charge for candlemaking).

Candle Mill Village is Vermont's oldest candle shop and its attraction, besides the beautiful surroundings and good shopping, is the dip-your-own-candle room. While many historic villages and restorations have demonstrations of old-fashioned candlemaking, not many allow you to try it yourself.

Norman Rockwell Exhibit (ages 10 and up)

3772 Route 7A, Arlington, Vt.; (802) 375–6423; www.normanrockwellvt.com. Open daily May through October from 9:00 A.M. to 5:00 P.M. and November through April 10:00 A.M. to 4:00 P.M.; closed January. Admission: $.

Inside an 1875 historic church, former Rockwell models and friends show your family

The **King's Pines**

When Vermont and New Hampshire were colonial holdings of Great Britain, all large, straight, white pine trees were reserved for the king. These "King's Pines" were cut as masts for the Royal Navy, and it was illegal to cut one for any other use. Timber surveyors who found stands of tall straight pines more than 18 inches in diameter marked them with three ax cuts in the shape of an arrow to identify them as the king's.

around the exhibits of *Saturday Evening Post* covers, illustrations, and printed works, with a fifteen-minute film. A gift shop, of course, completes the picture.

Fisher-Scott Memorial Pines (ages 6 and up)
Red Mountain Road, Arlington, Vt. Shortly after crossing the Battenkill River, look for Red Mountain Road on the left. About 0.2 mile from Route 7A, look for a widened area on the left where you can pull the car off the road. Follow the short trail. Free.

Although the forests that cover much of Vermont and New Hampshire seem to have been there forever, most of them are actually later growth. Nearly every inch of both states has been cleared for farms or cut for timber at least once since its settlement. But on this hillside is a rare stand of huge first-growth trees. They were here when the first colonists carved their farms out of the wilderness and have remained largely because the hillside is too steep for timbering or farming. In colonial times, trees this size would have been reserved for masts for the Royal Navy. See how many people it takes to hug one of these giants.

Where to Eat

Alldays and Onions, 519 East Main Street, Bennington, Vt.; (802) 447–0043. Open 8:00 A.M. to 9:00 P.M. Monday through Saturday. Healthy, well-prepared sandwiches and main dishes are served in a casual, cafe-like setting where families will feel right at home. The dinner menu offers sophisticated choices, such as scallops in a Dijon tarragon sauce and grilled fresh tuna with chili soy sauce. $–$$

Arlington Dairy Bar, Route 7A, Arlington, Vt.; (802) 375–2546. The usual ice cream plus dogs and burgers. $

Blue Benn Diner, 102 Hunt Street, Bennington, Vt.; (802) 442–9877. An absolute must for the diner enthusiast—real American diner food at real prices, and the atmosphere doesn't have to try to be authentic. Along with the usual meatloaf and roast pork dinners, you'll find some unexpected south-of-the-border and other "exotic" dishes. $

Vermont Steak House, 716 Main Street, Bennington, Vt.; (802) 442–9793. Open May through mid-October. Good food and prices with children's menu. $–$$

Wagon Wheel Restaurant, Historic Route 7A, Arlington, Vt.; (802) 375–9508. Family favorite for locals. $–$$

Your Belly's Deli, 100 Pleasant Street, Bennington, Vt.; (802) 442–3653. Great sandwiches, generous portions, nice relaxed atmosphere. $

Where to Stay

The Autumn Inn, 924 East Main Street, Bennington, Vt.; (802) 447–7625. Comfortable inn with steakhouse on premises, plus snack and soda machines, coin-op laundry, and cable TV. Adjoining rooms available. $–$$

Best Western New Englander Motor Inn, 220 Northside Drive, Bennington, Vt.; (802) 442–6311 or (800) 528–1234. Children under 12 stay **free, free** continental breakfast, cable TV, restaurant and lounge on premises. Outdoor pool. $$

Candlelight Motel, Historic Route 7A, Arlington, Vt.; (802) 375–6647 or (800) 348–5294; www.candlelightmotel.com. Children under 5 stay **free.** Spacious rooms, cable TV, **free** breakfast, pool, family rates, quiet setting. $–$$

Cutleaf Maples Motel, 3420 Route 7A, Arlington, Vt.; (802) 375–2725. Home-cooked breakfasts available. Fireplace, **free** cribs, e-mail access, cable TV, **free** coffee, bus stop nearby. $ for family rooms

Darling Kelly's Motel, Route 7 South, Bennington, Vt.; (802) 442–2322 or (877) 447–1364. Continental breakfast included. Offers a pool, cable TV; pets allowed if you call ahead. $–$$

Green River Inn, 2480 Sandgate Road, Sandgate, Vt.; (802) 375–2272 or (888) 648–2212; www.greenriverinn.com. This out-of-the-way inn is quiet and comfortable, offers special events and children's programs, and has a gourmet restaurant on site that uses local and inn-raised ingredients. $$

Hill Farm Inn, 458 Hill Farm Road, Arlington, Vt.; (802) 375–2269 or (800) 882–2545; www.hillfarminn.com. Beautiful views over Battenkill River. Offers full country breakfast; cottages available; families welcome. $$–$$$

For More Information

Arlington Chamber of Commerce, Booth on Main Street, P.O. Box 245, Route 7A, Arlington, VT 05250; (802) 442–5494; www.arlingtonvt.com.

Bennington Chamber of Commerce, One Veterans Memorial Drive, Bennington, VT 05201; (802) 447–3311 or (800) 229–0252; www.bennington.com.

Manchester and Dorset

The visual beauty of its setting, with Mount Equinox rising directly behind it, would set Manchester, Vermont, apart even if its streets weren't lined with fine mansions of the very rich who made it their summer home in the 1800s. Many of these estates are still private homes; others have become fine inns.

Manchester Center is known for its outlet shops, and several outlet malls feature everything from clothing to furniture. Late summer and early winter bring the best sales.

Robert Todd Lincoln's Hildene (ages 7 and up)

Route 7A, Manchester Village, Vt.; (802) 362–1788; www.hildene.org. Open daily 9:30 A.M. to 4:00 P.M., mid-May through October. Admission: Guided tours $$; grounds pass: $$; age 5 and under free.

Abraham Lincoln's son, Robert Todd, first visited Manchester as a child one summer while his father was busy in the White House. Todd, his brother, and their mother stayed at the Equinox, which even then was a fine resort worthy of a first family. The whole family, president included, planned to return the next summer, but a night at the theater put an end to their plans. Todd did come back to Manchester often, however, first as the guest of his law partner, who owned the fine home that is now Ormsby Hill Inn. Todd liked Manchester summers so much that he built his own estate behind his partner's, overlooking the wide valley and the mountains. He surrounded it with gardens, which have been restored and are open to visitors, along with the mansion.

Abraham Lincoln's tall silk hat is there, along with other family mementos. The house is quietly grand, with an unusual organ that works like a player piano, and a huge bathtub in which the even more huge President William Howard Taft was once stuck. (He had to be pulled out by the serving staff.) Interesting here, too, is a chance to see the servants' rooms and the kitchen where they worked.

Around Christmas the home is open for candlelight tours, which include a trip up the long driveway in a horse-drawn sleigh. These are in the early evening, by reservation only, and are suitable for children who will not get too antsy waiting in the long line for their turn to board the sleigh.

Cross-country ski trails crisscross the woods and meadows below the house, with some of the best scenery of any in the southern part of the state.

Bushee Battenkill Valley Farm (ages 3 and up)

Richville Road, Manchester, Vt.; (802) 362–4088. Open June through October, weekends only. Admission: $–$$.

Not exactly a petting zoo, the farm is a working family venture of the Bushees and their three children. But the animals seem always ready for visitors. They include a Vietnamese pig, chickens, goats, rabbits, cows, a horse, a pony, llamas, and sheep. You can watch milking or wool processing—whatever is happening in each season. It's wheelchair-accessible.

The Equinox Spa (ages 12 and up)

Route 7A, Manchester Village, Vt.; (802) 362–4700 or (800) 362–4747. Fees vary depending on services selected.

A spa may seem like a strange destination for a book on family travel, but families come in all sizes and shapes. The health spa in the backyard of the Equinox recalls its origins as a hotel built around a source of pure spring water. We suggest a trip here as a very good bonding weekend for a mother and pre-teen or teenage daughter. The spa staff is helpful, good-humored, and friendly, recognizing that you are there for a vacation as well as a healthy interlude. A large indoor pool, saunas, massage and herbal therapies, and fitness

Scenic Drive

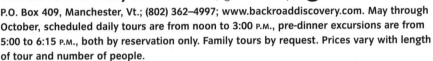

Equinox Skyline Drive, Route 7A, Sunderland, Vt.; (802) 362–1115. Open May through October. Toll for car and driver $$, plus $ per passenger. The 5.2-mile drive up to the top of Mount Equinox is steep and winding, but it's paved all the way. At the top, you can see four states and Canada (Quebec). It is a breathtaking place to look at fall foliage.

equipment are in an encouraging atmosphere that prompts you to use them. The hiking, cross-country ski trails, and snowshoe trails that ascend the slopes of Mount Equinox, directly behind the inn, are worked into the spa experience. It's a good introduction to keeping in shape and a nice way to share quality time and girl-talk.

Backroad Discovery Scenic Tours (ages 5 and up)

P.O. Box 409, Manchester, Vt.; (802) 362–4997; www.backroaddiscovery.com. **May through October, scheduled daily tours are from noon to 3:00 P.M., pre-dinner excursions are from 5:00 to 6:15 P.M., both by reservation only. Family tours by request. Prices vary with length of tour and number of people.**

Lively tour guides will show you and your family around Manchester and the surrounding areas. They will bring you out on beautiful back roads to find out-of-the-way waterfalls, abandoned marble quarries, perfect foliage viewing areas, and other neat unknown spots you'd never find on your own. Their Jeeps and four-wheel-drive vehicles carry a maximum of seven people, so these are highly personalized tours. We think of them as Vermont safaris, because you never know when you'll see a moose or deer on one of the wooded roads or tracks they explore.

Manchester Recreation Area (all ages)

Route 30, Manchester Center, Vt.; (802) 362–1439. Open daylight hours. **Free.**

A public recreation park, with swings, slides, a picnic area, basketball courts, tennis courts, and a swimming pool with lifeguard on duty. The Recreation Department also offers Summer Day Camp Programs with arts and crafts, camping, and field trips.

Windhill Horses and Tack Shop (ages 4–7)

North Road, Manchester Center, Vt.; (802) 362–2604. Various fees.

Pony rides are designed for small children, trail rides for older ones. In the winter they offer sleigh rides.

Riley Rink (ages 2 and up)

Hunter Park Road, off Route 7A, Manchester Center, Vt.; (802) 362–0150 or (866) 866–2086; www.rileyrink.com. Hours vary; call ahead for availability. Admission: $.

An Olympic-size rink with 35,000 square feet of ice provides plenty of room for skaters to learn and practice or just to play on the ice. Nonskating parents will appreciate the warm room to sit in while watching the kids. Skate rentals are available, and there is a concession stand.

American Museum of Fly Fishing (ages 10 and up)

Route 7A at Seminary Avenue, Manchester Village, Vt.; (802) 362–3300; www.amff.com. Open weekdays year-round except holidays, 10:00 A.M. to 4:00 P.M. Admission: $, students with ID free.

Older kids who love to fish might enjoy seeing the exhibits here, which look at the history and evolution of the sport, as well as the crafts and art that are associated with fly fishing. You may be surprised at how old the sport is; rods, reels, and flies shown here date from the 1500s. Much of the books, photos, art, and equipment in the museum was once owned and used by famous people, such as Daniel Webster and presidents Herbert Hoover and Dwight Eisenhower.

Girls who are squeamish about fishing because of the worms, have no fear: This is fly-fishing territory. But unless fishing is your thing, you might want to go shopping instead.

Emerald Lake State Park (all ages)

Route 7, North Dorset, Vt.; (802) 362–1655. Admission: $, under age 4 free. Season passes are available for admission to all state parks.

Interconnected trails and abandoned roads offer 6 miles of walking in this 430-acre park that surrounds a lake. But more people come here for the swimming beach, picnic area with tables and fireplaces, boat and canoe rentals, playground, and campground. A free booklet describes the half-mile nature trail. Naturalists lead frequent tours exploring its environment and wildlife habitats.

COOL Facts

North America's first commercial marble quarries opened in Dorset in 1785, and they cut more than 15.5 million cubic feet of stone during the next 150 years. The Jefferson Memorial in Washington, D.C., is built of Dorset marble. So were the columns for the New York Public Library, and you can still see the leftovers from that cutting. They are in front of the parking lot for the **J. K. Adams** workshop, on Route 30 south of Dorset.

Public Swimming

- **Emerald Lake State Park,** Route 7, East Dorset; (802) 362–1655. The large lake has swimming and fishing as well as boat rentals. Admission: $.

- **Manchester Recreation Area,** Route 30, Manchester Center; (802) 362–1439. Pool open daylight hours June through August. Day admission $–$$. Residents of Manchester and Dorset pay half price.

Merck Forest and Farmland Center (ages 5 and up)

Route 315, Rupert, Vt.; (802) 394–7836; www.merckforest.com. From Route 30 in East Rupert, turn west onto Route 315. Admission: free, with fees for certain programs and events.

Miles of walking and cross-country ski trails crisscross the woods and meadows of this working organic farm. A well-labeled nature trail, farm animals, a maple sugarhouse, and regular weekend family programs and activities focus on farming and the environment.

Slate Quarry (ages 7 and up)

Route 153, at the north end of West Pawlet, Vt. Free.

There's something fascinating about quarries, but we hesitate to suggest visiting most of them with children because of their steep, unrailed sides and the deep water they hold. However, this one is clearly visible from the road, which passes through the middle of it. The town was built in the 1890s to house the workers for the quarries; be sure to look at the slate roofs, often in patterns of different-colored stone.

Mach's General Store (all ages)

Route 30, Pawlet, Vt.; (802) 325–2149. Open Monday through Saturday 7:00 A.M. to 6:30 P.M., Sunday 8:00 A.M. to 12:30 P.M. Free.

Along with being a good place to buy picnic supplies, the store is worth a stop to look through the glass top of the cabinet in back. There you can see straight down into the chasm cut by the brook that runs far below.

Where to Eat

Candeleros, Route 7A, Manchester Center, Vt.; (802) 362–0836. Billed as "a Mexican cantina," this traditional Tex-Mex restaurant specializes in guacamole that is prepared tableside. A children's menu is available, and they are open seven days a week for lunch and dinner. $–$$

Garlic John's, Routes 11 and 30, Bromley Mountain Road, Manchester Center, Vt., (802) 362–9843. Offers informal Italian cuisine, a children's menu, and take-out. $$

Mach's Brick Oven Bakery, Route 30, Pawlet, Vt.; (802) 325–6331. Serves lunch and snacks, including pizza, and sells fresh-baked bread and goodies. $

Manchester Pizza House, Manchester Shopping Center, Manchester Center, Vt.; (802) 362–3338. Call ahead for orders ready when you get there. This pizza came highly recommended by several ski magazines, and we agree. Specializing in standard fare plus gyros, homemade pasta, and fresh-from-the-oven grinders. Open until 10:00 P.M. weekdays, 11:00 P.M. weekends. They deliver to the Manchester area. $

Mulligan's Manchester, Route 7A, between Manchester Village and Manchester Center, Vt.; (802) 362–3663. Children welcome in this relaxed pub-style restaurant with a bargain-priced children's menu. Great appetizer menu and sandwiches, plus plenty of entrees. Weekend entertainment. $–$$

Peltier's Store, Route 30, Dorset, Vt. A good place to stop for picnic makings or snacks. $

Sirloin Saloon, intersection of Route 11 and Route 30, Manchester Center, Vt.; (802) 362–2600. Open for dinner only. Full children's menu, plus steaks, live Maine lobster, salad bar, homemade desserts, and entrees tailored for health. Voted "Best Steakhouse in Vermont." $$

The Station Restaurant, off Route 30, Pawlet, Vt.; (802) 325–3041. Has a lunch counter and tables, serving three meals daily in an old railway station. $

Where to Stay

Manchester is one of the priciest places to stay in Vermont. Perhaps you can mitigate this somewhat by finding great bargains at the outlet stores, but if you are looking for budget rooms, you might be better off looking farther north or in the Bennington area to the south.

Barrows House, Main Street, Dorset, Vt.; (802) 867–4455 or (800) 639–1620; www.barrowshouse.com. Spreading over a large property, this nine-building inn is a favorite of families. The dining room has a children's menu. $$

The Equinox, Route 7A, Manchester Village, Vt.; (802) 362–4700 or (800) 362–4747. Manchester Village is dominated by the façade of The Equinox, a grand old hotel beautifully restored to its regal elegance. A full-service resort, it offers everything from a golf course and cross-country ski center to its own school of falconry. Children under 12 stay **free,** but there is a charge of $10 for a crib or rollaway bed. Kids will be interested to know that Abraham Lincoln's children once stayed here (see Robert Todd Lincoln's Hildene, early in this section). $$$

FourWinds Country Motel, 7379 Historic Route 7A, Manchester, Vt.; (802) 362–1105 or (877) 456–7654; www.vtweb.com/four winds. Nice, large rooms; coffeemaker, refrigerator, and hair dryer in-room; cable TV; gorgeous mountain views from front and back patios; outdoor pool; continental breakfast included; packages available. $$

Inn at West View Farm, Route 30, Dorset, Vt.; (802) 867–5715 or (800) 769–4903; www. innatwestviewfarm.com. This rambling country inn was among the first farms in Vermont to welcome summer guests. It still offers warm hospitality to families, and its outstanding dining room specializes in dishes using locally grown products. $–$$

Manchester View Motel, north of Manchester Center, Vt., on Route 7A; (802) 362–2739; www.manchesterview.com. A cross between a hotel and a motel, with the best of each. Rooms are spread among several buildings, each with mountain views. Half the rooms have a fireplace, many have a whirlpool tub, and all are individually decorated. Family suites are a real bargain. During Manchester's "Prelude to Christmas," they offer three nights for the price of two. $$

Marbledge Motor Inn, Route 7, East Dorset, Vt.; (802) 362–1418; www.marbledge inn.com. Large rooms and efficiencies with special packages available, home-cooked meals at their restaurant, children's menu, cable TV, country store next door. $–$$

Olympia Motor Lodge, Route 7A North, Manchester, Vt.; (802) 362–1700 or (888) 3–OLYMPIA; www.olympia-vt.com. Nice countryside setting with good mountain views, heated pool, tennis courts, and cable TV. Includes golf privileges at Manchester Country Club. Sit out on the back deck and watch the deer and wild turkeys graze in the yard. $$

Silas Griffin Inn, 178 South Main Street, Danby, Vt.; (802) 293–5567 or (800) 545–1509. A fine Victorian home, but not over-decorated or frilly. A full breakfast each day is included. The inn has a heated outdoor pool and a six-person heated whirlpool outside as well. $$–$$$

Weathervane Motel, Historic Route 7A, Manchester, Vt.; (802) 362–2444 or (800) 262–1317; www.weathervanemotel.com. Huge rooms with dressing rooms, refrigerators, coffeemakers, cable TV. In-ground heated pool; continental breakfast included. $$

Wiley Inn, Route 11, Peru, Vt.; (802) 824–6600 or (800) 843–6600; www.wileyinn.com. Large family rooms, children's playground, heated pool, and outdoor hot tub, ten minutes from Manchester. $$

Camping

Emerald Lake State Park, Route 7, East Dorset, Vt.; (802) 362–1655. The park has 105 campsites (including 36 lean-tos), with toilets, showers, swimming, and fishing. Boat rentals are available at the lake. $

For More Information

Manchester and the Mountains Chamber of Commerce, 5046 Main Street, Manchester Center, VT 05255; (802) 362–2100; www.manchesterandmtns.com.

Annual Events

APRIL

Easter at Stratton, Stratton Mountain, Vt., (802) 297–2200. A parade and Easter egg hunt. The golden egg contains a **free** season pass for Stratton for the next year.

MAY

Taste of the Village, White House of Wilmington, Vt., (802) 896–6037, first weekend of the month. Proceeds benefit the Wilmington Congregational Church Restoration Fund. Features dinner and a fashion show, complete with door prizes.

Annual Lip Sync Concert, Memorial Hall Center for the Arts, West Main Street, Wilmington, Vt., (802) 464–8075, late May. Held to raise money for Project Graduation. Admission: $$

Memorial Day Weekend Open House at Adams Farm, Wilmington, Vt., (802) 464–3762. Two-day open house with puppet shows, Vermont history lectures, demonstrations of spinning and weaving, agricultural education, pony rides, and more.

The Great Duck Race, at the Deerfield River, downtown Wilmington, Vt., (802) 464–5618, Memorial Day Weekend. Proceeds go to the Make-a-Wish Foundation. Before and after the ducks are let loose at noon, there are plenty of great activities, including a barbecue, bake sale, face painting, and more than a hundred prizes.

Vermont Children's Festival, on The Green, Weston, Vt.; www.westonvt.com.

JUNE

Children's Fishing Program at Tadingers Orvis, Wilmington, Vt., (802) 464–1223, early June. For kids 12 and up. Teaches casting and stream reading. Reservations required. Admission: $$$$

Ethan Allen Days, Arlington, Vt., (802) 375–6144, mid-June. Includes a reenactment of a Revolutionary War skirmish.

Vermont Theatre Company, "Shakespeare in the Park," Wilmington, Vt., (802) 464–8411, varied shows in late June.

JULY

Independence Day at Baker Field Party and Fireworks, Wilmington, Vt., (802) 464–8092, July 4. Includes live entertainment, vendors, and food. Donations accepted to support fireworks.

Moonlight in Vermont, Adams Farm, Wilmington, Vt., (802) 464–3762, first weekend in July. Enjoy the barbershop quartet and hayride. Reservations highly recommended.

Farmin' for the Fourth at Adams Farm, Wilmington, Vt., (802) 464–3762, first weekend in July. Features 1800s games and prizes, historical farming workshops, and farming activities.

Independence Day Encampment and Display, the Living History Museum, Hogback Mountain, Marlboro, Vt., (802) 464–5569, first weekend in July. Reenactment of both Civil and Revolutionary War camps, including demonstrations of weapons, music, and re-creation of battle scenes.

"Celebrate Kids" at Mount Snow, West Dover, Vt., (802) 464–3333 or (800) 245–7669. Fun and games, including a treasure hunt, held at the resort.

Annual Wardsboro Parade and Street Fair, Wardsboro, Vt., (802) 896–6405, July 4. This is the oldest street fair in the state, occurring since 1949. Watch the parade of fire trucks, tractors, antique cars, bands, and floats. Plenty of food, games, crafts, and more.

Independence Day Parade, Londonderry, Vt., (802) 824–8178. This parade—one of the state's oldest—ties up Route 11, so be prepared.

Hometown Fourth of July, Bennington, Vt., at Willow Park, (802) 477–3311, July 4. Features food, entertainment, children's games, popcorn, and a fireworks display.

Washington County Band Concert, at Robert Todd Lincoln's Hildene, Manchester, Vt., early July, (802) 362–1788. Picnics on the lawn. **Free.**

Old Home Day, Jamaica, Vt., (802) 874–4160, late July. The whole town welcomes back former residents with a street fair, barbecue, parade, and general merrymaking.

Vermont State Chili Cookoff and Salsa Too, Mount Snow Resort, West Dover, Vt., (802) 464–3333 or (800) 245–7669, last weekend of July. Plenty of chili- and salsa-tasting fun to add to the midsummer heat. Enjoy the games, live music, and dancing.

AUGUST

Living History Time Line, the Living History Museum, Marlboro, Vt., (802) 464–5569, first weekend in August. Scenes reenacted from Roman times to today. Music and fun.

Old Home Week Celebrations, Wilmington, Vt., (802) 464–1446 or (877) 887–6884, second week of August. Includes activities at Adams Farm, Mount Mills Boat Ride, a barbecue at Bakers Field, dances, parades, **free** concerts, and a pig and beef roast.

Revolutionary War Days, Living History Museum, Marlboro, Vt., (802) 464–5569, third weekend in August. Demonstrations and reenactments from the American Revolutionary War.

Garlic Festival, Wilmington, Vt., (802) 368–7147, last weekend of August. Includes music and festivities for all ages.

Dulcimer Daze, Memorial Hall Center for the Arts, Wilmington, Vt., (802) 368–7437 or (802) 464–8411, last weekend in August. Concert and workshops.

Bondville Fair, Bondville, Vt., (802) 297–1882, late August. This is the oldest continually held fair in Vermont.

Battle of Bennington, Living History Museum, Marlboro, Vt., (802) 464–5569, last weekend of August. Reenactment of this important battle. Includes children's activities and music.

SEPTEMBER

Moonlight in Vermont—Evening Hayride and Puppet Show at Adams Farm, Wilmington, Vt., (802) 464–3762. Features the No Strings Marionettes. Reservations are required.

Adams Farm Barn Dance and Bonfire Party, Wilmington, Vt., (802) 464–3762, third weekend in September. Offers the fire and a dance; music is by a local band. Takes place among the animals of the farm.

OCTOBER

Oktoberfest, Mount Snow Resort, West Dover, Vt., (802) 464–3333 or (800) 245–7669, first weekend of October. Traditional German fare, real oompah bands, and chairlift rides up the mountain.

Hildene Farm, Food and Folk Art Fair, Manchester Village, Vt., (802) 362–1788, early October. Farm exhibits, a farmers' market, pony rides, and old-fashioned county fair contests, such as horse- and ox-pulling and a tractor pull.

DECEMBER

Prelude to Christmas, Manchester, Vt., (802) 362–2100. A pathway of 3,000 luminarias. The Regional Tree Lighting on December 1 begins the festivities.

Festival of Lights, Arlington, Vt., (802) 375–2800, the second weekend of December. Arlington celebrates St. Lucia Days, and the town is taken over by Nordic decorations, events, and delicacies.

Dorset Christmas, Dorset, Vt., (802) 867–5747, early December. Tree lighting in the center of the village, with a carol sing.

Winter Solstice Gathering, Merck Center, Rupert, Vt., (802) 394–7836. Sleigh rides, snowshoeing, animal tracking, winter astronomy, and maple sugaring.

The Dorset Players present their Christmas play at the playhouse in Dorset (802) 867–5570, during the first two weekends in December. Children under 12 admitted **free;** adults $$. Buy tickets well in advance.

Candlelight tours at Robert Todd Lincoln's Hildene, Manchester Village, Vt., (802) 362–1788, late December. Includes a sleigh ride to the mansion.

First Night at Stratton, Stratton Mountain, Vt., (802) 297–2200, December 31. This is a giant party and torchlit parade, ending with fireworks.

The Center of Vermont

The northernmost section of the Green Mountain National Forest covers the center of the state in green, both physically and on a map. Outlining the eastern boundary is Route 100, The Skiers' Highway, stringing together some of the legendary names in Vermont skiing: Killington, Sugarbush, and Mad River Glen. At the foot of the western slopes of these mountains are the attractive towns of Middlebury and Brandon. Here too are the city of Rutland and its surrounding towns, known for their marble production.

Rutland, Killington, and Plymouth

One of the largest ski resorts in the east, Killington is famous for its six mountains, interconnected by a system of trails and lifts. Although it is covered in The Connecticut Valley chapter, Okemo is not far south of Killington on Route 100, close enough for skiers to enjoy both on a single trip.

Wilson Castle (all ages)

Business Route 4, ½ mile west of intersection with Route 3. Take a right onto West Proctor Road, Proctor, Vt.; (802) 773–3284; www.wilsoncastle.com. Open daily late May through mid-October, 9:00 A.M. to 6:00 P.M., with the last tour starting at 5:30. Admission: $–$$, children under 6 free.

This spectacular nineteenth-century castle is something you would expect to find while touring Europe, but a rare find indeed for a secluded town in Vermont. The outside view of the castle alone is breathtaking; the edifice is constructed from English brick and marble, which marches around the arches and up to the turret. The castle is set on 115 acres, which are also home to a carriage house and stables, as well as beautiful fountains and a birdhouse for resident peacocks.

THE CENTER OF VERMONT

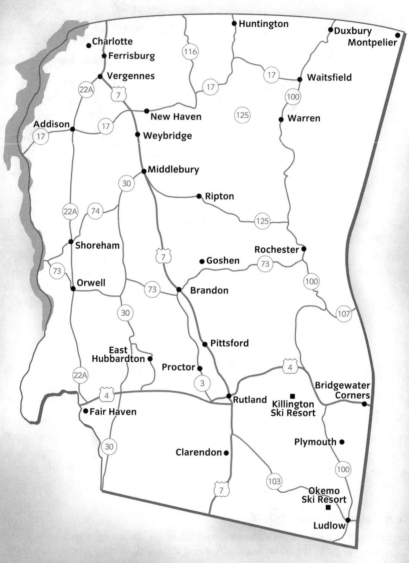

The thirty-two-room estate, home to the Wilson family for several generations, is furnished with an eclectic mix of European and Far Eastern antiques. Each room has its own unique atmosphere and furnishings, as well as striking wood wall panels. The Grand Reception Hall's walls are made of Honduras mahogany, while the library is paneled with black cherry wood that offsets the bronze-and-tile fireplace and the Tiffany chandelier. The drawing room holds one of the castle's most prized possessions, the Louis XVI Crown Jewel case, as well as a Louis XV Papal chair. The music room's atmosphere is perfectly orchestrated with a concert-quality reed organ and with lyre designs decorating every detail down to the elegant chairs.

One of the neatest parts of the castle is the fact that it is still looked after and protected by the famed Swiss Guard, who have been respected for centuries and hold such important positions as guards to Vatican City and the Pope. If you are in the area, a visit here is an absolute must—the kids will be thrilled at the sheer grandeur and storybook feel of the old castle while you enjoy the subtle nuances and priceless antiques.

Vermont Marble Exhibit (ages 8 and up)

62 Main Street, Proctor, Vt.; (802) 459–2300 or (800) 427–1396; www.vermont-marble.com. Open daily May through October 9:00 A.M. to 5:30 P.M., and November through April Monday through Saturday 9:00 A.M. to 4:00 P.M. Admission: $–$$, under 15 free.

At the Vermont Marble Exhibit, which is one of the area's most popular attractions, you get to learn all about the marble industry and see marble sculptors at work. In addition to marble exhibits of all sorts, there is also an enormous mural that explains the earth's crust and mineral formation, as well as planetary relationships. Exhibits also include the history of the area as it relates to the local marble industry.

New England Maple Museum (ages 6 and up)

Route 7, Pittsford, Vt.; (802) 483–9414; www.maplemuseum.com. Open daily 8:30 A.M. to 5:30 p.m. late May through October, 10:00 A.M. to 4:00 P.M. March through late May and November through mid-December. Admission: $.

This maple museum does more than show the sugaring process, which can be witnessed at any sugarhouse. Here your family will learn about the history of maple sugar and how the Native Americans discovered the sweet sap and turned it into the yummy confection we know today.

Killington Ski Area (all ages)

Killington Access Road, off Routes 100 and 4, Killington, Vt.; (802) 422–3333 or (800) 621–MTNS. Ski season from mid-November through mid-April. Lift tickets vary; many packages are available.

This is an enormous ski area that covers six mountains and offers more than 170 trails. One of the greatest family-oriented programs here is the Perfect Turn "Learn to

Ski/Snowboard" program. The ski school guarantees your lessons and allows students to learn in their own special area with lifts just for them. This is a great way to be confident that your children will be safe and feel secure while getting their private or group lessons. Childcare and kiddie ski schools are available, as well as a nursery for younger non-skiers.

Mountain Meadows Munchkins (ages 6 months and up)

Route 100, Killington, Vt.; (802) 775–1010; www.mtmeadowslodge.com. Open 7:30 A.M. to 8:00 P.M. Full day $$$$; additional children in the same family receive 10 percent discount.

This is a new twist on daycare. This unique children's center explores nature and the arts and introduces children to the care of farm animals. No more than fourteen children are here at any time, so each one gets full attention and plenty of space in the playground, at the water table, in the library, and at the dress-up trunk. Each day's activities include feeding the barnful of animals. Feeding the children themselves is a high priority, too, with wholesome, low-fat, low-sugar meals (three a day are offered) plus healthy snacks.

Killington Adventure Center (ages 10 and up)

Resort Village, Killington Road, Killington, Vt.; (877) 458–4637. Open daily late June through Labor Day 10:00 A.M. to 5:00 P.M.; late May through late June and September through mid-October weekends only 10:00 A.M. to 5:00 P.M. All-day passes $$$$; other activities priced separately.

Taking the lead in converting formerly winter-only ski areas into year-round vacation resorts, Killington has a bang-up package of activities at its adventure center. These include waterslides, skateboarding, in-line skating, a climbing wall, a gondola, and mountain biking. These attractions are convenient to lodgings in the resort center but are open to the general public. Rental equipment is available.

COOL Facts

When Calvin Coolidge was vice president of the United States in 1923, the job had very few responsibilities. The vice presidency in those days was little more than an "insurance policy" in case the president died in office. So in August, Calvin Coolidge went back to his boyhood home in Vermont to help his father get in the hay crop. He was there when word came that President Warren G. Harding had died in California. So Calvin's father administered the oath of office at the kitchen table of the Coolidge farmhouse at 2:47 in the morning. Later, when someone asked him why he thought he had the authority to swear in his son as president, Coolidge replied with Yankee practicality, "I didn't know I couldn't."

Killington K1 Gondola (all ages)

Resort Village, Killington Road, Killington, Vt.; (877) 458–4637. Operates late June through Labor Day daily 9:00 A.M. to 5:00 P.M.; late May through late June and September through mid-October weekends only 9:00 A.M. to 5:00 P.M. Round-trip fare: $$–$$$, age 5 and under free; one-way ride: $$; family discount available.

Although many people use the gondola for access to mountain biking and mountain boarding trails, others simply ride to the top for the fun of the trip and the beautiful views of the Green Mountains. The ride is 1¼ miles to the top of a 4,241-foot mountain. From the summit you can see into five states and Canada. While there you can have lunch at the Killington Peak Restaurant.

President Calvin Coolidge State Historic Site (ages 6 and up)

Route 100A, 6 miles south of Route 4, Plymouth Notch, Vt.; (802) 672–3773. Open daily 9:30 A.M. to 5:30 P.M. from late May through mid-October. Admission: $$, under age 14 free.

This historic site is not just a little building with a few neat artifacts—this is literally a town full of history, which you can tour all or part of. Among the houses is the actual birthplace of America's thirtieth president, Calvin Coolidge, still furnished in 1920s New England decor, as it was when he lived here. There is also a visitor center where you can find out lots of information on Coolidge. Other sites to visit include the Wilder house (where you can get a yummy cup of chowder or some fresh-baked bread), the Plymouth Cheese Factory, a one-room schoolhouse, the Union Christian Church, the Plymouth Post Office, and the Plymouth Cemetery.

Hubbardton Battlefield (ages 6 and up)

East Hubbardton Road, East Hubbardton, Vt. (off Route 4); (802) 273–2282. Interpretive center open late May through October, Wednesday through Sunday 9:30 A.M. to 5:00 P.M.; battlefield open all year. Admission: $, under age 14 free.

While not nearly as well known as the Battle of Bennington, it was actually the Battle of Hubbardton that made victory at Bennington possible. American troops withdrew from Fort Ticonderoga and Mount Independence (see next section, Right in the Middlebury) in July 1777, and the British, sure of their ability to defeat the ill-equipped local militia, took chase. At Hubbardton, the American rear guard found a good defensive position behind a hilltop and turned on their pursuers. They defeated the British, protecting the main colonial army which, consequently, was able to regroup at Bennington and defeat the British there, turning the tide of the war.

This important battlefield is open to walk around, although it is best to visit when the interpretive center is also open. Here you will find a detailed map of the field, as well as displays and exhibits on the history and significance of this spot. You can also pick up a "walking tour" guide to the battlefield, or you may choose to read the informational signs posted around the site. Frequently throughout the summer and fall, you will find reenactors in encampments, reliving the lives of the soldiers who fought here.

Clarendon Gorge ⊛

Route 103, Clarendon, Vt.; no phone. Open daylight hours. Free.

Kids will love the swinging bridge that carries them across this gorge; parents may not be so happy with it. If you are uneasy with heights, perhaps it would be better to cross the bridge one adult at a time, children firmly in hand so they don't set it swaying by running. Your best view of the deep gorge is from the bridge itself. Underneath the bridge are potholes and formations of waterworn rock.

Where to Eat

Blanche and Bill's Pancake House, Route 4, Bridgewater Corners, Vt.; no phone. Breakfast—and we mean real breakfast—is served 7:00 A.M. to 2:00 P.M., along with equally hearty lunches. $

Fair Haven Inn, 5 Adams Street, Fair Haven, Vt.; (802) 265–4907. Open daily for lunch and dinner; known for its Sunday dinner special—a full dinner for $12.95. Early-bird dinner bargains from 5:00 to 6:00 P.M. weekdays. $–$$.

Seward's Family Restaurant, 244 North Main Street (Route 7), Rutland, Vt.; (802) 773–2738. A standard menu of well-prepared dishes and a warm, family-friendly atmosphere. $

Sweet Tomatoes Trattoria, 88 Merchants Row, Rutland, Vt.; (802) 747–7747. A warm, modern Italian atmosphere and a chef who insists on the freshest ingredients make this a winner. Pizza lovers come for the big wood oven, but the menu doesn't stop there. It includes choice after choice of wood-grilled meats and vegetables, along with sparkling pasta combinations. $–$$

Where to Stay

Cortina Inn, Route 4, Killington, Vt.; (802) 773–3333 or (800) 451–6108; www.cortinainn.com. A modern building with well-decorated and spacious rooms. Public gathering places abound, and the many children who visit the inn invariably gather in one of these or at the indoor pool. Parents will appreciate the health club and spa. A shuttle takes skiers to the slopes, and the resort has its own restaurant. $$

The Country Squire Motel, Routes 7B and 103, North Clarendon, Vt.; (802) 773–3805 or (888) 604–7298; e-mail: Eamangels@aol.com. This is a comfortable motel that is kid-friendly. It's just 4 miles south of Rutland in a quiet location. Continental breakfast included. Family rate: $ includes two adults and two children.

Green-Mont Motel, 138 North Main Street, Rutland, Vt.; (802) 775–2575 or (800) 774–2575. Swimming pool; two-bedroom unit available; cable TV; microwaves and VCRs available at no charge. $–$$

Holiday Inn, Centre of Vermont, 476 Route 7 South, Rutland, Vt.; (802) 775–1911 or (800) 462–4810. Full-service hotel with indoor pool, exercise room, and restaurant on premises. Children under 12 stay and eat for free. $$–$$$

The Inn at Rutland, 70 North Main Street, Route 7, Rutland, Vt.; (802) 773–0575 or (800) 808–0575; www.innatrutland.com. Children welcome at this 1890s Victorian B&B. Breakfast included, phones, TV, private baths, ski and bike storage. $–$$

Mountain Meadows Lodge, Thundering Brook Road, Killington, Vt.; (802) 775–1010.

Families are the main clientele of this attractive lodge, which offers a licensed childcare service, baby-sitting, and on-site sports activities, along with a petting farm. All members of the family will want to participate in cross-country skiing, snowshoeing, kick-sledding, or canoeing and hiking. In the winter, the lodge offers dogsled rides, not an easy activity to find. $$

For More Information

Killington and Pico Area Association, P.O. Box 114, Killington, VT 05751; (802) 773–4181 or (800) 337–1928.

Rutland Region Chamber of Commerce, 256 North Main Street, Rutland, VT 05701; (802) 773–2747 or (800) 756–8880; www.rutlandvermont.com.

Right in the Middlebury

In the center of this region, beneath the Green Mountains, sits Middlebury, a college town with a relaxed air of gentility and history. In summer the town retains its intellectual and literary air with a notable writer's conference at Breadloaf, where Robert Frost spent many summers writing.

Middlebury Snow Bowl (all ages)

Route 125, Ripton, Vt.; (802) 388–4356. Season runs December through March. Lift tickets $$$$ weekends, $$$ weekdays for adults (the lowest in Vermont).

This mountain is a particularly great place for a family who wants to ski together. Even from the top of the mountain, you can find a full range of trails for all skill levels. The thirty-two trails cover more area than you expect and offer some very challenging courses. The base lodge is small-town friendly, and the food is really good here, with a home-cooked flavor. Rentals and child care are available, and Vermont students ski on weekends for weekday prices.

Texas Falls (all ages)

Route 125, Middlebury Gap, Vt.; no phone. Daylight hours. Free.

Because of its walkway and log bridge, Texas is one of the few Vermont waterfalls that is really safe for kids to explore. It is quite impressive, especially when you stand on the bridge after a heavy rain and watch the torrents rip through the gorge right under you. Bring your picnic to enjoy at the tables beside the river just above the falls.

Mount Independence (ages 6 and up)

Catfish Bay Road, Orwell, Vt.; (802) 948–2000. Open daily late May through mid-October 9:30 A.M. to 5:00 P.M. Admission: $$, under age 14 free.

Mount Independence includes not only a visitor center (which explains the fort's importance during the Revolution), but it also has four walking trails on which you can experience the historic sites yourself. The trails are well marked with plaques that explain the events and the fort's connections with its sister fort, Fort Ticonderoga. The trails encompass a total of 400 acres and are used for cross-country skiing in the winter. Trail maps with more information are available at the visitor center. There is always something new to discover, too, as new artifacts are being dug up nearly every day.

Carillon (all ages)

Route 74, Teachout's Lakehouse Store and Wharf at Larabees Point, Shoreham, Vt.; (802) 897–5331. Daily from Father's Day through Labor Day, cruises leave at 10:30 A.M., 12:30 P.M., and 2:30 P.M. Fare: $–$$.

The *Carillon* is a 60-foot boat that was designed just for this cruise. It tours Lake Champlain from Larabees Point to Fort Ticonderoga and Mount Independence. You may choose between a two-hour and a one-hour tour, the shorter of which leaves from Mount Independence. If you are taking the longer cruise from Shoreham but want to look around Mount Independence, take one of two earlier cruises and get off there, then pick up the next boat when it comes through. The boat itself is lovely, and the cruise is great fun even if you're not a history buff.

Blueberry Hill Cross-Country Center

Forest Road #32, Goshen, Vt.; (802) 247–6735 or (800) 448–0707; www.blueberryhillinn. com. Open when snow conditions permit, usually mid-December through March. Day rates: $$–$$$.

Miles and miles of trails wind along the ridge and through the woods of Moosalamoo, with views over the valley to the Adirondacks. No "gerbil cage" skiing here—you can ski for days and never repeat a trail. Snowshoes and skis are available for rent (and are included in winter packages for guests at the inn).

University of Vermont Morgan Horse Farm

74 Battell Drive (2½ miles from downtown Middlebury), Weybridge, Vt.; (802) 388–2011. Open daily with tours on the hour May through October 9:00 A.M. to 4:00 P.M. Admission: $, age 4 and under free.

Admission to the Morgan Horse Farm includes a guided tour of the main barn and a fifteen-minute video about these special horses and the farm itself. The Morgan horse is the state animal of Vermont and is obviously highly celebrated here on the working farm. Your family is welcome to stay and picnic by the fields or even watch training sessions.

Where to Eat

The Brandon Inn, on the Village Green, 20 Park Street, Brandon, Vt.; (802) 247–5766. An innovative menu in a casual tavern setting in the back of the hotel, where families will feel quite comfortable. $–$$

Neil & Otto's Pizza Cellar, 11 Merchant's Row (in the cellar of the Baptist Church), Middlebury, Vt.; (802) 388–6774 or 388–6776. The variety of pizzas is astonishing, and the prices are too. $

Storm Cafe, Frog Hollow, Middlebury, Vt.; (802) 388–1063. Servings are big, but the restaurant is very small. $–$$

Vermont Home Bakery, the Old Hancock Hotel, Routes 100 and 125, Rochester, Vt.; (802) 767–4976. Breakfast dishes, served all day, include all the old favorites and some new ones such as venison sausage. Lunch and dinner are hearty and up to date at this casual corner store with a bakery and restaurant. $

Where to Stay

Blueberry Hill Inn, Forest Road #32, Goshen, Vt.; (802) 247–6735 or (800) 448–0707; www.blueberryhillinn.com. Most inns of such distinction look tense when you mention arriving with children. Not this one. In fact, the owners' daughter Britta looks positively disappointed when guests arrive without playmates for her. When children arrive, she'll whisk them off to her secret garden, with its leafy little hedge rooms and a tepee made of bean vines. True to the property's name, blueberries abound in its beautiful gardens and find their way into the breakfasts and dinners. The cuisine is stylish, artfully presented, and made with impeccably fresh local ingredients. Dinner and breakfast are included. $$–$$$

Liberty Hill Farm, 511 Liberty Hill Road off Route 100, Rochester, Vt.; (802) 767–3926; www.libertyhillfarm.com. A real working farm, where you can stay for a farm vacation. You may take part in the daily activities as much as you like, or simply treat the place as a B&B. Breakfast and dinner are included; children stay for less than half price. $

Moffett House Bed & Breakfast, 69 Park Street, Brandon, Vt.; (802) 247–3843. A fine Victorian home has been converted into a relaxed B&B with beautifully decorated rooms and a host who really enjoys her guests. $$

Along the Lake

Although it is much narrower here than farther north, Lake Champlain is still a formidable body of water, forming the border with neighboring New York. It defines the region, and many of the sites you will want to see are in some way influenced by its presence. An entire museum examines the lake's maritime past, including its crucial role in the War of 1812.

Chimney Point State Historic Site (ages 7 and up)

7305 Route 125 at Champlain Bridge, Addison, Vt.; (802) 759–2412. Open Memorial Day through Columbus Day, Wednesday through Sunday from 9:30 A.M. to 5:00 P.M. **Free.**

This is a good place to learn about the Native Americans of the Champlain area, as well as the history of the settlers at Chimney Point. The museum is inside an eighteenth-century tavern on the shore of the lake, and it includes several displays.

Lake Champlain Ferries

Off Route 7, Charlotte, Vt.; (802) 864–9804; www.ferries.com. Operates April through December. Fare per car: $$ one way, $$$ round-trip. Extra for passengers.

These ferries will bring you to New York and back, a short but interesting boat excursion for passengers. To make a round trip, you can take your car across on this ferry, drive north, visit Ausable Chasm in New York, and return to Burlington from Port Kent via another ferry. If nothing else, it's a lot more fun for the kids than a bridge, and those are pretty far away.

Lake Champlain Maritime Museum at Basin Harbor
(ages 6 and up)

Basin Harbor Road, Vergennes, Vt.; (802) 475–2022; www.lcmm.org. Open daily early May through mid-October 10:00 A.M. to 5:00 P.M. Admission: $–$$, age 5 and under **free.**

Your kids may want to run away to sea after visiting this museum, which extends from the shore into the actual waters of Lake Champlain. Many of the boats shown were recovered from the bottom of the lake, and as they work, shipbuilders, blacksmiths, and other craftsmen tell stories of the many shipwrecks in these sometimes violent waters. If all these stories don't scare you, you can rent sailboats, rowboats, canoes, and kayaks at the museum and explore the water yourself. Frequent programs feature special aspects of the maritime history of the lake; in early June an entire weekend is devoted to a kid's maritime festival.

Rokeby Homestead (ages 5 and up)

Route 7, Ferrisburg, Vt.; (802) 877–3406; www.rokeby.org. Open Thursday through Sunday, mid-May through mid-October, with tours at 11:00 A.M., 12:30 P.M., and 2:00 P.M. Admission: $–$$.

The Underground Railroad, by its nature, was kept a secret, so it's difficult to document with certainty which of Vermont's many homes, inns, and other buildings were stations on the road to freedom. Rokeby is one of the few with irrefutable documentation. The Robinson family—including the writer and naturalist Rowland Robinson and his descendants—lived here from the late 1700s to the 1960s. The home contains exhibits that cover this entire period, and you can tour the eight outbuildings on the farm of this famous family.

Where to Eat

Roland's Place, Route 7, New Haven, Vt.; (802) 453–6309. The freshest produce from local farms, in the hands of a brilliant French chef—how can you go wrong? The service and hospitality match, and children are always welcome. Early dinners, from 5:00 to 6:00 P.M., are an outstanding bargain. $–$$

Where to Stay

Emersons' Bed and Breakfast, 82 Main Street, Vergennes, Vt.; (802) 877–3293. A warm and inviting Victorian home right downtown. $$

Roland's Place, Route 7, New Haven, Vt.; (802) 453–6309. Three homey guest rooms are upstairs over the restaurant, with a child's room attached to one. $–$$

Mad River Valley

The Mad River may seem benign enough in the summer, but in the spring it rushes through the valley in a torrent. Its valley is a center for skiing and winter sports, although it is still farming country, as the giant barns and silos beside Route 100 will show. One of Vermont's rare remaining round barns is here.

Sugarbush Ski Resort (ages 4 and up)

Sugarbush Access Road, Warren, Vt.; (802) 583–6300 or (800) 53–SUGAR; www.sugarbush. com. Open mid-November through mid-April. Rates in value season (before December 15 and after April 2) are lower, and multiple-day tickets offer discounts in high season.

This large resort, which offers all of the expected perks of a mountain this size, is also very focused on children and families. The Perfect Kids program is divided into the Microbears (age three), Minibears (ages four–six), Sugarbears (ages seven–twelve), and the Catamounts (ages thirteen–sixteen). Each group gets a full- or half-day learn-to-ski program, including rentals, lunch, and supervision. A special area called Family Adventure Land has an entire lift and seventy-five acres set aside as a safe place for families to ski together. There are also plenty of special family events planned throughout the season. This ski area offers 110 trails on three mountains; about half the trails are intermediate.

Mad River Glen

Route 17, Waitsfield, Vt.; (802) 496–3551; www.madriverglen.com. Open mid-November through late March. Half-day, season, and student passes are available.

This skier-owned mountain is sought out by adventure skiers and is very popular with those who like to challenge themselves. This dedication to the sport of skiing has kept this a snowboard-free mountain. The mountain's reputation and 2,036-foot vertical drop often discourage less-experienced skiers, although there is a section just for beginners where they won't feel intimidated by hotshots whizzing by. Also, the beginner will never get stuck having to take a trail that is above his or her skill level, since trails merge into only the same or easier levels. Experts, however, will find this the most challenging mountain in New England and will surely want to buy a bumper sticker with their motto "Ski it if you can." Ski instruction, rentals, and daycare are available.

Palmer Sugar House (ages 6 and up)

Palmer Lane, Waitsfield, Vt.; (802) 496–3696. Open in February and early March. **Free** to visit.

This is a great place to stop by and have some traditional sugar-on-snow, with fresh-made donuts on the side. You can also watch the maple sugaring process and admire the 1840s farmhouse that still stands much as it did back then. You may also buy some of their own syrup and candies to take home with you.

Green Mountain Audubon Nature Center (ages 6 and up)

Sherman Hollow Road, Huntington, Vt.; (802) 434–3068. Trails open daylight hours. **Free.**

The nature center has displays and a library of nature guides and trail leaflets to help you identify the plants and trees you'll see on the trails. One trail passes through ten different species of ferns; another has a rope guide for the visually impaired. A regular schedule of programs is designed for families and includes field trips, hikes, full-moon walks, and a summer ecology camp for children. In March, they have **free** sugaring parties on Sunday afternoons, or you can watch the sugaring operation any day and follow the self-guided trail at their sugarhouse.

Where to Eat

American Flatbread Kitchen, Lareau Farm, Route 100, Waitsfield, Vt.; (802) 496–8856. Pizzas hot from a wood-fired oven are served on weekends only. $–$$

The Common Man Restaurant, German Flats Road, Warren, Vt.; (802) 583–2800. New American and European specialties in the relaxed setting of a renovated barn. $$

Where to Stay

Grunberg Haus, Route 100, Duxbury, Vt.; (802) 244–7726 or (800) 800–7760; www.grunberghaus.com. Your kids will love this cozy Alpine-style lodge at first sight. The cottages along the hillside are also a nice option. Overnight stays in either include an excellent breakfast. Snowshoes are available for guests. $–$$

The Inn at Round Barn Farm, East Warren Road, Waitsfield, Vt.; (802) 496–2276. Stylishly decorated rooms are large and have fireplaces, whirlpools, or steam baths. The round barn is an architectural treasure, one of few remaining in the state, and it has been beautifully restored. Inn guests have **free** use of the cross-country trails. $$

Lareau Farm Country Inn, Route 100, Waitsfield, Vt.; (802) 496–4949 or (800) 833–0746. Rooms in the rambling farmhouse are homey and comfortable, with private or shared baths. $–$$

Sugarbush Village, Waitsfield, Vt.; (802) 583–3000 or (800) 451–4326. Condos at the foot of the ski slopes have fully equipped kitchens and up to five bedrooms. A shuttle bus takes skiers to the slopes, sports facilities, restaurants, and other places in the Sugarbush community. $$–$$$

Annual Events

AUGUST

Addison County Fair, Route 17, New Haven, Vt., (802) 545–2557, mid-August. The state's largest agricultural fair with youth activities and a children's barnyard.

SEPTEMBER

Vermont State Fair, Rutland, Vt., (802) 775–5200, early September.

Vermont Sheep and Wool Festival, Killington, Vt., e-mail: allwool@aol.com, late September. Sheep, goats, llamas, alpacas, and angora rabbits will be on hand. Hands-on activities for children.

DECEMBER

Coolidge Christmas Open House, Plymouth Notch, Vt., (802) 672–3773, early December.

Champlain's Shores and Ski Country

L ake Champlain is so big that it dominates Vermont's western border for nearly half the length of the state. On clear days you can see the mountains of upstate New York across even its widest point, but on hazy days there are places where it seems like an ocean, prompting many people to call it "New England's West Coast."

The area's history includes pivotal battles in the War of 1812, smuggling, major stations in the Underground Railroad, and New England's only Confederate raid during the Civil War.

Burlington and Shelburne

Burlington—Vermont's largest city (39,000 population)—rises in gentle layers, from the eastern shore of Lake Champlain to the hilltop campus of the University of Vermont. From there you can see the western slopes of the Green Mountains, just minutes beyond.

At the crossroads of commerce on the lake and land routes between nearby Montreal and New York, Burlington has been a thriving center since Ethan Allen and his wife retired there after the Revolution and Ethan's brother chose it as the site for the new university in 1791. But for all its long history, Burlington is very much a city of the here-and-now. The brick-paved Church Street Marketplace is free of vehicle traffic and is lined with 160 of the city's smartest shops, cafes, and restaurants.

Leahy Center for Lake Champlain (ages 3 and up)
Beside the Boathouse, 1 College Street, Burlington, Vt.; (802) 864–1848; www.echovermont. org. Open daily mid-June through August, weekends year-round, 12:30 to 4:00 or 5:00 P.M., depending on business. Admission: $$, age 2 and under free.

Children will learn about the lake and the animals and plants that live there—and have fun in the process—through interactive exhibits. Not just computer screens to sit in front of, but live critters to touch and ways to interpret the lake through crafts and art. Archaeology of the many shipwrecks is usually included in the changing interpretive activities.

CHAMPLAIN'S SHORES AND SKI COUNTRY

Flynn Theater (ages 4 and up)
135 Main Street, Burlington, Vt.; (802) 863–5966. Ticket prices vary with performance.

Performing arts are at the heart of Burlington's cultural life, and they take center stage at the Art Deco Flynn Theater, where the likes of ballet dancer Mikhail Baryshnikov have performed in the two decades since it was restored and reopened. Programs may include anything—Broadway musicals, vocal soloists, ballet, jazz—with a good selection of them aimed at families and children. On average, the Flynn has three different events a month, which is especially surprising since they are not the only performance venue in town. The City Hall across the street has its own resident theater companies, and the University has an active schedule as well.

Robert Hull Fleming Museum (ages 5 and up)
61 Colchester Avenue (University of Vermont campus), Burlington, Vt.; (802) 656–0750. Open September through April, Tuesday through Friday 9:00 A.M. to 4:00 P.M. and weekends 1:00 to 5:00 P.M. Open May through Labor Day Tuesday through Friday noon to 4:00 P.M. and weekends 1:00 to 5:00 P.M. Admission: $–$$.

The University's museum is as eclectic as the city itself, with everything from European and Middle Eastern to Vermont artists represented. Kids will want to head straight for the Egyptian mummy, but antiques-loving parents will want to stop at the outstanding collections of early American furniture.

Spirit of Ethan Allen II (ages 3 and up)
Spirit Landing, Burlington Boathouse, College Street, Burlington, Vt.; (802) 862–8300; www.soea.com. Tours depart daily mid-May through mid-October, at two-hour intervals 10:00 A.M. to 4:00 P.M. Fare: $–$$. Reservations are essential.

The *Spirit of Ethan Allen II* cruises on Lake Champlain, with ninety-minute sightseeing trips throughout the day. You can combine some of these with lunch or dinner. At noon and at 2:00 P.M., a buffet lunch is served on the cruise. Along with their regular dinner cruises, they offer Monday Feast Afloat dinner cruises ($25.95), with a buffet of Tex-Mex, Polynesian, and Italian dishes. These trips are longer, from 6:30 to 9:30 P.M., so on a pleasant day you'll see the sun set over water (a rare sight for New Englanders, who are used to seeing it rise, not set, over water). Tuesdays are "Lobstah-on-the-Lake" clambake days, with lobster, chowder, steamers, and corn on the cob for $34.95.

Lake Champlain Ferries (ages 4 and up)
Boathouse, College Street, Burlington, Vt.; (802) 864–9804. Operates daily on a regular shuttle basis. Passenger fare $ one-way, $$ round-trip; car and driver $$ one-way, $$$ round-trip.

These little ferries leave from Burlington, Grand Isle, and Charlotte to cross the lake to the New York side. Although they are primarily designed to carry cars, they make a great passenger excursion, with views of the lake and the two mountain-backed shorelines. Kids are made much of, and older ones will enjoy a look into the pilot house to see the operations.

Ethan Allen Homestead (ages 4 and up)

Route 127 in Burlington (take North Avenue Beaches exit and look for the tiny sign for a right turn); (802) 865–4556; www.ethanallenhomestead.com. Open mid-May to mid-October, Monday through Saturday 10:00 A.M. to 5:00 P.M. and Sunday 1:00 to 5:00 P.M. Admission: $–$$, family rate $$$.

Two centuries ago, the famous Vermont leader Ethan Allen moved to this farmstead, where he raised crops and livestock. Begin at the Interpretation Center to learn about the life and exploits of this cheeky Vermonter and about the Revolution, in which he played an important part. Be sure to follow the interpretive trails in the **Wetlands Nature Center,** where signs and a self-guiding brochure will help you identify the many birds and plants you will see.

Shelburne Museum (ages 3 and up)

Route 7, Shelburne, Vt. (10 miles south of Burlington); (802) 985–3346; www.shelburnemuseum.org. Open daily late May to mid-October, 10:00 A.M. to 5:00 P.M. Admission: $$–$$$, under age 6 free.

Forget what you usually picture when you hear the word museum. This is really a collection of buildings and other things too large to be kept in the collector's home, including a steamboat. These are filled and furnished with more collections, creating a compendium of Americana that has something for all interests and ages.

Kids will prefer the early toys and dolls, brightly painted horses from carousels, horse-drawn sleighs and carriages, a covered bridge they can walk through, a train station and locomotive with private railcar, the lighthouse, and, of course, the steamship *Ticonderoga,* high and dry after arriving by special rail track. And they will certainly want to see the 500-foot handmade model of a circus parade. That's only the beginning of the more than 80,000 artifacts here, which also include an outstanding collection of early New England quilts and painted tin and woodenware.

As if this weren't enough, the museum includes an art gallery that would do credit to a much larger city, with French and American Impressionists, Winslow Homer, and even Rembrandt represented. The museum sprawls over forty-five acres, so don't forget the stroller, and plan to spend the day. The gardens make a nice place to relax, and craft demonstrations break the tedium of static displays.

Shelburne Farms (ages 3 and up)

Harbor Road, Shelburne, Vt.; (802) 985–8686; www.shelburnefarms.org. Tours daily June through mid-October, 9:30 A.M. to 3:30 P.M. Admission: $$, age 2 and under free.

The barns here are grand, with turrets and thick stone walls, grander by far than many mansions. The house—a "cottage" as it was called—is now an uppity-scale hotel, which you can't tour unless you're staying there. You can see cheese being made, as well as hand-crafted furniture in progress, and see the gardens. Small children will like this 1,400-acre working "gentleman farm" for its children's farmyard, where they can sometimes try

Burlington Area **Parks** and **Beaches**

- **Battery Park,** downtown off Pearl Street on the lake shore, was where the defensive battery kept British ships at bay during the Revolution. Today the views of the lake are still filled with boats, but they are harmless sailboats. Sunday- and Thursday-evening concerts are free here in the summer.

- **North Beach,** North Avenue (off Route 127), has a tower with good lake views, along with public beaches and campsites. It's open mid-May to mid-October.

- **Blanchard Beach,** Flynn Avenue (off Route 7, south of town), has changing rooms and other facilities, along with (usually) ample parking.

- **Red Rocks Park,** Queen City Park Road, South Burlington, also has changing facilities and parking.

milking a cow. Tours in an open hay wagon last ninety minutes, a little long for tots young enough to be excited by the petting farm. We suggest that you stop to ask exactly what you will see happening that day and decide accordingly.

Vermont Teddy Bear Company (all ages)

Route 7, Shelburne, Vt.; (802) 985–3001 or (800) 829–2327; www.vermontteddybear.com. The showrooms are open Monday through Saturday 10:00 A.M. to 6:00 P.M., Sunday 10:00 A.M. to 5:00 P.M. Last tour starts at 4:00 P.M. Admission: free, tours $.

This is teddy-bear-lovers' heaven. Not only can you see and squeeze all the various creations, but you can get just the feel you like by stuffing your own. It's a very clever idea, and virtually irresistible, so be prepared to get one for each kid and an extra for yourself. Pick out your own bear, fill for just the squishiness you want, and someone will sew it up

Champ, the Lake's Own Sea Serpent

First reported by the explorer Samuel de Champlain in July of 1609, Champ has turned up now and then ever since. Champlain described a serpentlike creature as big around as a barrel and about 20 feet long, with a horse-shaped head. Newspaper accounts have reported similar details. Once an entire sightseeing excursion boat described seeing the creature surface. You'll find information on scientific investigation and sightings at the nature center at Button Bay State Park or in the Lake Champlain Maritime Museum.

for you. Don't worry about finding one you like; you can choose from bears with just about every personality, many with themes to match sports and hobbies.

Tours show the whole process of making the bears, whose arms and legs move on joints and whose faces are created in appealing detail.

Where to Eat

Butler's, 70 Essex Way, Essex Junction, Vt.; (802) 878–1100. Cuisines from all over the world inspire New England Culinary Institute students. Fine dining, with a children's menu that exceeds most. $$

Five Spice Cafe, 175 Church Street, Burlington, Vt.; (802) 864–4045. Pan-Asian influences mix to create a healthy menu with a faint New England accent. It's "exotic," but kids always find something they like here—or at least have fun trying to learn to eat with chopsticks. $–$$

Our Daily Bread, Bridge Street, Richmond, Vt. (east of Burlington on Route 2); (802) 434–3148. Cafe and bakery with very few tables, but a good selection of healthy sandwiches you can carry off for a picnic. Calzones are big and well-filled, and cookies are delicious. $

Windjammer, Route 2, just east of I–89 exit 14E, Burlington, Vt.; (802) 862–6585. Casual style, healthy menu options, and a children's menu make this popular with families. $–$$

Where to Stay

Countryside Motel, Route 7, Shelburne, Vt. (south of Burlington); (802) 985–2839; www.countrysidevt.com. A very small property with only twelve rooms, all efficiencies and with **free** movies. Outdoor swimming pool. $$

The Inn at Essex, 70 Essex Way, Essex Junction, Vt.; (802) 878–1100. Stylish and new, this hotel with country-inn decor is run by the New England Culinary Institute, whose students are always eager to please and are terrific with children. Indoor pool. $$

Radisson Hotel Burlington, 60 Battery Street, Burlington, Vt.; (802) 658–6500 or (800) 333–3333. No surprises, but a nice property with large rooms, cribs, a swimming pool, and full services. $$

For More Information

Lake Champlain Regional Chamber of Commerce, 60 Main Street, Burlington, VT 05401; (802) 863–3489; www.vermont.org.

Smugglers Notch and Jeffersonville

The Green Mountains, which have been rising steadily from the Massachusetts border many miles to the south, reach their highest point just east of Burlington, at the summit of Mount Mansfield. This mountain forms one side of Smugglers Notch, a mountain pass that was indeed used to transport illegal contraband during the early years of the nation, when Vermonters were cut off from their natural trading partners in Canada by Jefferson's Embargo Act.

Smugglers' Notch Resort (all ages)
Route 108, Smugglers Notch, Jeffersonville, Vt.; (802) 644–8851 or (800) 451–8752; www.smuggs.com.

We've visited a lot of places designed for families, and we've never stayed at one that has been more successful in creating a self-contained center for both parents and children. In the winter it offers a rare combination of world-class skiing and family activities and facilities. All ages, skiers or not, will be comfortable and well-entertained.

For skiers, "Smuggs" offers two mountains with separate lift systems and base lodges, connected by ski trails and a shuttle bus. This busy bus takes guests to the swimming pool, spa, Nordic ski center, restaurants, and all the other pleasures of the compact village at the feet of the two mountains. The skiing is superb, with state-of-the-art grooming. Ski rates for day guests on weekends: adults, $48; ages seven–seventeen, $34; under age seven **free.** Lower on weekends.

For kids who don't ski (or those who ski only occasionally), there is a state-of-the-art childcare center, Alice's Wonderland. This amazing facility is so beautiful that you may have trouble convincing kids to leave it so they can ski. Each age group has its own area; there's even a nursery for babies and darkened rooms for toddler naps. The toys and activities are mind-boggling, both indoors and out. For nervous parents or just to peek at the kids when they don't know it, there is a one-way window so you can visit anonymously any time during the day.

In addition to skiing Smuggs' own two mountains, skiers staying two or more nights can also use their lift tickets at Stowe's three mountains. Adding the terrain of one of New England's best-known ski capitals brings the available total to 107 trails. You can get to Stowe by skiing over the top of the mountain, as you would in the Alps. This mountain-to-mountain trail link is the only one in the East. Ride the lift to the top, then follow the Nordic trail along Vermont's highest pond, in a saddle between the two summits. A brief and easy climb brings you over the mountain, where the view of the two valleys alone is worth the climb. To get back, reverse the process and ski to your own condo door.

Go by yourself or on one of Smugglers' many guided adventures. Along with the over-the-top trip, there are day adventures for skiers, snowboarders, and outdoor enthusiasts of all ages, who can try ice-fishing or snowshoeing or horseback riding. Those who don't love snow can take painting or rug-hooking lessons or try other crafts, or even visit Montreal on a day tour. Skates can be rented at the outdoor rink at the Nordic ski center.

The ski school is first-rate, with lessons tailored to each skier's skills and weaknesses (even in group lessons), making it an excellent place to introduce kids to skiing. For those families who must take children out of school to have a winter vacation together, Smuggs offers not just a quiet place to study, but well-trained staff to support them, too. So if your teen is stymied by an algebra problem, there's help at hand.

But their success has not been limited to ski season. Summer brings a whole new set of activities: hiking, climbing, kayaking, tennis, nature programs, kids' camp, and more. Like the winter programs, these are designed to allow all family members, whatever their age, to enjoy the sports and activities they love or learn new ones. It's in the concept, and in the numbers: eight heated pools, five waterslides, life-size pick-up-sticks games, night spiker volleyball, even an autumn program that amuses the kids while parents go leaf-peeping without a chorus of "are-we-there-yets" from the back seat. While the whole area is there to explore, you could easily spend a vacation without ever leaving the village.

Scenic Drive: **Smuggler's Notch**

Route 108, Jeffersonville, Vt.

New England's notches are not the same as passes or gaps—mere low places in a chain of mountains where a road or trail can make its way through. Although notches serve that purpose, they are by definition glacially scoured, and you can usually see this in their deep bowl-shaped southern sides. Smugglers Notch was formed by glaciers, but in a different way, and even now geologists are not sure exactly how. But however it came to be, Smugglers is one of the most dramatic New England notches, its road climbing steeply to a top passage that is so strewn with giant boulders that the road must snake between them. The passage is so narrow that RVs, trucks, and trailers are not allowed over it; they would be unable to make the sharp turns between the boulders that line its sides. At the top, look for the few spaces where you can park between them, and climb up the short trail to the south for sweeping views of northern Vermont, New York, and Canada.

To get to Smugglers Notch, follow Route 108 from either end (from Route 15 in Jeffersonville or from Route 100 in Stowe). Snow plows can't make it through this road, so it closes in the winter.

Summer Fun University (ages 6–17) 🎯

Smugglers' Notch Resort, Route 108, Jeffersonville, Vt.; (802) 644–8851. Prices vary with age and program.

Specialized programs are designed to build confidence and teach outdoor skills without forgetting that a vacation should be fun. Professional golf instruction begins as early as age six, junior tennis camp is aimed at ages ten to seventeen, overnight hikes are for ages six to ten, and a three-day guided discovery trip—Meadows, Wetlands, and Forests—introduces six- to twelve-year-olds to canoeing, fishing, and beaver ponds. Ropes, Boats, and Boards, for ages ten to seventeen, teaches rope-climbing, kayaking, canoeing, orienteering, and mountain-boarding in an action-packed week. Adventure Rangers programs, which combine some of these activities (on a less intensive basis) with water sports, crafts, and hiking, are included in all lodging packages. A "Big Kids Camp," for adults ages eighteen and over, gives parents and older siblings a chance to join in the fun, too.

Living Machine Wastewater Treatment Plant (ages 8 and up) 🧑‍🔬

Smugglers' Notch Resort, Route 108, Jeffersonville, Vt.; (802) 644–8851. Free.

Older kids who have begun to study environmental sciences can return to school with a great subject for a report. Smugglers' Notch Resort has taken its highly environmentally sensitive policies a step further. The plant's three-stage process includes a large greenhouse of tropical and subtropical plants, which purify the resort's wastewater. The odorless greenhouse is surrounded by a deck with signs describing the treatment process. You can visit even if you are not staying there, as part of one of several tours of the resort.

Green River Canoe (ages 5 and up) ⚠️

Route 15, Jeffersonville, Vt.; (802) 644–8336; e-mail: vtcabins@sover.net. Trip prices: $$$$. Reservations are necessary.

The Lamoille River is an idyllic stream as it winds and gurgles across Vermont in the shadow of the Green Mountains. A canoe is the best way to appreciate it, and it's not a hair-raising experience because the valley is pretty flat. The mountain views change constantly, from good to better, as you paddle downstream. Green River Canoe takes small groups of six in canoes on guided tours, which begin with canoe-handling instruction. You need not have ever set foot in a canoe to enjoy these trips in safety, and all equipment, including flotation vests, is included. The Wetlands and Wildlife tours concentrate on the river's environment, particularly rich in birds. Sunset trips paddle to within sight of beavers, and another trip explores the Native Americans' lore and their use of wild plants.

Johnson Woolen Mills 🔒

Route 15, Johnson, Vt.; (802) 635–2271; www.johnsonwoolenmills.com. Open Monday through Friday 8:00 A.M. to 5:00 P.M., Saturday 9:00 A.M. to 4:00 P.M., and August through March also on Sunday 11:00 A.M. to 4:00 P.M.

Valley farmers once brought their wool here to have it spun and made into cloth, which led the mill to begin making warm woolen pants in the late 1800s. By the 1900s they'd added the jackets, shirts, and vests they still make, along with blankets, mittens, and hats. At their shop in the original mill, you'll find factory-store prices and remarkable bargains on seconds.

Vermont Horse Park (ages 3 and up)

Route 108, Smugglers Notch, Jeffersonville, Vt.; (802) 644–5347. Open daily, rides scheduled by reservation. Prices vary.

The horse park offers private or group sleigh and hayrides, pony rides for children, and trail rides on paths that meander through quiet forests. All rides are in both summer and winter. Their sleighs hold from four to sixteen passengers, with bench seats or hay, and rides are about forty-five minutes.

Where to Eat

The Green Mountain Bakery and Cafe, Smugglers' Notch Resort; (802) 644–8851. Open for breakfast, lunch, and afternoon snacks. $

Hearth and Candle Restaurant, Smugglers' Notch Resort; (802) 644–8090 (in-resort ext. 1260). Open daily 4:30 to 9:30 P.M. A cozy New England-style building offers separate dining rooms for families and for adults wanting a quiet, romantic evening. Appetizers, entrees, and desserts have a European flair, with several heart-healthy entrees and fish dishes. Children's menu begins at $3.95. $$

The Mountain Grille, Smugglers' Notch Resort; (802) 644–2247 (in-resort ext. 2247). Open daily for breakfast, lunch, après-sports, and dinner. A comfortable setting with mountain views invites families with children to enjoy American cuisine. A Little Smugglers' dinner buffet offers children under 12 a full meal priced at one-half their age. $

Riga-bello's Pizzeria, Smugglers' Notch Resort; (902) 644–1141 (in-resort ext. 1141).

Open daily 11:00 A.M. to 10:00 P.M. Fresh-baked pizza, pasta dishes, and Italian specialties, as well as stuffed breads, calzones, fresh salads, and garlic bread tempt families with made-on-premises hearty meals. Takeout available and delivered to condominiums. $

Where to Stay

Smugglers' Notch Resort, Route 108, Smugglers Notch, Jeffersonville, Vt.; (802) 644–8851 or (800) 451–8752; www.smuggs. com. Modern slopeside condos have fully equipped kitchens, fireplaces, entertainment centers, and whirlpool tubs in spacious, beautifully maintained units that range in size from studios to five-bedroom homes. Package plans include lifts, lessons, and extras, including access to the pool, teen center, theater, and activities, even allowing Christmas and New Year's stays at non-holiday rates. Summer from $1,029 for a family of four on a five-night package, winter from $1,740 for a family of four on a five-night package. Resort packages include sports and activity programs.

The Islands and North of Burlington

Once you cross the long bridge to the islands, you feel a world away from Burlington's stylish bustle. Small villages, farmland (apple orchards cover a good part of the islands), and a gentle landscape are all backed by water vistas, dotted with sailboats.

Between Burlington and the Canadian border on the mainland side, the area is still dominated by the lake, with a delta rich in bird life and long miles of shoreline.

West Swanton Orchards, Cider Mill, and Farm Market (all ages) 🔒

Route 78 west, about 4 miles from Swanton, Vt.; (802) 868–7851. Open June through October; apples are ready late August through mid-October.

Take the kids into the orchard to pick their own apples, or buy them at the stand. Vermont honey, maple syrup and candy, cider, pies, and baked goods are also for sale here, but apple-picking is the main attraction for kids.

Lake Carmi State Park (all ages) 🍁

Route 236, Enosburg Falls, Vt.; (802) 933–8383. Open mid-May to mid-October. Free.

An attractive recreation area on the shores of Lake Carmi, the park has a swimming beach with changing facilities, a campground, and an excellent nature trail with an unusually large variety of wildflowers. The trail is level and covers several habitats, including a deep cedar forest where you can see how the roots have formed a web to stabilize a former bog. Kids will like it mostly because it's a little spooky. The park has a good series of nature programs run by staff naturalists.

Swimming **Beaches**

- **Sand Bar State Park,** Route 2, Milton, Vt. (at bridge to South Hero); (802) 372–8240. The park has a long beach on Lake Champlain, a picnic area, and public boat access, making it popular with Burlington residents.

- **Kamp Kill Kare,** off Route 36, St. Albans Bay, Vt.; (802) 534–6021. Kamp Kill Kare is also on the mainland, near St. Albans. It has boat access to Burton Island State Park, where there are nature trails.

- **Knight Point State Park,** North Hero, Vt.; (802) 372–8389. This park has a sand beach, as does Alberg Dunes State Park, farther north in Alberg; (802) 796–4170. Grand Isle State Park, also on the islands, has swimming only for campers; (802) 372–4200.

Water Sports

North Hero House (Route 2, North Hero, Vt.; 802–372–8237), has become the islands' center for sailing, small boats, canoeing, and kayaking. They offer equipment rentals, instruction, and little regattas. Boat rentals include Hobi-Cats, Sunfish, and Skates, and regular sailing programs teach adults and children the basics of boat handling. These programs are open to the public.

North Hero State Park (all ages)
Lakeview Drive (off Route 2), North Hero, Vt.; (802) 372-8727. **Free.**

On Lake Champlain, the park has a long beach of tiny round pebbles, part of which is roped off while the rare map turtles that breed there are nesting. Other wildlife, including painted turtles and deer, are often seen here. Bring plenty of mosquito repellent to discourage the less attractive wildlife that also favor the well-forested park.

Family Kayak Tours (ages 6 and up)
North Hero House, Route 2, North Hero, Vt.; (802) 372-8237; www.northherohouse.com.

Three-day guided kayak experiences on Lake Champlain explore its islands, shoreline, or the bird-rich marshlands of the Missisquoi Delta. No one needs to have kayaking experience as the first day is spent learning how to paddle and focusing on water safety and how to help other paddlers in the water. The second and third days are spent exploring the lake, whose shore varies from rocky cliffs to quiet beaches. Knight Island is a long-but-easy paddle away, and stops there include hearty box lunches prepared by the inn's chef. Lodging and other meals are at the inn. Younger paddlers are in tandem kayaks with parents; older children learn to handle their own craft. Rates are $519 per adult; children priced according to age and accommodations. Rate includes two nights' lodging, all meals, kayaks, safety equipment, instruction, guides, and gratuities.

Hermann's Royal Lipizzan Stallions of Austria (all ages)
Route 2, North Hero, Vt.; (802) 372-8400. Performances Thursday through Sunday from early July to Labor Day. Admission: $$–$$$, under age 6 **free.** On Friday evening, two children are admitted **free** with each adult.

The lakeshore is the summer home of the famous performing horses descended from the same stock as the Spanish Riding School in Vienna. Their balletlike routine is enchanting to watch, even for kids who are not horse-crazy. You can stop at the farm for a visit any day.

J & M Ladd Families Farm (ages 3 and up)
Alburg Springs Road (off Route 78), Alburg Springs, Vt.; (802) 796–4566. Milking daily at 4:00 P.M., tours by reservation. Free.

Just seeing cows milked is a unique experience for children who have never been to a dairy farm, but there's nothing like getting to try it for themselves. That's what the Ladds, sixth-generation Vermont dairy farmers, will let them do on a tour of their "Dairy of Distinction." They'll also get to see the food mixed—just the right amount of each nutrient to keep the cows healthy—in a drum that looks like a giant cement mixer. After visiting the huge milking barn, with conveyor belts to carry away the waste, they can visit the milk room and see how milk is processed and stored.

Where to Eat

The Country Pantry, Junction of Route 104 and Route 128, Fairfax, Vt.; (802) 849–6364. Open for three meals daily, with enormous breakfasts (the Belgian waffles are wonderful). $–$$

Hero's Welcome Deli, Route 2, North Hero, Vt.; (802) 372–4161. Open 6:30 A.M. to 8:30 P.M. daily. Good, fat sandwiches on wholesome breads, made to order. $

Jeff's Maine Seafood, 65 North Main Street, St. Albans, Vt.; (802) 524–6135. Open for dinner only, Tuesday through Saturday. The take-out section and daytime retail shop are brimming with good picnic choices, or you can dine on Maine lobster and other seafood that arrives fresh from the boat every other day. $$

Northern Cafe, Route 2, Alburg, Vt.; (802) 796–3003. From BLTs and grilled cheese sandwiches bursting with aged Vermont cheddar to ostrich burgers, the menu is filled with old favorites and a few surprises. Cafe tables and booths, friendly service, great pies. $

North Hero House, Route 2, North Hero, Vt.; (802) 372–8237. Dinner daily 5:00 to 9:00 P.M. Separate dining rooms provide fine dining in an atmosphere where families will feel comfortable. The chef has a gift with seafood, whether it's crab cakes, mussels, or salmon. Children's menu and early bird prix fixe specials (5:00 to 6:00 P.M.) at $15. $–$$

Where to Stay

Berkson Farms Inn, Enosburg Falls, Vt.; (802) 933–2522. At this working dairy farm, you and your children can participate in the daily activities and chores if you so desire. If your children have never greeted the source of their morning milk up close and personal, here's their chance: They can even learn how to milk a cow. Rooms are comfortable and furnished in Victorian antiques; not all rooms have private baths, which only accents the sense of being part of the family. Rates are by the night or by the week; the weekly rate includes all meals and is a real bargain. $–$$

North Hero House, Route 2, North Hero, Vt.; (802) 372–8237; www.northherohouse. com. Recently restored and redecorated with antiques, feather comforters, and elegant details, the comfortable hotel rooms in the main inn are smaller than those in the lakefront building across the street. Many rooms in both buildings have views over the lake, and everyone has access to the private beach below. The dining room is excellent, and a number of water sports programs are available for all ages. (See "Family Kayak Tours," earlier in this section.) $$

Camping

Grand Isle State Park, Route 2, Grand Isle, Vt.; (802) 372–4200. Campsites are on a sloping shore overlooking the lake, some open, some wooded. The park has swimming for campers only. $

Lake Carmi State Park, Route 236, Enosburg Falls, Vt.; (802) 933–8383. The park's 178 campsites include 35 with lean-tos and a number with wheelchair access. A swimming beach at the lakefront has changing facilities. $

Maple Grove Campground, Route 104, Fairfax, Vt. (south of St. Albans); (802)

849–6439. Pleasant, open sites in a grove of tall maple trees. No swimming pool or rec center, which means it attracts a quieter group of campers, but children are welcome and campers have pool privileges at a nearby campground. Sites for both tents and RVs, some with wheelchair access. $

North Hero State Park, Lakeview Drive (off Route 2), North Hero, Vt.; (802) 372–8727. More than a hundred campsites, none with trailer hookups, are well spaced in the lakeside woods. Some have lean-tos and are wheelchair accessible. Bring mosquito repellent. $

Stowe

Stowe made its name before skiing was a widely popular sport, when it was one of a handful of New England mountains with a way to get skiers to the top. And although it is still one of the legendary names—synonymous with skiing—its ski facilities are not among the largest or even the most glitzy. The mountain remains largely the domain of serious skiers, while the town has remained a mecca for those looking for a winter getaway. But don't overlook Stowe in the summer or fall, when outdoor sports of different kinds abound and the town is just as pretty dressed in green or in orange and red. Stowe's Main Street is lined with upscale boutiques, mixed in with everyday shops filling the needs of the people who live there.

Stowe Recreation Path (all ages)
Begins in the center of the village, paralleling Route 108 (Mountain Road), Stowe, Vt.; (802) 253–7205. Free.

Stowe has created an exceptional corridor from its very center through its loveliest landscapes and up the side of the mountain that brought it fame. And the nicest part of it is that people use it—a lot. In any season you are sure to meet walkers, cyclists, runners, skiers, skaters, snowshoers, or families out for a stroll with their strollers. Fast travelers look out for the slower traffic, cars slow down for the few road crossings, and the town meets the tourists on this 5-mile stretch of pavement. The path runs along the river, and from it you can reach lodging and dining along Mountain Road and enjoy an ever-changing display of mountain vistas. You can rent bicycles at Stowe Hardware Store on Main Street, near the start of the path.

Gondola Skyride (ages 4 and up)

Stowe Mountain, Mountain Road (Route 108), Stowe, Vt.; (802) 253–3000. Operates daily 10:00 A.M. to 5:00 P.M. from mid-June through mid-October. Fare: $$–$$$.

Travel inside a giant bubble car to the top of Mount Mansfield, Vermont's highest elevation. Sweeping views reach as far as 70 miles, into Canada and the Adirondacks in New York. From the top you have access to hiking trails, including the Mount Mansfield portion of the Long Trail, which spans the length of the state along the spine of the Green Mountains.

Stowe Mountain (ages 4 and up)

Mountain Road (Route 108), Stowe, Vt.; (802) 253–3000; www.stowe.com. Open mid-November through April, weather permitting. Rates vary.

Perhaps the best-known ski resort in Vermont, Stowe has been synonymous with skiing since the sport's early years. Still primarily a "skier's mountain," Stowe is not an especially good resort for beginners. More than half its trails are classified as intermediate, and comparatively few are suitable for learning skiers. That said, it is a friendly place, with good ski instruction even if it isn't set up for children as well as many other resorts are. Stowe Resort does offer a children's day camp for ages six to twelve.

Ice-Skating and Sleigh Rides

- **The Jackson Arena,** on Park Street in Stowe, has a public rink, where rental skates are available. Call (802) 253–6148.

- **Charlie Horse Sleigh and Carriage Rides,** at Topnotch Resort in Stowe, has a Currier and Ives–style sleigh that carries two adults and one child, as well as larger sleighs for group rides. You do not have to be a guest at the resort to enjoy the sleigh rides, which are offered daily 11:00 A.M. to 4:00 P.M. from mid-November through February. Call (802) 253–2215.

- **The Stowehof Inn,** on Edson Hill Road, has two antique Victorian-era sleds, each of which carries two adults and one child. Their half-hour rides at twilight and throughout the evening, 4:00 to 9:00 P.M. daily, include a warm-up drink after the ride. If you'd like to combine a ride with dinner at the resort, you can get a package price. You will need a reservation for sleigh rides. Call (802) 253–9722.

- In Morrisville, **Apple Cheek Farm** has a two-horse, ten-passenger open sleigh that carries passengers through a lantern-lighted forest. Hot drinks and a farm tour are included with the ride. Call (802) 888–4482.

In-Line Skate Park (ages 10 and up)

Mountain Road (Route 108), Stowe, Vt.; (802) 253–3000. Open daily 10:00 A.M. to 5:00 P.M., mid-June through Labor Day, same hours Saturday and Sunday mid-May to mid-June and September through Columbus Day weekend. All-day rate: $$; half-day $.

Facilities for beginners and experienced skaters include pipes, ramps, a slalom course, and a speed track. Protective gear, which is required, is available for a rental fee of $5.00.

Stowe Alpine Slide (ages 6 and up)

Mountain Road (Route 108), Stowe, Vt.; (802) 253–3000. Open daily 10:00 A.M. to 5:00 P.M., mid-June through Labor Day, same hours Saturday and Sunday early June and September through Columbus Day weekend. Single ride $$.

The slide is approached by the Spruce Mountain chairlift, the same one used for skiers in the winter. The slide is equipped with a braking system for speed control (which older children usually decline to use, but which most parents who ride it will be glad to find). The views from the top of the slide are wonderful.

Sage Sheep Farm (ages 2 and up)

West Hill Road, Stowe, Vt.; (802) 253–8532. Open Wednesday through Sunday noon to 5:30 P.M., mid-June through mid-October. Admission: free, charge for tea.

Small children will love the woolly sheep, while parents will enjoy the herb gardens of this mountainside farm. Surrounding the shop, which is filled with tasteful wool and herb crafts, is a wide veranda that the owner designed after those on ranches in her native Australia. She serves afternoon tea there, overlooking the gardens. A pot of tea with either a sweet plate, a savory plate, or a veggie plate is $5.00. The sweet plate, kids' favorite by far, has English scones with jam and cream, along with cookies and tea cakes.

Trapp Family Lodge (all ages)

Trapp Hill Road (off Mountain Road), Stowe, Vt.; (802) 253–8511 or (800) 826–7000; www.trappfamily.com.

If your kids have never heard of Maria von Trapp, the Trapp Family Singers, or *The Sound of Music* before they arrive, they will certainly know the whole story before they leave. Built by the von Trapp family and welcoming families ever since, this all-season resort combines Alpine kitsch with a very forward-looking environmental vision—all, of course, set to the sound of music.

Most of the seasonal activities are available to those who are not staying at the resort. In the winter there's cross-country skiing on some of the finest trails in all of New England, many of them overlooking the Green Mountains across the wide valley. *Snow Country* magazine called it "simply the finest cross-country ski resort in the United States." More than 50 miles of cross-country trails are divided almost evenly between carefully groomed and tended routes and back country trails designed for explorers.

Snowshoeing, which is too often an afterthought activity, really gets its due here, with good trails and several places that are snowshoe-hiking destinations. Trails lead to the sugarhouse, to the stone Werner's Chapel, and to Slayton Pasture Cabin, built of logs and set in the woods on a hillside. It's about an hour's walk, uphill most of the way, but on snowshoes you're not in anyone's way if you stop to admire the snow-covered woods while you catch your breath. Hot drinks and a lunch of hearty soups, sandwiches, and Austrian pastries are served in front of the fire. You can't get lost, but it's fun to join a group for a guided trip.

Sleigh rides and maple sugaring (see the Sugar House entry that follows) provide less strenuous activities in the winter. Summer programs are well designed for families to enjoy together or separately and are tailored to children of various ages. Outdoor activities include fishing, swimming, birding, hiking, nature walks, and llama treks.

Trapp Family Lodge Sugar House (ages 4 and up)
Trapp Hill Road (off Mountain Road), Stowe, Vt.; (802) 253–8511 or (800) 826–7000; www.trappfamily.com. Free.

Just as it was used in the 1950s, when the von Trapp family tapped the maples behind the lodge, the sugarhouse continues using the old, entirely sustainable methods. They tap 1,000 trees, gathering all the sap on sleighs pulled by Belgian horses. Lodge guests can take part, and non-guests can watch the sap boiling at close range from a gallery. Sleighs take visitors to the sugarhouse, or you can go on skis or snowshoes. The von Trapps use buckets instead of plastic tubing, horse power to collect the sap, and the wood from thinning their woodlot to fire the evaporator. This is one of the few places where you can watch these traditional methods in real use; most places only have a few token trees to show the old way. On Saturday afternoons they have sugar-on-snow parties, and during sugar season there are special weekend packages for families.

Meadow Concerts (all ages)
Trapp Family Lodge; Trapp Hill Road (off Mountain Road), Stowe, Vt.; (800) 24–STOWE. Late June through August. Admission: $$–$$$$.

Bring a picnic dinner to the von Trapps' meadow and watch the sunset as you eat to the strains of music. It is a long-standing family tradition here and a good way to introduce children to music without the constraints of a concert hall.

Lake Elmore State Park (all ages)
Route 12, Lake Elmore, Vt. (east of Morrisville); (802) 888–2982. Open mid-May through Columbus Day. Admission: $, under age 4 free.

A swimming beach, picnic area, and boat rentals are at the day-use area, along with hiking trails. One of these trails leads up Mount Elmore to the fire tower.

Where to Eat

Gracie's, Main Street, Stowe, Vt.; (802) 253–8741. Burgers and sandwiches at lunch and heaping plates at dinner. The long menu has several selections for kids. It's open until midnight daily, in case you feel like sneaking out for a late snack. $

McCarthy's, Mountain Road, Stowe, Vt.; (802) 253–8626. Open 6:30 A.M. to 3:00 P.M. Locals eat breakfast and good healthy lunches here. They have special menus for kids and many low-fat and low-cholesterol choices. $

Miguel's Stowe Away, Mountain Road, Stowe, Vt.; (802) 253–7574. Open 11:30 A.M. to 3:30 P.M. for lunch and 5:30 to 10:00 P.M. for dinner. Mixing the ingredients and cooking styles of Mexico with those of New England really works here, and so do the very reasonable prices. $

Stowe Farmer's Market, Mountain Road, Stowe, Vt.; (800) 24–STOWE. Open Sunday 11:00 A.M. to 3:00 P.M. May through October. Locally produced picnic ingredients include fresh-baked breads, cheese, country sausage, and fruits. You can reach the market from the Recreation Path.

The Whip Bar and Grill, the Green Mountain Inn, Main Street (Route 100), Stowe, Vt.; (802) 253–7301 or (800) 253–7302; www.genghis.com. Selections range from old-fashioned corn chowder to shepherd's pie baked in a giant potato, with many vegetarian and heart-healthy selections. Kids will keep busy looking at the menu, filled with old photographs of Stowe, including the Mount Mansfield Stage and the electric railroad. $–$$

Whiskers Restaurant, Mountain Road, Stowe, Vt.; (802) 253–8996. The bike rack at its back gate invites you to stop in from your wanderings on the Recreation Path, and you will at least want to look at the brilliant gardens, in bloom until October. You can eat on the terrace amid lupines, poppies, irises, and daisies. The lunch menu has salad plates and sandwiches; dinner is extensive, with plenty of kids' favorites. Desserts are heavenly. $–$$

Where to Stay

The Gables, 1457 Mountain Road (Route 108), Stowe, Vt.; (802) 253–7730 or (800) GABLES–1; www.Stoweinfo.com/saa/gables. Hospitality radiates from this comfortable and unpretentious family-owned inn. Some rooms have fireplaces and whirlpool tubs. Kids immediately feel like part of the family. Breakfast will last you all day. The Gables is only a few yards from Stowe's Recreational Path. $–$$

Golden Eagle Resort and Motor Inn, Mountain Road (Route 108), Stowe, Vt.; (802) 253–4811 or (800) 626–1010. In the summer this attractive inn facing Mount Mansfield offers families a Summer Children's Program, and in the winter they treat kids to a Kids' Night Out twice a week, with pizza, a movie, and popcorn. Add an indoor pool, game room with an under-the-sea theme, and ponds to provide fishing in the summer and skating in the winter. Both restaurants have children's menus, even at breakfast, and children under 12 stay **free.** Rooms are large, some with efficiency kitchens; family suites are available as well. $$

Green Mountain Inn, Main Street (Route 100), Stowe, Vt.; (802) 253–7301 or (800) 253–7302. Children are treated well in this cheery country inn overlooking the center of Stowe. Parents will appreciate little details like canopy beds, whirlpool baths, terry robes, and electric fireplaces, and no one will want to miss afternoon cider and fresh-baked cookies in the lobby. Breakfast includes all the old favorites plus some surprises, such as crepes filled with whole pistachios and ricotta. A complimentary health club is in the rear wing of the inn, and a trolley runs from the door to the mountain. Special winter packages include a snowshoe picnic or a sleigh ride. $–$$

Trapp Family Lodge, Trapp Hill Road (off Mountain Road), Stowe, Vt.; (802) 253–8511 or (800) 826–7000; www.trappfamily.com. Well-decorated rooms overlook the valley views or the forest behind the lodge. Rates in high season include breakfast and dinner. While some children may not appreciate the live harp music in the dining room each evening, they will like the evening sing-alongs for guests. $$–$$$

Camping

Lake Elmore State Park, Route 12, Lake Elmore, Vt. (east of Morrisville); (802) 888–2982. Open mid-May through Columbus Day. The campground has forty-five tent/trailer sites and fifteen lean-to sites. No sites have hookups. A swimming beach is also at the park.

For More Information

Stowe Area Association, Main Street or Box 1320, Stowe, VT 05672; (800) 24–STOWE. This is one of the friendliest and most accommodating information centers we have visited.

Waterbury

Not nearly as cute as its neighbor to the north, Waterbury is not without its own charms. For one thing, the train stops here, bringing visitors from New York City and other points south into the heart of the Green Mountains. I–89 runs past it, so most people arriving in the area come via Waterbury. Along its main street, which is also Route 100 (known here as "The Skiers' Highway"), are distinguished old Victorian homes.

Ben and Jerry's Ice Cream Factory (ages 3 and up) 🍴 🔒 🎫
Route 100, Waterbury, Vt.; (802) 244–5641. Open daily year-round. Factory tours $.

You won't travel far in Vermont before someone tells your kids about Ben and Jerry's factory in Waterbury. Somehow, the message always seems to center on "free ice cream." At risk of heresy, we'll set the record straight. You pay for a factory tour, at the end of which everyone gets a small sample. That's not exactly free ice cream for you, but it is for the kids. And we warn you, that sample will whet kids' appetites for more, available for a fee at the handy ice-cream counter. Perhaps we take too narrow a view; clearly this doesn't discourage most people, as the place is always mobbed.

Cold Hollow Cider Mill (ages 5 and up)

Route 100, Waterbury Center, Vt.; (802) 244–8771 or (800) 327–7537; www.coldhollow.com. Open daily 8:00 A.M. to 7:00 P.M. July through October, 8:00 A.M. to 6:00 P.M. November through June. **Free.**

Watch cider being pressed from Vermont apples year-round, with **free** samples. You can also sample Vermont cheddar and find other apple products, including apple butter and cider jelly. Maple candy and syrup and other specialty foods are sold in the shop and bakery.

Little River State Park (all ages)

Route 2, west of Waterbury, Vt.; (802) 244–7103 (in winter (802–479–4280). Open mid-May through mid-October. Admission: $, under age 4 **free.**

Little River is one of our favorite Vermont parks, set beside a large lake created by a dam. Swimming and boating are popular activities, and the park offers nature tours via boat. A wide variety of other nature programs fill the park schedule, including "wild edibles" walks, canoe trips, meet-the-trees walks, and evening wildlife shows. The interpretive booklets are especially good; they explain the geology as well as the plant and animal life. After following the Stevenson Brook Trail, kids may spend the rest of their trip there looking for the curious little round stones in the riverbed. These are not water-worn rocks; they are calcium deposits that formed around small stems in the mud of the brook bed. Cellar holes on the trail tell the land's farming history, although the former fields and pastures are now deep forest.

Thursday Concerts (all ages)

Rusty Parker Memorial Park, Main Street, Waterbury, Vt.; (802) 244–7352. Summer only, 6:30 P.M. each Thursday.

The music can be anything from bluegrass to a brass band, but it will always be lively. Bring lawn chairs or a blanket and picnic dinner to enjoy on the lawn while the music plays.

Where to Eat

Arvad's, Main Street, Waterbury, Vt.; (802) 244–8973. An informal local spot that can get crowded and noisy later in the evening but serves good food. Sandwiches are on good breads from their own bakery, and dinner specialties include several to please young palates. $–$$

Tanglewoods, Guptil Road (off Route 100 North), Waterbury, Vt.; (802) 244–7855. The New American menu relies a lot on south-west flavors, but blends them adroitly with local ingredients. Families will feel comfortable in the warm, relaxed atmosphere. $–$$

Where to Stay

1836 Cabins, Route 100, Waterbury, Vt.; (802) 244–8533. Attractive cabins scattered through pine woods give more privacy for families than hotel rooms do, along with a chance to cook your own meals. These have good kitchens. $–$$

Grunberg Haus, Route 100 South, Duxbury, Vt.; (802) 244–7726 or (800) 800–7760. See page 92 for a description of this nearby inn with cabins. It's about halfway between Waterbury and Waitsfield. $–$$

The Old Stagecoach Inn, 18 Main Street (Route 2), Waterbury, Vt.; (802) 244–5056 or (800) 262–2206. In the quiet center of town, this historic coach stop has large, well-furnished rooms, warm hosts, and wonderful fresh-baked breakfast pastries, in addition to cooked-to-order entrees to begin your day right. Occasionally, on weekends, they serve an equally good fixed-price dinner. $–$$

Camping

Little River State Park, Route 2, west of Waterbury, Vt.; (802) 244–7103 (in winter 802–479–4280). Campsites, some overlooking the lake, are well spaced and wooded. A busy schedule of nature programs, canoe trips, and boat tours on the reservoir are fun and help interpret the natural history of the area. $

Annual Events

JANUARY

Lake Elmore DogSled Races, north of Stowe, Vt., (800) 24–STOWE, early January. Mushers of all ages (even preschoolers) from all over New England compete.

Stowe Winter Carnival, (800) 24–STOWE. An extravaganza celebrating winter, with an accent on active sports.

FEBRUARY

Smugglers Notch Area Winter Carnival, Smugglers Notch, Vt., (802) 644–8851, early February. Nordic races, snow sculptures, food, snowshoe hikes, and social activities.

APRIL

A Sunrise Service and Children's Celebration, Mount Mansfield, Stowe, Vt., (800) 24–STOWE, Easter. This event is followed by an Easter egg hunt.

The Vermont Maple Festival, St. Albans, Vt., north of Burlington, (802) 524–5800, mid-April.

Lake Champlain Balloon and Craft Show, Essex Junction, Vt., (802) 899–2993. Craft show, hayrides, fireworks.

AUGUST

Champlain Valley Fair, Essex Junction, Vt., (802) 878–5545. Agricultural exhibits and entertainment.

SEPTEMBER

Harvest Festival, Shelburne Farms, Shelburne, Vt., (802) 985–8686.

Old-Fashioned Harvest Market, Underhill, Vt., (802) 899–3369. Farmers market, flea market, food.

The Northeast
Kingdom
and
Border Country

A lthough the largest geographically, the three counties of the Northeast Kingdom include vast areas of wilderness and relatively small populations. These will appeal to the traveler who likes open space, wild landscapes, and still more open space. This part of the state looks different, and it largely avoids the done-up tidiness and self-consciousness of some of the southern regions. This is ragtag farmland, miles of timber country, and tough-times towns. It is also beautiful, wild, and filled with moose, loons, and other wildlife.

Montgomery and Jay Peak

Montgomery has two separate village centers: one clustered around its green and another with a tiny business district along its single street. Jay Peak has brought tourism to Montgomery, but its distance from the major population centers means that the region is seldom crowded. An easygoing, small-town atmosphere prevails here, and with its proximity to the border, you may hear French spoken as often as you do English.

Jay Peak (ages 4 and up) 🎿 🍽️ 🛏️
Route 242, between Jay and Montgomery, Vt.; (802) 988–2611 or (800) 451–4449; www.jay peakresort.com. Open late November through April, weather permitting. Rates vary.

Vermont's northernmost ski mountain is very close to Canada, and many of its skiers are from across the border. Back-country and adventurous skiers love its eighteen glades, two chutes, and hundreds of acres of off-trail skiing. Jay has a vertical rise of more than 2,100 feet and more than fifty trails, and it consistently gets the greatest natural snowfall of any ski area in the East. It's not unusual for the area to get more than 300 inches in a season. Families staying at the resort can take part in a wide variety of activities in addition to skiing. Weekly snowshoe walks are led by a staff naturalist, and you can rent the snowshoes

THE NORTHEAST KINGDOM
AND BORDER COUNTRY

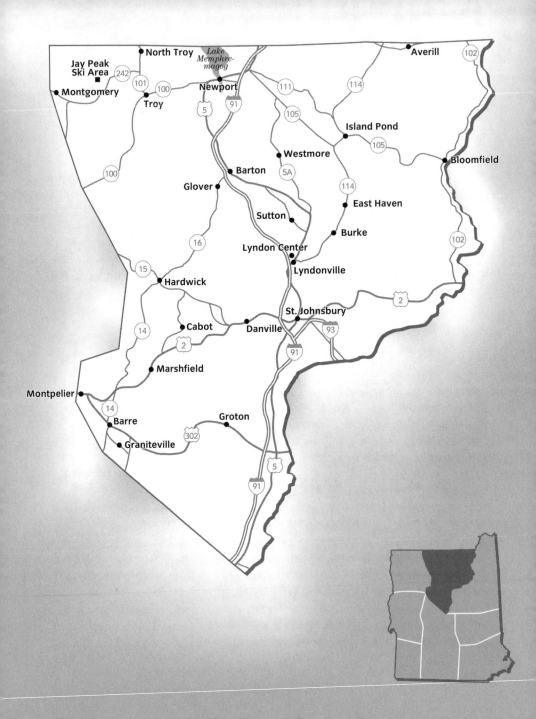

there. The ice-skating rink is lighted for evening use, and skate rentals are available. Also offered are rides on the snow cats (snow grooming machines) and trips to a working dairy farm. Evening sledding parties include a campfire and marshmallow roast. Programs for teens feature snow volleyball, movies, bowling, skating parties, and dances.

Jay Peak Aerial Tramway (ages 4 and up)

Route 242, between Jay and Montgomery, Vt.; (802) 988–2611 or (800) 451–4449; www.jay peakresort.com. Operates daily late June through Labor Day and during foliage season, every half hour from 10:00 A.M. to 5:00 P.M. Fare is $$. Canadian funds are accepted at par value.

In summer, Vermont's only aerial tramway carries sightseers, hikers, and walkers to the top of the mountain. (Maximum family rate is $30.) From the top you can descend on a self-guided Mountain Ecology Nature Trail; pick up the trail guide at the resort's welcome center at the base. The trail takes about 1½ hours, traversing coniferous forests and passing an alpine pond whose fragile ecosystem is examined. Because it's downhill, the trip is suitable for little people whose short legs would tucker out on the uphill climb.

Hazen's Notch Cross-Country Ski Area

Route 58, Hazen's Notch, Vt.; (802) 326–4799; www.hazensnotch.org. Open snow permitting. Day passes are $$.

More than 15 miles of groomed trails and 72 miles of back-country trails are snow-covered even in the mildest of winters. The views from many of them are splendid, overlooking the valley and the mountains.

Godfrey's Sugarhouse (ages 4 and up)

Gibou Road, Montgomery, Vt. (off Route 118 just south of town); (802) 326–4775. Free.

Watch their open evaporation process as they boil down the sap in the old-fashioned way. The sugaring season here extends well into April because of the northern location.

Covered Bridges (ages 5 and up)

Pick up local free map (available almost everywhere) showing all locations. Free.

Seven covered wooden bridges span the brooks and rivers of Montgomery, a record no other Vermont town exceeds. Three of them span gorges. The bridges were built from the 1860s to 1880s, and several are still in use today. You should avoid the trails that lead close to the banks of the bridges spanning gorges if you are traveling with small children, but you can view the waterfalls and rocky sides safely from the bridges themselves.

Rose Apple Acres Farm (ages 3 and up)

East Hill Road, North Troy, Vt.; (802) 988–2503. Reservations required. Rates vary.

A twelve-passenger sleigh makes thirty-minute sleigh rides, and passengers can warm up with hot cider or cocoa afterward. In case there isn't enough snow, they have a wagon as a backup. In the summer the farm also offers hayrides.

Where to Eat

Buon Amici, North Troy, Vt.; (802) 988–2299. Closed Tuesday. You and your kids will feel at home immediately in this cheery Italian-American restaurant. The menu is filled with all the kids' favorites. $

J.R.'s Restaurant and Pub, Main Street, Montgomery, Vt.; (802) 326–4682. Open from 6:30 A.M. to 10:00 P.M. The sandwiches here are hefty and inexpensive, and the dinner menu is innovative, with plenty of small-plate options for kids. The cafe atmosphere in the front is preferable for families, we think; the back is more publike. $–$$

Kilgore's General Store, Main Street, Montgomery, Vt.; (802) 326–3058. You shouldn't miss the magnificent soda fountain here, which extends in vintage glory along one side of the store. Breakfasts and lunches are excellent, and you can eat them from stools at the counter or in a cozy cafe area overlooking the river. Hours of the store vary widely, but the cafe is open daily for breakfast, lunch, and dinner. $

Where to Stay

Inglenook Lodge, Route 242, between Jay and Montgomery, Vt.; (802) 988–2880 or (800) 331–4346; www.jaypeakresort.com. Perched on the mountainside a mile from the base lodge, this contemporary lodge has a swimming pool and whirlpool tub, roomy public areas, and a giant fireplace with a sunken lounge, where everyone gathers in the evening. $$–$$$

Phineas Swann B&B, Main Street, Montgomery, Vt.; (802) 326–4306. The two genial gentlemen who own this B&B have succeeded in creating an atmosphere that is casual, classy, camp, and comfortable all at the same time. They welcome children over age 6, not because they don't like younger ones, but because they worry about them being hurt on some of the Victorian furniture, whose carved edges are just at eye level. The new suites in the carriage house behind the main building are just right for families, roomy with whirlpool baths and fireplaces. Breakfasts and afternoon tea are both worth planning your day around. $$–$$$

Rose Apple Acres Farm, East Hill Road, North Troy, Vt.; (802) 988–2503. A working farm with livestock, including goats, sheep, cattle, and a team of Belgian horses. $.

For More Information

Jay Peak Area Association, Route 242, Jay, VT 05859; (800) 882–7460.

St. Johnsbury, Lyndonville, and Burke

After you've traveled along the back roads of the Northeast Kingdom, St. Johnsbury will look like a big city. Although the niceties of its fine Victorian architecture may be lost on the children, they are sure to enjoy its outstanding museum. To the north of "Saint Jay," as locals call it, are the town of Lyndonville and its clutch of outlying "Lyndon" villages and another group of villages with "Burke" in their names. Winter sports are king here, with cross-country skiing, dogsledding, and a major snowmobile artery crossing at the general store in East Burke.

Fairbanks Museum (ages 4 and up)

Main Street, at the corner of Prospect Street, St. Johnsbury, Vt. (Main Street is not the main route that goes through the downtown business section—that's Railroad Street—but the older town center that runs parallel to Railroad Street, at the top of the hill.); (802) 748–2372; www.fairbanksmuseum.org. Open Monday through Saturday 9:00 A.M. to 5:00 P.M. and Sunday 1:00 to 5:00 P.M. Admission: $–$$, family rate $$$ (up to 3 adults, no limit on number of children).

If your kids are used to the spiffy new hands-on interpretive museums that are shy on artifacts and long on computer screens, they will be delighted with this old-fashioned building with its galleries and cabinets filled with curiosities. This is not to say that the exhibits are all static or lack the interactive element that draws kids in. But it's a more self-motivated interaction and combined with lots of things that are just plain fascinating to look at. They'll immediately see the giant polar bear, but we'd begin with the bizarre collection of Victorian "bug art," which includes portraits of Washington, Lincoln, and others. That will get the kids looking for the other cool stuff that's scattered throughout. The building itself is beautiful, trimmed in carved red sandstone, with an oak barrel-vaulted ceiling and an upper arcade gallery.

Be sure to look at the wildflower identification table, where fresh examples of wild plants currently in bloom are shown and identified. This is a good way to learn the names of those you will see blooming by the trails and roadside as you travel.

Interactive exhibits look at Vermont's wetlands and their inhabitants and the Children's Nature Corner, open June through August. Upstairs are the cultural and ethnographic collections from Asia, Africa, and the South Pacific, collected by Victorian travelers. Look here, too, for the original snowflake photographs by the Vermonter who invented the technique of filming these intricate crystals.

Downstairs is the Northern New England Weather Center, the U.S. weather station where for one hundred years the details of Vermont's varied and interesting weather have been recorded. And from here, since radio communications have made it possible, the weather forecasts have been broadcast to northern New Englanders. If your kids have listened to Mark Breen or Steve Meletsky and their "Eye on the Sky" as they ate breakfast each morning, they'll enjoy looking through the big glass window into the studio Breen and Meletsky broadcast from.

Fairbanks Planetarium (ages 4 and up)

Main Street, at the corner of Prospect Street, St. Johnsbury, Vt. (Main Street is not the main route that goes through the downtown business section—that's Railroad Street—but the older town center that runs parallel to Railroad Street, at the top of the hill.); (802) 748–2372. Shows are Monday through Saturday at 11:00 A.M. and 1:30 P.M., Sunday 1:30 P.M. in July and August. The rest of the year, open Saturday and Sunday only for shows at 1:30 P.M. Admission: $.

What separates this from most other planetarium shows is that it does not depend on a "canned" recorded or computerized narration. A real live person actually talks, and often integrates other nature subjects—or history or local legend—into the astronomical show. These spirited programs can change day to day, depending on some current phenomenon, the weather, or a particular astronomical event. Whatever subject works its way into the program, the show will be fresh and lively.

The Wildflower Inn (all ages)

Darling Hill Road, Lyndonville, Vt.; (802) 626–8310 or (800) 627–8310; www.wildflowerinn. com. The inn is a center for family-oriented activities, many of which are open to non-guests. Fees vary.

Although it revolves around the inn, the world that the O'Reillys have created on their Vermont hillside is an attraction of its own. They've taken their property far beyond a place to stay and made it a four-season place to play as well.

The idea began when they grew tired of being sent to dreary motels when they traveled with their family of several children, so they set out to create a fine inn that not only welcomed children but provided a place for them to have a vacation of their own, with and independent from their parents.

They began with a stunning setting, part of an old estate farm where views stretch across the valley to the facing hillside farms. Gardens alive with color fill the spring, summer, and fall foreground. The swimming pool is set in the midst of these gardens, with one of the finest views of any we've swum in.

A barnful of baby animals waits to be petted, and there's a sledding hill (sleds are provided), lighted skating rink, basketball court, large playground, batting cage, pitching machine, playhouse, and playroom. This bright corner room is filled with games and has a trunkful of costumes.

The cross-country ski center has more than 10 miles of cross-country ski trails (**free** to inn guests) that wind through meadows and woods along the hilltop property. A series of weekend winter carnivals in March includes skating parties, winter-related contests for all ages, and dogsledding.

Sleigh rides or hayrides are available regularly, depending on the season. A fifteen-passenger sled is drawn by Belgian draft horses for a thirty to forty minute ride across the meadows, where you can look down into the valley and out across the other hills.

For the kid- and parent-friendly lodging and dining aspects of the inn, see the "Where to Stay" section.

Vermont Children's Theater (ages 8–13 participating, ages 3 and up spectators)
Darling Hill Road, Lyndonville, Vt.; (802) 626–8310 or (800) 627–8310; www.vtnek.com. Mid-July and August. Tickets are $–$$.

This twenty-year-old theater produces two musical shows each summer. One is always a well-known Broadway show and the other is written especially for actors ages eight to thirteen. Performances are in the 200-seat barn theater, where you can also watch rehearsals in the afternoons.

Laplant's Sugar House (ages 5 and up) 🌀
Route 5, Sutton, Vt., 3 miles north of West Burke; (802) 467–3900. Sugar House open March through mid-April, 9:00 A.M. to 5:00 P.M. Sleigh rides seasonal, by reservation. Rates vary.

This old-fashioned 1,000-bucket sugar bush still uses the old-time methods, which are much more romantic even if they are a lot more work. The sap is collected in buckets hanging on the trees instead of miles of ugly plastic tubing. We know it's not as efficient, but it's nice to see the buckets and the team of Belgian horses that hauls the sap to the sugarhouse. You can visit their bush and sample some syrup at the sugarhouse during sugaring, a season that usually lasts from March to mid-April. During the rest of the winter, the Laplants give sleigh rides with their team of Belgians. Day and evening rides end with a warm-up snack and a cup of hot cocoa or cider.

Maple Grove Maple Museum (ages 6 and up)
Route 2, east of St. Johnsbury, Vt.; (802) 748–5141. Open Monday through Friday, 8:00 A.M. to 2:00 P.M. Last tour begins at 1:00 P.M. Museum admission free; factory tour $, under age 12 free.

More than eighty years ago, when two women began making maple candy in the family kitchen at their farm, their little cottage industry turned into the largest manufacturer of maple candies in the world. The sugarhouse museum shows the process of tapping trees, gathering the sap, and boiling it into syrup. Historic tools, equipment, and candy-making utensils and molds are displayed.

While all this is pretty dull for younger kids, the factory tour will get their attention as they see mind-boggling quantities of candy taking shape.

Ice-**Skating**

An indoor rink in Lyndon Center, at the Fenton Chester Arena, rents skates; (802) 626–9361. Wildflower Inn has an outdoor skating rink, which is lighted for night skating, on Darling Hill Road, Lyndonville; (802) 626–8310.

Where to Eat

Cindy's Pasta Shop, Route 5 North, St. Johnsbury, Vt.; (802) 748–4848. As you might expect from the name, you'll find a wide variety of pasta here, served up plain or fancy. $

Miss Lyndonville Diner, Route 5, Lyndonville, Vt.; (802) 626–9890. Tasty, no-nonsense dishes like roast turkey, liver and onions, baked fresh haddock, a hot turkey sandwich, a three-decker club. Nothing fancy, and cheery service. $

Northern Lights Book Shop and Cafe, 378 Railroad Street, St. Johnsbury, Vt.; (802) 748–4463. Open 8:00 A.M. weekdays, 9:00 A.M. weekends, to 5:00 P.M. and for dinner until 8:30 P.M. Wednesday through Saturday only. Wholesome and hearty sandwiches, rich home-style soups, good chili, and many vegetarian options. At dinner there's a bistro menu, with plenty of healthy options for kids. The book shop has a large children's section. $

River Garden Cafe, Route 114, East Burke, Vt.; (802) 626–3514. Serves lunch and dinner Tuesday through Sunday. A bright cafe setting with an up-to-date menu. Kids will find several appealing dishes, including several pasta choices. Ours just devour the bruschetta. $–$$

Wildflower Inn, Darling Hill Road, Lyndonville, Vt.; (802) 626–8310; www.wildflower inn.com. At the other end of the spectrum is this stylish dining room and simply smashing menu. Early dinners have a special— very special—children's menu, complete at $5.95. $$

Where to Stay

Hansel and Gretel Haus, off Route 114, Box 95, East Haven, Vt.; (802) 467–8884. Almost hidden in the woods, this cottage really is the color of rich gingerbread. Next door to the B&B is a shop with animated German clocks and imported German Christmas decorations.

The Wildflower Inn, Darling Hill Road, Lyndonville, Vt.; (802) 626–8310; www.wild flowerinn.com. Planned with families in mind, this hilltop inn provides every detail. Well-decorated rooms and suites, the latter with kitchenettes and bunk beds in many, are geared to providing space for everyone. Thoughtful touches delight kids—morning pancakes in teddy-bear or other shapes, a separate dinner menu of their favorites (including drink and dessert, $5.95), baby animals to pet, a miniature house to play in. An early children's dinner is designed so parents can join them over an appetizer, then enjoy their own dinner later. Kids, meanwhile, are entertained at evening programs or asleep in nearby rooms. See the listing for this inn in the attractions section for other activities at this family-friendly place. $$

Other local B&Bs: information is available at (800) 377–1212.

For More Information

Burke Area Chamber of Commerce, P.O. Box 347, East Burke, VT 05832; (800) 377–1212.

Lyndon Area Chamber of Commerce, P.O. Box 886, Lyndonville, VT 05851; (802) 626–9696.

Northeast Kingdom Chamber of Commerce, 30 Western Avenue, St. Johnsbury, VT 05819; (802) 748–3678 or (800) 639–6379.

Northeast Kingdom Travel & Tourism Association, P.O. Box 465, Barton, VT 05822; (800) 884–8001 or (802) 525–4386; e-mail: info@travelthekingdom.com.

The Far, Far North

Miles and miles of northern coniferous forest, punctuated by lakes and ponds and broken by a few elevations, characterize this area north of the St. Johnsbury region. Stretching along the Canadian border, these towns have a distinctly French accent that increases as you travel north. Be on the lookout for moose, both because seeing them is an unforgettable experience and because they are a hazard for night and twilight drivers.

Brighton State Park (all ages)
Off Route 105, Island Pond, Vt.; (802) 723–4360. Open mid-May through Columbus Day weekend. Admission: $, under age 4 **free.**

The trails at the park, especially the half-mile Northeast Kingdom Nature Trail, show the impact of logging on the north country and the ability of nature to regenerate quickly after cutting.

Along the nature trail you will see the one remaining giant tree that escaped logging early in the century, possibly because it was too small then. Evidence has been found at the point of land called Indian Point that suggests it was used by Native Americans. You can visit this lovely spot on a trail about a mile long. The nature trail begins at the small park museum, well worth a stop to learn about the flora and fauna you'll see on the trails. The park has a nice play area and a swimming beach with bathhouses for day visitors. Campers enjoy the evening nature programs, led by resident naturalists, who also lead day hikes and other activities in which noncampers can join in.

Maidstone State Park (all ages)
Off Route 102, Bloomfield, Vt.; (802) 676–3930. Open mid-May through Labor Day. Admission: $, under age 4 **free.**

Loons nest on the lake here, a glacial pond surrounded by thick spruce forest. Swimming beaches have picnic facilities and rest rooms, but no other facilities. One beach is reserved for day use, the other for campers. By following the Moose Trail between camping areas A and B to the crest of a hill, you can still see the huge boulders dropped as the

COOL Facts

Look in Brighton State Park—and elsewhere—for the "walking trees" whose roots are aboveground as though they were standing on tiptoe. This tells you that the tree originally grew out of the stump of an older tree that was cut. The original stump rotted away, leaving the roots above ground, where they grew bark and continued to support the new tree.

Moose Watching

As you travel along Route 105 between Island Pond and Bloomfield, or along Route 155 north of Island Pond, look for low, wet places along the roadsides. If you park along the road next to some of these in the early evening, you are likely to see moose. In fact, you may spot other cars sitting there waiting for them too, as moose-watching is popular even with the locals who see them frequently.

If you do see moose, be sure to keep the children in the car and stay within a very few steps of the car yourself. Bring the animals closer with binoculars or a telephoto lens, and remember that those gangly legs can carry them very fast if they are alarmed. They have no fear of you or your car, which is just another small animal to them.

glaciers melted. The shorter trail along the pond may bring loon sightings or at least a good look at a beaver house.

Quimby Country (all ages)

Forest Lake, Averill, Vt.; (802) 822–5533; www.quimbycountry.com. Open mid-May through mid-October.

Picture a summer camp for the entire family, with individual cabins, family-style meals in a common dining room, and activities scheduled throughout the day and evening. Of course, you don't have to take part, but your kids will want to follow their upbeat counselors into every new adventure. Swimming at the lakefront beach, fishing, paddling in canoes or rowing in rowboats, and looking for moose (sure to turn up) will occupy lazy summer and fall days for your family, just as they have many families before you—for more than a century. In fact, most of the people you'll meet here have been coming since they were kids and can count the generations that came before them. The woodsy, rustic atmosphere is just the right setting. Rates in the summer are about $400 a day for a family, including all meals and a fully supervised activity program for kids.

Bread and Puppet Museum (ages 7 and up)

Route 122, Glover, Vt.; (802) 525–3031. Open daily 10:00 A.M. to 5:00 P.M. June through October. Free; donations welcome.

The sight of 12-foot-tall people with outsized heads could be frightening for small children; it's almost overwhelming for adults to enter the upper level of this backstage storehouse and see the figures hanging above. Older kids will be interested in how these huge creatures move and perform. Smaller shows have replaced the big annual one of years past, and they take place every Sunday at 3:00 P.M., mid-July through August. Kids and adults alike will enjoy performing their own plays with the smaller puppets available for their use.

Where to Eat

Jennifer's Restaurant, Cross Street, Island Pond, Vt.; (802) 723–6135. Good, hearty, and plain, the food here includes the old favorites—hot sandwiches with gravy and fries, deli sandwiches, and heaping plates of pancakes and eggs for breakfast. Prices will make you wonder if you've stumbled back into another decade. $

The Willough Vale Inn, Route 5A, Westmore, Vt.; (802) 525–4123; www.willoughvale. com. The Tap Room is a casual publike place, and the Main Dining Room, overlooking Lake Willoughby, is a bit more formal, but still kid-friendly. $–$$

Where to Stay

Lakefront Motel, Cross Street, Island Pond, Vt.; (802) 723–6507. Right in town and right on the lake, a good place for people who bring boats or canoes on vacation with them. In the winter it's a haven for snowmobilers. $–$$

The Willough Vale Inn, Route 5A, Westmore, Vt.; (802) 525–4123; www.willoughvale. com. Views over Lake Willoughby decorate the windows of the inn rooms and four lakefront cottages, which are furnished in handcrafted furniture. The easy atmosphere is family-friendly. $$

Camping

Brighton State Park, off Route 105, Island Pond, Vt.; (802) 723–4360. Open mid-May through Columbus Day weekend. Campsites are nicely spaced and separated, all in the woods surrounding a tree-lined pond. More than twenty of the sites have lean-to shelters, all of which are wheelchair accessible; one is reserved exclusively for that use. A swimming beach and evening nature programs make this park popular with families. $

Maidstone State Park, off Route 102, Bloomfield, Vt.; (802) 676–3930. Open mid-May through Labor Day. Tent and trailer sites have no hookups, and thirty-seven of the sites have lean-tos. A swimming beach is reserved for camper use. $

For More Information

North Country Chamber of Commerce, The Causeway, Newport, VT 05855; (800) 698–8939 or (603) 237–8939; www.north countrychamber.org.

Along Route 2: Groton, Cabot, and Danville

Between St. Johnsbury and Montpelier, Route 2 strings together some very pretty countryside, including one of our favorite state parks. South of Route 2, Route 302 forms a wedge, like a badly cut slice of pie. Barre and Graniteville, the center of Vermont's granite quarries, have another kind of mountain view: mountains of granite chippings and slag that rise beside the road. The contrast between this largely immigrant industrial Vermont and the idyllic rolling hills to its east is almost startling, but each has attractions you'll want to visit with your children.

Danville Morgan Horse Farm (ages 4 and up)

Joe's Brook Road, Danville, Vt. (leave Route 2 in Danville on Brainerd Street, at the village green, and bear left onto Joe's Brook Road); (802) 684–2251. Open daily 9:00 A.M. to 3:00 P.M. Free.

Stretching along a hillside with fine views of the White Mountains across the river, is a farm where they raise Vermont's own breed of horse, the famous Morgan. You can visit the farm any day and see these horses or even help feed them if you arrive at the right time.

Cabot Creamery (ages 5 and up)

128 Main Street, Cabot, Vt.; (802) 563–2231 or (800) 837–4261; www.cabotcheese.com. Open 9:00 A.M. to 5:00 P.M. daily June through October, Monday through Saturday 9:00 A.M. to 4:00 P.M. February through May and November and December. Tours every half hour. Admission free; guided tours $, under age 12 free.

At the best-known creamery in Vermont you can sample all their varieties with or without a tour to see cheese being made. The tour is interesting; maybe your kids will get to see the very yogurt that will become Ben and Jerry's frozen yogurt the next day.

Groton State Forest (all ages)

Route 232, between Groton and Marshfield, Vt.; (802) 584–3820. Open mid-May through mid-October. Free.

A vast area of state lands lies between Route 2 and Route 302. In it are several different recreation areas, each with its own attractions. Park publications show the trails and facilities at each, along with lists of plants and birds you may see, and its history from the logging and railway days.

A very nice nature center explains the geologic history in very graphic ways, as well as displaying samples of the various kinds of local stone (which make up the floor of the center). A nature trail begins at the Nature Center, explaining more about the landscape and habitats.

Hawks often circle over Owl's Head, an elevation you can reach by a trail from its base or by a ten-minute climb up stone steps from the end of a road. The geology at the top is quite dramatic, with contrasting stripes of rock crisscrossing through the granite.

Frequent nature programs and walks are led by resident naturalists. Along with the trails and nature interpretation, you'll find swimming and boat rentals.

Rock of Ages Quarry (ages 4 and up)

Graniteville Road (follow signs from Route 302), Graniteville, Vt. (east of Barre); (802) 476–3119; www.rockofages.com. Open Monday through Saturday 8:30 A.M. to 5:00 P.M., Sunday noon to 5:00 P.M. May through October. Stonecutting open Monday through Friday 8:00 A.M. to 3:30 P.M. Shuttle tours Monday through Friday 9:30 A.M. to 3:00 P.M. June through mid-October. Admission free; shuttle fare $.

The sheer size of the hole left by the extraction of granite here over the past hundred years boggles the mind. Tours show the various steps in drilling, blasting, and lifting the stone out of the ground, as well as the cutting and finishing process that turns this high-quality fine-grade granite into the world's premier monuments.

Bragg Farm Sugarhouse and Gift Shop (ages 5 and up)
Route 14, East Montpelier, Vt.; (802) 223–5757 or (800) 376–5757. Open year-round, daily 8:30 A.M. to 7:00 P.M. Free.

Guided tours in season show how maple sugar is made, or you can see it all on their video. At the shop you can buy the candy, syrup, and maple ice cream.

Where to Eat

Bob's, Route 302, Groton, Vt.; (802) 584–3225. Generous portions of Italian and other favorites are served in the modest cafe or for takeout. $

Danville Restaurant and Inn, Route 2, Danville, Vt.; (802) 684–3484. Family-run and family-friendly, serving a mainstream menu. $–$$

Where to Stay

The Hollow Inn and Motel, Route 14 (south of intersection with Route 302), Barre, Vt.; (802) 479–9313. Large rooms in the inn or motel units, some with kitchenettes, are in a nicely landscaped hilltop setting with pleasant swimming pool area. Children under 12 stay free. $$

Camping

Groton State Forest, Route 232, between Groton and Marshfield, Vt.; (802) 584–3820. Open mid-May through mid-October. Several camping areas offer open and wooded sites. $

For More Information

Central Vermont Chamber of Commerce, Steward Road, Barre, VT 05641; (802) 229–5711.

Annual Events

JANUARY

Northeast Kingdom Sled Dog Races, Wildflower Inn, Lyndonville, Vt., (802) 626–8310, early January.

FEBRUARY

Heavenly Kingdom Weekend, Barton, Vt., Route 5 (north of Lyndonville and just off I–91), (802) 525–1137, mid-February. A family festival, with sledding, ice-fishing, and ice sculpture.

MAY

Annual Spring Festival, Hardwick, Vt., (802) 472–6555, late May. Features a parade, horse-pulling, and a barbecue.

JULY

Old Time Fiddlers' Contest, Shepherd's Field, Hardwick, Vt., (802) 472–5501, late July. More than sixty contestants.

SEPTEMBER/OCTOBER

Northeast Kingdom Fall Foliage Festival, Cabot, Peacham, Barnet, Groton, and elsewhere, (802) 563–2472, late September/early October. A day of events in each town.

The
White
Mountains

New Hampshire's White Mountains are cut by notches, giant glacial scours that left depressions in the mountain chains. Early trails that followed these notches were replaced by roads. These roads and are now lined with historic sites and natural attractions, as well as a few created just for the tourists that have been coming here since the mid-1800s. Here you will see New England's tallest mountain, vast pine and hardwood forests, and a wide variety of rock formations begun by glaciers and continued by the rivers that flow from the mountains. Mountain views predominate, punctuated by some grand old resort hotels and ski areas. The mountainsides are webbed with rushing mountain streams that break into waterfalls at the slightest chance.

Way up North

Make way for the moose in this narrow triangle at the top of New Hampshire with the Connecticut River (which forms the border with Vermont) on the west and the Maine border on the east. Canada's Quebec province forms New Hampshire's border at the very top. Although you can see moose farther south, they are most common here, and a drive at evening or on a cloudy summer day is quite likely to bring sightings.

Christies' Maple Farm and Museum (ages 3 and up) 🐕 🏕

Route 2, Lancaster, N.H.; (800) 788–2118; www.RealMaple.com. Open daily. Free tours.

The Christie family invites visitors to tour their maple museum and sugarhouse to learn all about how maple syrup is made. Stop by to have some pancakes, too, drenched in the pure New Hampshire maple syrup. You may also enjoy a free tasting of the different grades of maple syrup and creams. There is a picnic area here, where you can get some great views of Mount Washington and the Presidential Range.

THE WHITE MOUNTAINS

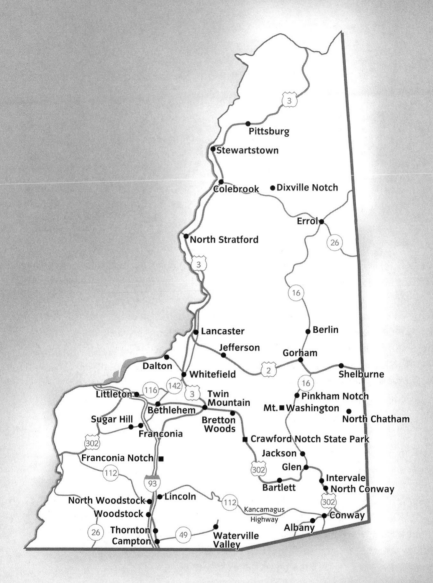

Mount Prospect Tower and Lodge (ages 3 and up)
Route 3, near Lancaster, N.H., at top of Mount Prospect; (603) 788–4004 or (603) 788–3155. Mid-June through Labor Day, open Tuesday through Sunday, Memorial Day through mid-October open weekends only, 10:00 A.M. to 6:00 P.M., plus special programs. Admission: $, under age 18 free.

The tower and lodge are part of the 420-acre Mount Prospect State Park. The round stone tower is neat for any kid to look up at, especially if he or she is into fairy tales, but the lodge is where you will find more educational stuff to interest the older kids. Inside, the lodge offers a great deal of White Mountains historical information, as well as wildlife displays that specialize in birds. There are also displays that discuss the history and role of Senator John Wingate Weeks, who was instrumental in preserving many parts of the area. Lectures and other programs are offered as well; call ahead for subjects and times.

Moose Watching near Dixville Notch (all ages)
Aside from The Balsams Grand Resort Hotel, the road between Colebrook and Errol (which climbs over Dixville Notch) is surrounded by wilderness. Just over Dixville Notch, a wild, narrow pass between jagged rocks, moose are such a common sight that a viewing platform has been built beside Route 26. This enables moose-watchers to see out over the low, wet area where moose feast on aquatic plants in the evening.

Moose Alley (all ages)
Another place that is almost certain to turn up moose is along Route 3 between the village of Pittsburg and the Canadian border. Look in low, muddy places beside the road that show signs of trampling, and drive with extra caution.

Across the Border to Canada (all ages)
Route 3, Pittsburg, N.H. Free.

After tracing the path of the Connecticut Lakes, the main road crosses into the province of Quebec. It's fun to add a foreign country to a trip, and this crossing usually has a shorter

Preserving our Forests

John Wingate Weeks was a U.S. senator and cabinet member who put his positions to good use. He was able to pass the Weeks Law, which established the government's right to purchase natural areas like forest land in an effort to protect the plants and animals and preserve these beautiful areas for future generations. His influence on the White Mountains area is still remembered today. He commissioned the construction of the tower and lodge at the top of Mount Prospect and rebuilt the old carriage road so that visitors could easily drive to the top of the mountain to enjoy the beautiful views.

line of vehicles waiting for inspection than the more frequently used routes. Do remember that the longest lines are on the other side as the rigorous security is for those entering the United States. When stopped for customs formalities, tell the guards you're just going over so the kids can say they have been to Canada.

To return to the United States, you may be asked to show proof of citizenship. You should carry a copy of your birth certificate, passport, naturalization papers, or a green card with you, unless your driver's license states your place of birth. It is also a good idea to have children's birth certificates along, although we have never been asked for them. Your car will be searched on the return trip, so be sure you are not carrying any fruit or vegetables, even if you took them out of the country only a few minutes before.

For even the shortest drive into Canada, you should have a statement from your automobile insurer to prove you have insurance coverage. These statements are easy to get; with a simple phone call they can fax or mail you one. Without one, even a tiny accident with no more than scratched fenders can result in having your car impounded until you prove that your liability insurance covers the damage.

The Foolish Frog (ages 5 and up)

Route 3, North Stratford, N.H.; (603) 636–1887. Open May through October, without set hours. Admission Free, **donations welcome (they support expansion of the collection).**

You probably never thought about how universal the frog is, nor how common a design motif it is throughout much of the world. But the owners of this little museum have, and their collection must reach a thousand examples. Indonesian frog deities are side-by-side with bouncy rubber frogs, frog baby bibs, and carved jumping-jack frogs. Fun to explore, the collection also contains some very nice wooden toys based on a frog motif, which are for sale. Your kids will never look at a bullfrog through the same eyes again after visiting this engaging little museum.

Moose Manners

When you spot a moose beside the road, remember that moose are not like creatures in a zoo, but wild animals in an environment where they have no real predators. They are not afraid of you or your car—not even your SUV or pickup truck. Unless you should happen to be between a mother and calf, they will probably ignore you completely if you are quiet, keep your distance, and move slowly. They are more nervous if they have a calf with them, especially if you get near it. They move with surprising speed—those awkward-looking long legs can carry them at 35 miles per hour. Keep children inside the car and stay within a few steps of your car yourself so you can get inside quickly should the moose take a disliking to you. Use your zoom lens or binoculars instead of your feet to bring the animals closer to you.

Beaverbrook Falls (all ages)

Route 145, about 2½ miles north of Colebrook, N.H. Route 145 is signposted "Clarksville" where it leaves Route 3. Free.

If you leave Route 3 to travel between Colebrook and Pittsburg on this smaller road, you can't miss this 35-foot waterfall on the east side of the road. After a rain, or in the spring runoff, it's pretty impressive; any time at all it's a pretty waterfall and a good place for a picnic. Tables are in a small grassy park at its base. Locals use the pool at its base as a swimming hole, although there is no supervision, of course.

Wilderness Ski Area (ages 3 and up)

Route 26, Dixville Notch, N.H.; (800) 255–0800 in New Hampshire, (800) 255–0600 elsewhere. Skiing and other snow sports are free to guests of The Balsams Grand Resort Hotel.

This small but well-tended and well-groomed ski area is family-oriented, with gentle terrain and dependable snow even in very mild winters. Five-day packages bring lodging, dining, and skiing into family budget range at $500 per person. Along with downhill skiing are cross-country trails and snowshoeing, with special programs for children. The Ski Learning Center offers private and group coaching in alpine, cross-country, and telemark skiing and snowboarding. Tiny Turns and Snow Farm programs are aimed at children ages three to six. Programs for skiers ages seven to twelve are aimed at building skills and confidence along with safe skiing habits, without losing sight of the first goal of skiing: having a good time. So remote is this ski area and so friendly and intimate its atmosphere that you will feel comfortable letting older children ski by themselves.

Six Gun City & Fort Splash Waterpark (ages 4 to 12)

Route 2, Jefferson, N.H.; (603) 586–4592. Open weekends May through mid-June, then daily through Labor Day weekend, 9:00 A.M. to 6:00 P.M. Admission: $$$ (which includes all rides and activities), under age 4 free with an adult.

Six Gun City is plenty of fun for the entire family. It is locally owned and operated by a family who has put a great deal of effort into the entire experience, and you will be impressed. The park is set up in sections that include the homestead and an Indian camp, as well as a fort. Every ten to fifteen minutes, Main Street is subject to play shoot-outs and holdups in the spirit of the "Old West" mystique. Kids really get into the spirit of these and plenty of other activities.

The two waterslides are age-appropriate. The 250-foot Tomahawk Run is for older children, and the Cheyenne Falls waterslide is for smaller fry. All ages can play on bumper boats or take log boats on the Timber Hollow Sawmill ride. At the sleigh museum, adults will admire the impressive collection of more than a hundred horse-drawn vehicles, each of which has been restored and maintained (at great cost) to ensure not only appearance but also authenticity and historical integrity.

The Old Man of the Valley (all ages)
Route 2, Shelburne, N.H. (look for the sign and the pullout for parking); no phone. Daylight hours. **Free.**

This "old man" is a little-known geological face in the rocks, and it is easy to get to. A single rock stands beside the trail, one side of which is a clearly recognizable profile. A mini-hike from the parking lot will bring you to the formation, which is so distinct that you will want to get closer and make sure it's natural, not sculpted by a stone-carver.

Gorham Historical Society Museum (ages 6 and up)
Gorham, on the Common across from the Town Hall; (603) 466–5570. Hours vary (call ahead). **Free.**

Although historic societies don't tend to be too exciting for children, this one may spark their interest. The museum is housed in an old railway station, so the emphasis of many displays is on this important part of the town's history. Kids might also enjoy viewing the prehistoric "television sets"—stereoscopic viewers, which were a family's way to remember their vacation before cameras and camcorders. Guests to the museum are welcome to use the old stereoptic cards, but be sure to supervise children's use, since these are valuable antiques today.

Northern Forest Moose Tours (ages 6 and up)
Northern Forest Heritage Park, 961 Main Street (Route 16), Berlin, N.H.; (603) 752–7202; www.northernforestheritage.org. Open daily Memorial Day through September, just before sunset (time varies with season). Admission: $$–$$$.

This tour is a great way to get to the best moose-spotting places in the area without getting lost. After boarding the van at the parking lot, you will be shown a video called *The Trees Still Grow,* which gives you some historical perspective on the area. It focuses especially on the logging and papermaking industry, which has affected the moose's habitat. The van is air-conditioned, and the tour lasts for about three hours. There is a guarantee that if you do not see a moose, you can get a raincheck, and this informative tour sure beats wandering back roads aimlessly while trying to peer out the window. It's not likely that you will be disappointed with this tour as it has boasted success rates as high as 97 percent. Feel free to bring cameras or camcorders, as well as your own car seat if you are bringing a small child. Food and beverages are not allowed.

Chester Eastman Homestead (ages 6 and up)
Route 113, North Chatham, N.H.; (603) 694–3388; www.cehfarm.com. Call ahead for special events and reservations. Chore Time 3:00 to 5:00 P.M. Most events **free;** $$ for Chore Time.

The Chester Eastman Homestead is home to Steve and Jeanne Eastman, who have restored the farm to its appearance in the early days of its operation. Although it did spend about fifty years out of the family, in 1966 the family bought back the farm that was originally settled by grandfather Chester Eastman in 1796. A detailed diary of the farm was kept from 1883 until 1917, which has proven invaluable to the Eastmans in restoring a nineteenth-century feel.

The farm is not open to the public every day but does invite visitors to special events and will open the farm for groups and families who are interested. Guests may choose activities tailored to their own special interests. Here you can experience life as it was in the nineteenth century, practicing cow-milking and butter churning, spinning wool and washing clothes, plowing the fields using the family's Percheron draft horses, shelling and grinding corn, or learning to cook.

Seasonal events include Maple Syrup Days in the spring, Fall on the Farm during harvest time, and the Winter Ice Harvest. The farm also hosts an ice-cream social (with homemade ice cream) and Logging Day, which shows how the forests were felled before the big machines were invented. You can also join the family as they milk their cow, feed the pig and chickens, and make a little ice cream during Chore Time. Most of their programs and events end with a sleigh ride or hayride drawn by their horses, and you may schedule a ride for your family even if the farm isn't operating. Charters cost $5.00 per person with a $25.00 minimum.

Forest Lake State Park (all ages)

Route 116, Dalton, N.H. (west of Whitefield); (603) 837–9150. Open 9:00 A.M. to 8:00 P.M. on weekends from Memorial Day through the last week of June and on the two weekends after Labor Day. During the rest of the summer, open every day during the same hours. Admission $, children under 12 and New Hampshire residents over 65 admitted free.

The small swimming beach with a bathhouse and picnic area is on a forest-ringed lake with a campground.

Where to Eat

Barbara's Little Restaurant, Route 116, Whitefield, N.H.; (603) 837–3161. Breakfast, lunch, and dinner are served every day of the week, all home-cooked and hearty. $

Lost Nation Natural Foods, Main Street, Lancaster, N.H.; (603) 788–4141. This place does not have sit-down eating but is a good place to get provisions for picnics. $

Midtown Restaurant, Route 3, Pittsburg, N.H.; (603) 538–6679. Serves three satisfying meals daily. $

Wilfred's Turkey Dinners, Main Street, Gorham, N.H.; (603) 466–2380. Yes, they serve a great turkey dinner, but they also have plenty of other homemade specialties to please the whole family. $–$$

Where to Stay

The Balsams Grand Resort Hotel, Route 26, Dixville Notch, N.H.; in-state (800) 255–0800, out-of-state (800) 255–0600. This grand hotel was one of the biggest and best of the White Mountains grand hotels, and it's one of the few still around today to tell the story. Central to all sorts of year-round activities, this is a wonderful family vacation spot. The building itself is impressive and unique, and inside you will love the ballroom, the movie theater, and especially the dining room, where everyone is treated like royalty. Three memorable meals a day are included in the room rate.

During the summer, families may like to take advantage of the special children's program Camp Wind Whistle (for ages 5 to 13) or Camp Wee Whistle (for ages 3 and 4). Both programs are available to guests at no extra charge. Children are divided into appropriate age groups and can join for a full day or half a day (9:30 A.M. to 12:30 P.M. and 1:30 to 4:00 P.M.), with lunch if you choose. The kids will spend their day hiking, playing games, swimming, participating in educational and nature activities, playing tennis, or taking tours of the kitchen with the head chef, as well as many other activities. One of our favorite parts of this is the weekly etiquette class. Children are also invited to dine with their counselors at any meal, where they will be tutored in choosing their own healthy meal and in table manners. Babysitting referrals are also available at no extra charge. $$–$$$.

The Glen, off Route 3, Pittsburg, N.H.; (603) 538–6500 or (800) 445–GLEN. This set of log cabins and main lodge are set back in the woods on the shore of a pretty lake. The owner is one of the best parts of this place. She will be eager to accommodate your needs as well as provide you with plenty of suggestions for little outings with your family in the raw nature of the North Kingdom. This is a particularly good place to stay if you want to be near some of the best moose-sighting spots up north. Prices may seem high, but they include three meals a day and tips, too. The Glen is open only from May through October. $$–$$$

Philbrook Farm Inn, 881 North Road, Shelburne, N.H.; (603) 466–3831. This inn is more out-of-the-way, but it offers a quiet, restful New England feel. The family atmosphere seeps into the warm, friendly service, and you will love the home-cooked meals served in their dining room. You may eat here if you are not a guest, but make reservations and bring cash because they do not take credit cards. $$–$$$

The Spalding Inn, Mountain View Road, Whitefield, N.H.; (603) 837–2572 or (800)

368–8439. Very friendly and warm, this family-owned inn is ideally laid out for families, with rooms in its low wings and in a separate converted carriage house and cottages. The inn has a swimming pool, tennis courts, and a bowling green. There's plenty of space, so you can explore the grounds, or perhaps play a game of croquet—a game that children catch on to quickly (they usually do better at it than their parents!). The chef loves a challenge and is sure to come up with something your children will love. Dining here is a treat, so you should reserve your family's table when you arrive. $$

Camping

Coleman State Park, off Route 26, Stewartstown, N.H.; (603) 237–4520. A small state park favored by fishing and canoeing enthusiasts. $

Forest Lake State Park, Route 116, Dalton, N.H. (west of Whitefield); (603) 837–9150. Well-spaced campsites spread around a lake with a swimming beach. $

Lake Francis State Park, Route 3, Pittsburg, N.H.; (603) 538–6965. This campground in the midst of the northern forest is rarely crowded, and moose sightings are almost certain. The lake is a favorite of canoeists and fishing enthusiasts. $

Lake Umbagog State Park, Route 26, Errol, N.H.; (603) 271–3628. The campground's thirty-eight campsites are suitable for tents, not RVs, and thirty more sites around the lake can be reached only by boat. The park is beloved by canoeists and kayakers and is the nesting place for osprey and eagles. $

For More Information

Connecticut Lakes Region Chamber of Commerce, Pittsburg , NH 03592; (603) 538–7118.

North Country Chamber of Commerce, Colebrook, NH 03576; (603) 237–8939 or (800) 698–8939.

Around Mount Washington

This area on the flanks of Mount Washington is almost circled by Routes 16 and 302 north of their split in Glen. On one side is Pinkham Notch and on the other Crawford Notch, one of the most scenic areas in the White Mountains. If the day is clear, you will see Mount Washington and other peaks of the Presidential Range ahead as you drive along the banks of the Saco River. At the Willey House, scene of the avalanche made immortal by Nathaniel Hawthorne in *The Ambitious Guest,* is a picnic area. Almost at the top of the long climb through the notch, Silver Cascade drops over a long series of ledges right beside the road. A nearby pull-out area offers a fine panorama southward back down the notch. At the head of the notch is the Victorian railway station, now a checkpoint for hikers and climbers.

Mt. Washington Auto Road (all ages)

Route 16, Pinkham Notch, Gorham, N.H.; (603) 466–3988. Open daily mid-May through late October 7:30 A.M. to 6:00 P.M., with shorter hours during the spring and fall. Toll is $$$ per car and driver, plus $$ for each additional adult and $ each child ages 5–15. By van $$$ per adult, $$ ages 5–12, under 5 free.

We recommend making sure your car can take this 8-mile, 12-percent grade climb (or better yet, take it out on a rental car). This is by far the least expensive and easiest way to get to the top of the famous mountain, and you will have the freedom to stay as long as you want to hike or explore the peak. The toll includes a bumper sticker ("This Car Climbed Mount Washington") and an audio tour on cassette.

Do remember that the mountain is often blanketed in a thick cover of fog, so if you can't see the top from the valley, you won't be able to see much from the top! On the way up, you'll pass several historic sites and geological formations. If you're driving up in June, stop by **Alpine Gardens,** where a great selection of wildflowers that are limited to certain elevations are in bloom. At the **Glen House Carriage Barns,** opposite the base of the

Blowing Up a **Storm**

At the top of Mt. Washington, observatory crews measured the highest winds ever recorded by man at 231 miles per hour on April 12, 1934.

Auto Road, you can see the sparse remains of one of the once-grand hotels. Also, you can explore the graveyard of vehicles of the past that brought tourists from those times up the mountain: the first coach, wagons, a Pierce Arrow, and others.

Glen Ellis Falls (ages 4 and up)
Route 302, Pinkham Notch, N.H. The parking for Glen Ellis is signposted from Route 302. Free.

A short walk from the parking lot takes you under the road and along a well-surfaced path to a flight of stairs. As you descend, you can stop at various levels to see a mountain stream drop over cascades, then plunge 65 feet through granite walls. Safety walls of local stone don't destroy the natural setting but do make viewing the falls safe.

Appalachian Mountain Club (ages 6 and up)
Route 302, Pinkham Notch, N.H.; (603) 466–2727. Prices vary with programs, some are free. You do not have to be an AMC member to take part in any program here.

Year-round programs and classes may be nature hikes, mountaineering classes, botany programs, photography workshops, or travelogues. Some programs are **free.** Classes require advance registration; a few are more intensive and include lodging. These programs are offered year-round, each suiting the weather and environment of its own season. The most unusual are the winter activities, which include family snowshoe adventures (one date is reserved for fathers and children, the rest are for all parents and children ages five to ten). The snowshoe adventures include the use of snowshoes for a fee of $39 adults and $17 children for nonmembers. A two-day adventure on snowshoes, for parents and their children ages eight to sixteen, includes building a snow shelter, and the price includes a night's lodging at the lodge. Even longer adventures are offered during school vacation weeks, with cross-country skiing, animal tracking, and winter ecology. Call for a schedule of activities for the time you will be there.

The **Trading Post** has a good selection of books, maps, and information about trails and wildlife. Be sure to see the giant relief map of Mount Washington. In the summer, a naturalist is on duty outside to introduce children and adults to the wildlife in the area.

Of special interest is the **Junior Naturalists Program,** for children ages five to twelve, which includes games and activities centered around the outdoors and nature subjects. The staff there can give you many suggestions for hikes just right for whatever ages your family represents—flat sneaker-hikes around a pond, a short uphill trek to a long waterfall, and even day-long climbs for the energetic.

Great Glen Trails (ages 4 and up)

Route 302, Pinkham Notch, N.H.; (603) 466–2333; www.mt-washington.com. Open daily 8:30 A.M. to 5:00 P.M. December through March and mid-May to mid-October. Prices vary with activity.

Great Glen Trails is a center for cross-country skiing, snowshoeing, ice-skating, bicycling, guided nature walks, archery, concerts, barbecues, and kite-flying, each in its own season. Rental bikes, skis, snowshoes, and Scandinavian-design kick sleds are available, along with a variety of strollers and sleds designed for carrying small children while you use the trails.

Jackson Falls (all ages)

Carter Notch Road, Jackson, N.H.; no phone. Daylight hours. Free.

Jackson Falls cascades down a long stairstep of flat ledges and may have been the scene of the first "bobsled" ride when a bunch of college boys decided to ride their sleigh down it one winter evening when the falls were frozen. Although it's beautiful in the winter when the falls turn to ice, we prefer it in the summer when we can cool our feet there and have a picnic on the ledges.

Mount Washington Cog Railway (all ages)

Off Route 302, Bretton Woods, N.H.; (603) 278–5404 or (800) 922–8825; www.thecog.com. Operates Saturday and Sunday in May, daily June through late October 9:00 A.M. to 3:00 P.M. (arrive ½ hour early). Reservations suggested.

While you are waiting to board the train, you can watch the puffs of smoke rise along the track above, as the other trains make their way up and down the mountain. Check out the old engines and other antique machinery in the yard, or visit the small museum and learn about the history of the railway and the area. Here you will find cutaway models of some of the first cog railway cars and engines, as well as information about the weather projects conducted at the top of the mountain. If you are not riding the train, there is a small admission price for the museum. It is open from May through October.

The Cog Railway has always been operated as a tourist train and was the first of its kind in the world. Its debut was on July 3, 1869, and it is the only remaining railway in the world still powered by coal. The trip takes about 1¼ hours each way; the round-trip is 3¼

Parking **Tickets**

The USDA Forest Service, which runs the **White Mountain National Forest,** now charges $5.00 per vehicle for a one-week pass. This pass is required to park your car in any of the roadside pull-outs or trailhead parking areas within the National Forest. Each place will have a notice warning you that parking without a permit will result in a hefty fine. You can buy these passes in several places around the White Mountains or in many of the parking lots themselves. To find the source nearest you, call (603) 528–8721.

miles long. (Rates are $49 for adults, $35 for children.) Be sure to sit on the left-hand side of the ascending train and the right side going down—the views are much better this way, and you'll get the greatest appreciation of Jacob's Ladder, a section of the track that has the second-highest grade in the world. At 37 percent, the grade of Jacob's Ladder leaves the back of the train car 14 feet lower than the front, and when a passenger stands up straight in the aisle, it looks like he is about to fall over!

The average grade of the Cog Railway is 25 percent, which is still enough to make all the trees look like they are growing at an angle. During the ride, passengers can see the rock-covered peaks of the alpine-like Presidential Range, as well as the landscape of the rest of the White Mountains. Don't forget to look down into the valley and see the red towers of the grand old Mount Washington Hotel. As the train climbs higher, the brakeman will show you the cairns used by Appalachian Trail hikers to find their way on the often-foggy trail that crosses the tracks. Along the entire ride, there is interesting commentary about the train, the region, and other neat facts.

Once at the top of the mountain, passengers have about twenty minutes to get off the train and explore. You may choose to visit the gift shop and cafeteria or to walk along the bridge to get a view of the surrounding mountains. Be sure to bring your camera so you can get your picture taken at the very top, above the lodge next to the altitude marker. If you would like to spend more time exploring the mountain and its trails, and perhaps make a side trip down to the Lake of the Clouds, you may choose to go back down on a later train, but remember that your seat is reserved only for the train on which you arrived. (They won't leave you stranded at the top, but you may have to stand, which isn't ideal if you have small children.)

Bretton Woods Mountain Resort (all ages) 👥 🍽 ⊖

Route 302, Bretton Woods, N.H.; (603) 278–3320; www.bretton woods.com. Open mid-November through mid-April, 8:30 A.M. to 4:00 P.M.

Bretton Woods' sixty-six trails cover 345 acres on West Mountain, Mount Rosebrook, and the newly opened Mount Stickney, which allows the resort to boast its title as New Hampshire's largest ski area. Snowmaking has 95 percent coverage, and night skiing is available. *Ski* magazine voted this resort #1 in grooming, family programs, and on-mountain food in New Hampshire. Rentals are available for all types of skis, snow tubing, ice-skating, and snowshoeing equipment. The Nordic Area offers 100 kilometers of trails, a warming hut, and lift-serviced cross-country trails. Bretton Woods is a full-service resort, so many different packages are available to accommodate every family's needs. Lift tickets range from $29 to $51 depending on age and day. Kids age five and under **free.**

Ski and snowboard instruction is available for groups or individuals of all ages and skill levels, and packages including rentals and lift tickets are also available. The Hobbit Program is designed for ages four to twelve (snowboarding suited for ages eight to twelve) and includes rentals, lessons, and lunch; it's available for full and half days. Ages five and under can participate in the Ski and Snowplay Program, which includes lunch, lessons, equipment, and an indoor nursery. Nonskiing kids from two months to five years can be enrolled in the Babes in the Woods Nursery for a full day, half day, or on an hourly basis, where they will be happily occupied with stories, games, and other indoor activities.

Moose Watching (ages 4 and up)

Route 302, between the Mount Washington Hotel and the head of Crawford Notch. Dawn, dusk, and cloudy days May through October are the best times. Free.

Along the road between the head of Crawford Notch and the Mount Washington Hotel are muddy areas, where the mud appears to be trampled by hooves. This is exactly what happened, and you can see the owners of those hooves doing it as they browse on aquatic plants. They are most often seen at dawn and dusk, although you should watch for them at any time of day.

The Mount Washington Hotel

Route 302, Bretton Woods, N.H.; (603) 278–1000; www.mtwashington.com. Daily tours. Free.

The grand demeanor of the hotel is reminiscent of a cruise ship, and this is actually what the architects were striving for when they designed the building. A full promenade "deck" swings around three sides of the hotel, offering views of Mount Washington and the Presidential Range from the comfort of cushioned wicker chairs. Kids may even be able to imagine this "ship" rising and dipping over the waving mountains. Inside, be sure to look up at the fine stucco work, all recently restored by an Italian master artist. There is not one nook of the hotel that does not ooze class.

While visiting the hotel, which is open to the public for daily historic tours, be sure to hear what they have to say about the hotel's past. One particularly memorable piece of the hotel's history was the Bretton Woods Monetary Conference in 1944. Like many other grand resort hotels, the Mount Washington Hotel had been closed during World War II. When world leaders realized the need to get together and figure out a worldwide currency exchange, their next challenge was to find a place large enough to hold everyone but also able to be secured for safety reasons. Because of its secluded location, the hotel was restored and reopened for the conference and became a part of history. You can still sit at the very same table where the united economic history of the world was decided. Rooms also bear the brass plates with names of the heads of state and royal family members from forty-four countries who stayed there.

Elephant's Head (ages 4 and up)

Route 302, at the head of Crawford Notch, Bretton Woods, N.H. Free.

From the trail around Saco Lake (from which the Saco River flows), look for a trail heading up to the forehead of Elephant's Head, the lifelike granite ledge that looks down into Crawford Notch. The top is a fine place for a picnic, but be careful here, as on all ledges. This is a favorite Saturday walk for local families.

Scenic Drive: Crawford and Pinkham Notches

A loop through the two eastern notches takes you all the way around Mount Washington, with access to a number of attractions on the way, including two ways of getting to the top of the mountain itself. You can begin anywhere, but we'll give the routes starting from Glen, at the intersection of Route 302 and Route 16. Follow Route 16 north through Jackson and Pinkham Notch to Gorham, turning west (left) on Route 2 to Jefferson Highlands. Turn south (left again) onto Route 115 and follow it into Twin Mountain. Another left onto Route 302 will take you past Bretton Woods and through Crawford Notch and Bartlett, and back to Glen.

Attitash Bear Peak (ages 3 and up)

Route 302, Bartlett, N.H.; (603) 374–2368. Open daily mid-June through mid-September and Saturday and Sunday until mid-October, 10:00 A.M. to 6:00 P.M. $$–$$$$

Attitash Bear Peak is a mountain resort that revolves around skiing and snow sports in the winter and a wide variety of outdoor activities in the summer. In addition to ski slopes, Attitash has an Alpine slide, waterslides for all age groups, horseback-riding along the Saco River, and a chairlift that runs in the winter for skiers and in the summer and fall for scenic 360-degree views. There is also mountain biking with a full rental shop, and the resort is host to several special events throughout the year. Vacation packages are available that include activities and lodgings.

Where to Eat

Many of the resort hotels in the area offer a variety of dining options, ranging from a single dining room to several restaurants.

Appalachian Mountain Club, Route 16, Gorham, N.H.; (603) 466–2727. The cafeteria here serves three meals daily, and it's a good place to stop for lunch in an area with few eateries. $

Fabyan's Station, Route 302, Bretton Woods, N.H.; (603) 278–2222. Serves lunch and dinner mid-June to mid-October and Thanksgiving to mid-April. Family-friendly restaurant in an old train station, with many

of its historic features intact. Children's menu, chicken, chili, and other American favorites. $

Munroe's Family Restaurant, Route 3, Twin Mountain, N.H.; (603) 846–5547. Monroe's is a favorite lunch stop for our family when we're "driving the circle" through Franconia and Crawford Notches. The burgers are good, and the menu offers some healthy non-fried lunch favorites. $

Top o' Quad Restaurant, Bretton Woods Ski Area, Bretton, N.H.; (603) 278–5000 or (800) 232–2972. You can get to this great restaurant by riding up on the chairlift or by taking the guest van to the top of the mountain (where you will enjoy the views as much as the food). Not always open, so it's wise to check. $–$$

Whitney's Inn, Route 16B, Jackson, N.H.; (603) 383–8916 or (800) 677–5737. The dining room operates as a restaurant for non-guests, who will appreciate the very good children's menu as well as the sophisticated treatments on the regular menu. $–$$

Where to Stay

The Bartlett Inn, Route 302, Bartlett, N.H.; (603) 374–2353 or (800) 292–2353. Families can choose between large inn rooms with shared baths or cottages with private baths, a fireplace, and kitchenette. Cross-country skiing at adjacent Bear Notch Touring Center. Close to many other attractions but set back in the woods for privacy and quiet. Kids under 12 stay **free,** and pets are welcome in cottages. $$–$$$

Carter Notch Inn, Carter Notch Road, Jackson, N.H.; (603) 383–9630 or (800) 794–9434. When staying here with your kids, be sure to request the room upstairs with the trap door and hiding space. This is a nice inn, very comfortable and friendly. $–$$

Eagle Mountain Resort, Carter Notch Road, Jackson, N.H.; (603) 383–9111. This is one of the last of the grand hotels, and it has maintained its integrity well throughout the years. Family dining, always a part of the grand hotel tradition, is a specialty here, and breakfast, lunch, and dinner are served by reservation. The cuisine here is focused more on traditional New England foods. They are known for their Sunday brunch. The classic porches add to the ambience of leisure, and the service never misses a beat. $$

Joe Dodge Lodge, Appalachian Mountain Club, Route 16, Gorham, N.H.; (603) 466–

2727. This hikers' hostel offers rustic lodging in family rooms and three buffet meals daily. $ (children's rates available for meals and lodging for those under 15)

The Mount Washington Hotel and Resort, Route 302, Bretton Woods, N.H.; (603) 278–1000 (information) or (800) 258–0330 (reservations); www.mtwashington. com. The Mount Washington is perhaps the grandest of the old hotels, both physically and in its level of service. Not one tiny detail will ever be left unattended, and the staff treats children with the same personal attention as they do distinguished foreign ambassadors. Kids will never forget this place. Many families have worked here for generations and take an almost proprietary pride in it. Breakfast and dinner are included in the price of your stay here. You have your choice of the main dining room, operated by award-winning chefs, or a quiet and cozy dinner at the Bretton Arms, the adjacent inn. We prefer the hotel's main dining room for dinner with children, because of atmosphere and the special children's menu. The hotel offers many services, living up to the resort tradition. A helpful concierge will get you a babysitter, make an appointment with the massage therapist, or set up your reservation for the Cog Railway. There are irons and full-size ironing boards in each room. In the evenings, there is live music, and the hotel often hosts performances of bands that recall the big-band and swing eras. Full recreational facilities include golf, tennis, hiking, skiing, horseback riding, mountain bike rentals, carriage rides, and a sports club. A kid's camp is available for both daytime and evening. $$–$$$

Wentworth Resort Hotel, Route 16A, Jackson Village, N.H.; (603) 383–9700 or (800) 637–0013. This hotel offers cottages outside of the main Victorian building. The cottages are designed for families, so this is a good choice if you like the convenience of a resort. The hotel has its own golf course and is also connected to a great selection of cross-country ski trails. Tennis and an excellent restaurant are on site. $$

Whitney's Inn, Route 16B, Jackson, N.H.; (603) 383–8916 or (800) 677–5737. Families are not just welcome at "Ma" Whitney's, they are the whole purpose of it. Large rooms, hearty family-style meals with a children's menu, and special kids' programs make everyone feel coddled and cared for at this year-round resort. In the summer there's a Wednesday night lobster cookout, and evening programs for kids give parents some time to relax together. Activities include swimming, paddleboats, downhill skiing, ice-skating, tennis, and lawn games, as well as a playground. Look for special summer and ski packages. $–$$

Camping

Sugarloaf Campground, off Route 302, Twin Mountain, N.H.; no phone. Sites at this National Forest campground are well spaced and separated, most set in the woods. The location couldn't be better, in the center of all the finest scenery and playgrounds of the White Mountains. $

For More Information

White Mountain Attractions Association, Route 112 at exit 32 off I–93, Box 10, North Woodstock, NH 03262; (603) 645–9889 or (800) 346–3687.

Pinkham Notch Visitors Center, Route 16; (603) 466–2727. For an event schedule, write AMC, P.O. Box 298, Gorham, NH 03581.

Near the Old Man of the Mountain

Franconia Notch packs several of New Hampshire's best-loved attractions into a tidy package. Above and below the Notch, you will find Interstate 93, but the Old Man of the Mountain's fragile brow looks down on a two-lane parkway through the notch itself. Popular vacation centers at North Woodstock and Lincoln are busy in summer and in foliage and ski seasons. North of the Notch, the towns of Franconia, Sugar Hill, Littleton, and Bethlehem offer more lodging and attractions of their own.

Old Man of the Mountain (all ages) 🍁

Route 3, Franconia Notch, N.H.; no phone. Daylight hours. Free.

In May of 2003, The Old Man of the Mountain, the stone profile that is New Hampshire's state symbol, slid into Franconia Notch. The overhanging ledges had defied the forces of gravity for too long, and despite the dedicated efforts of local volunteers who repaired cracks each year, nature finally won out. The familiar image is still very evident in the state, and almost as many people stop to see where it was as stopped to see "The Old Man" when he was still there. For children, this is an interesting example of how the earth changes, and a look at the cliff where the face once hung is a good accompaniment to the museum, below.

Old Man of the Mountain Museum (ages 8–16)

Route 3, Franconia Notch, N.H.; (603) 823–5563. Open daily June through mid-October 10:00 A.M. to 5:30 P.M. Free.

The museum, which is located in the same building as a nice gift shop that serves Bishop's ice cream, will interest children old enough to understand the geology that formed the profile. There are displays that explain the Old Man, as well as several historical displays about the history of the region.

Aerial Tramway (all ages)

Route 3, Franconia Notch Parkway, Franconia, N.H.; (603) 823–5563; www.cannonmt.com. Open daily mid-May through October; 9:00 A.M. to 4:30 P.M. in July and August. Round-trip fare: $–$$, age 5 and under free.

The Aerial Tramway begins at the head of Franconia Notch and climbs to the top of Cannon Mountain. Large cars suspended from cables carry passengers 4,200 feet to the top of Cannon Mountain, where trails circle the summit. You can look down into the notch to get a good view of how notches were scoured out by glaciers. On clear days you can see all the way to Canada. In the winter the tramway is used as a ski lift.

Cannon Mountain Ski Area (all ages)

Route 3, Franconia Notch Parkway, Franconia, N.H.; (603) 823–8800; www.cannonmt.com. Lift tickets for age 5 and under free.

Cannon Mountain is New Hampshire's tallest ski mountain, with 2,146 vertical feet. Ski and snowboard packages and programs are available. There are lesson packages that include rentals and tickets, group instruction or private lessons, or even small-group lessons for your family of up to three people. Kids ages five to twelve can be enrolled in the youth all-day program; kids ages three and four can spend the day in lessons (this includes rentals) and activities; or, you can opt for childcare that includes lunch for your little nonskiers. Other packages and programs can be tailored to suit your family's skiing abilities and ages. There is also a New England Ski Museum and plenty of places to get good food after you work up an appetite on the slopes. Cannon offers $5.00 off your ticket if you still have the previous day's ticket on your jacket, so don't be in a hurry to tidy up your jacket.

Echo Lake Beach (all ages)

Route 3, Franconia, N.H.; (603) 823–5563. Open daily mid-June through August. Admission: $.

This small, sandy swimming beach also has canoes and paddleboats for rent.

The Source of the **Mighty Merrimack**

The water that rushes through the Basin is part of the Pemigewasset River (named by the Abenaki, using their word for swift). It is the prime watershed for Franconia Notch, as well as for much of the land through which it flows downstream, draining more than 5,000 square miles. It begins at Profile Lake at an altitude of 1,900 feet, becomes the Merrimack River about 60 miles downstream, and then finally empties into the Atlantic Ocean after a 185-mile trip, at Newburyport, Massachusetts. On the way, the river once powered some of the largest mill complexes of the industrial era.

The Basin (all ages)
Franconia Notch Parkway (Route 3). Daylight hours. Free.

The river at this natural site looks like a giant had been playing with modeling clay. A natural pothole formed by melting glaciers was carved in the granite at the base of a small waterfall. As the water melted more than 25,000 years ago, it rushed over the stone ledge with such force that it caused a whirlpool in which bits of rock and sediment were caught and swirled around and around. These eventually carved the round hole that you see today, which is more than 30 feet in diameter and over 15 feet deep. The well-known author and naturalist Henry David Thoreau visited this site in 1839 and was struck by the marvel of its soft curves, imagining it the bathtub of a nature goddess.

The park has been designed to allow wheelchair and stroller accessibility to the small flume and some of the surrounding trails.

A short walk past the Basin is the cascading **Kinsman Falls,** which slides over a long set of sloping ledges. Although you should certainly guard small children here, older children will enjoy clambering up the ledges and sliding down some of the natural waterslides into the shallow pools. The flatter places along the falls are a favorite place to stop for picnics.

If you take the smaller trail off to the left marked **Baby Flume,** you will not only encounter a small, narrow canal and set of "steps" that the water has carved out, but you will also find more good summer splashing places. Another set of nature's waterslides, this area is full of little (and big) wonders of its own. There is one particularly impressive perpendicular rock that stands in the river as a perfect example of how glaciers dropped boulders in their path, which were later tumbled downstream by spring floodwaters. If the kids want to slide down the smooth rocks, be sure to test the depth and the speed of the water, although this is a relatively safe place to go wading.

The Flume (all ages)

Route 3, Franconia Notch State Reservation, N.H. After following the marked exit, watch carefully for a sign because the turn is abrupt and soon after the exit. Phone: (603) 745–8391. Open daily mid-May through late October 9:00 A.M. to 5:00 P.M. $–$$, under age 6 free.

The Flume is said to have been discovered in 1808 by "Aunt Jess" Guernsey when the 93-year-old woman was out fishing. Since then, it has been regarded as one of the most impressive natural sites of the area. If you have a problem paying admission to a state-owned natural site, as we sometimes do, once you see the extensive stairs and walkways built and maintained throughout your tour, you will understand. You should note that the flume is not stroller-friendly and that the short hike is nevertheless strenuous due to the sometimes steep incline and many stairs. If you want to shorten the walk a bit, a free bus will bring you from the visitor center to Boulder Cabin. Boulder Cabin has historical displays, restrooms, and a soda machine in case you didn't get a drink for the hike while you were at the visitor center.

As you go up through the flume, there are plenty of signs and informational plaques to tell you all about the formation of this deep chasm and about the ecology and wildlife of the area. You will pass Table Rock, which is 500 feet long and 75 feet wide, made of granite worn smooth by the water that rushes over its flat surface. You will also see the Flume Covered Bridge, which is one of the oldest covered bridges in the state. It was built during the 1800s to allow visitors to cross the river.

The Flume itself is a gorge cut by glacial runoff and now the Pemigewasset River. It is about 800 feet long, and its walls stand from 70 to 90 feet tall. The elevation at the top of the flume is 1,600 feet (kids will want to peek into the bear cave while you're up here). You should expect to take at least an hour for the hike up the Flume and back.

The visitor center at the base of the Flume is well equipped, with a cafeteria, clean restrooms, an information booth, wildlife and science displays, and even an interactive computer that tells you about the geology, weather, and nature of the notch.

A Little Geology

The Flume was formed around 200 million years ago and began with the cooling of the volcanic rock, which created fractures in the earth's crust. Frost and other forces continued to force rocks apart, and soon draining water was helping to erode the rock. As the river flows through today, the process of erosion continues to etch the canyon a little bit deeper each year.

Iron Furnace
(ages 6 and up) 🏛 🚡

Off Route 18, just after intersection with Route 117, Franconia, N.H. (near LaFayette Regional School). The hours for the little museum vary greatly. Free.

This iron furnace is the last one left in the state, and it was once an important element of the area's economy. The iron ore smelted here was taken from higher on the hill that rises behind the furnace (you have to be very careful hiking local trails because there are still open mine pits alongside them). The furnace was used until 1850. Today, there are informative plaques that explain the history and process of the furnace and smelting, as well as an overview of the iron industry. A small display building contains a scaled-down replica of this furnace, which will show the kids how it works on the inside.

Crossroads of America (ages 4 and up)

Bethlehem, corner of Route 302 and Trudeau Road, 2 miles east of Bethlehem Village, N.H.; (603) 869–3919; www.travel.to/cofa; e-mail: cofa@together.net. Open June 1 through foliage season, 9:00 A.M. to 5:00 P.M.; closed Monday. Admission: $.

Crossroads of America claims to have the world's largest ³⁄₁₆ scale model railroad on public exhibit. Painstakingly built with incredible attention to detail, this model has many tracks, switches, and cars that traverse a huge landscape. The train will go through tunnels in mountains, ride past towns and fields, and go over trellises. You can be the conductor, operating the train from its control platform and choosing its path, sounding the whistle as you wave hello to the tiny inhabitants of the miniature houses. The details and authenticity of this model are stunning, down to the specially designed lighting that simulates the passing of an entire day. There is also a museum of miniatures here, which includes background information on the miniature cars, trucks, airplanes, and other objects. Tours are given every half-hour.

The Rocks Estate (ages 4 and up)

Route 302, Bethlehem, N.H.; (603) 444–6228. From I–93 take exit 40 and travel east about 2 miles. Open year-round, during daylight hours with frequent weekend events. Admission prices vary from free to a few dollars for some events.

Built in the 1880s, The Rocks was the hobby farm of one of the owners of International Harvester and was known for its progressive farming methods. Today it belongs to the Society for the Protection of New Hampshire Forests and remains sustainable with a plantation of 55,000 Christmas trees. The Rocks sponsors a number of activities during the holiday season, as well as other special events. Most of these center around the seasons, local nature and wildlife, and traditional farming activities. The wildflower festival in June includes guided wildflower and "wild edibles" hikes and programs on the restoration of the estate's once-grand gardens. Halloween brings hay wagon rides and pumpkin carving, and Christmas tree–cutting is accompanied by free wagon rides. The farm's 6 miles of trails are used for hiking in the summer and for snowshoeing and cross-country skiing in the winter. Visitors are welcome to use the farm's picnic area.

Littleton Grist Mill (ages 4 and up)

18 Mill Street, Littleton, N.H.; (888) 284–7478; www.LittletonGrist Mill.com. Open daily May through December 11:00 A.M. to 5:00 P.M.; January through April Wednesday through Saturday 11:00 A.M. to 5:00 P.M. and Sunday to 3:00 P.M. Free.

Watch a working gristmill grind wheat and corn into flour, then go downstairs to see the giant waterwheel in action. Completely restored, but with an undershot wheel replacing the original overshot wheel that once ran the mill, the operating systems are easy to see and understand. The cog wheels are made of wood, with teeth more than 2 inches in diameter, and you can easily follow their path from the wheel outside to the big grindstones on the upper level.

On most days a miller is there to demonstrate and tell the mill's history. The original wheel powered an entire series of operations along the riverside that included a fulling mill, three gristmills, and several others. You can buy flour ground at the mill, along with miniature grindstones to use as paperweights, in the small shop. In the same mill is The Miller's Fare (see the "Where to Eat" section).

Where to Eat

Bishop's Homemade Ice Cream Shoppe, 78 Cottage Street, Littleton, N.H.; (603) 444–6039. Open mid-April through mid-October seven days a week. Incredible ice cream that you can't pass up—try one of their specialty sundaes. $

The Clam Shell, Route 302 at I–93 exit 42, Littleton, N.H.; (603) 444–6445. Casual atmosphere and rustic setting, with good food (especially seafood) and a children's menu. They also have carry-out. $–$$

Littleton Diner, 145 Main Street, Littleton, N.H.; (603) 444–3994. Diner food with a little more flair than some, served in a real old diner. $

The Miller's Fare, in the Grist Mill complex, 16 Mill Street, Littleton, N.H.; (603) 444–2146. Closed Monday. Located right next to the historic Grist Mill, this is a great place to make a stop. The deck looks out over the Ammonoosuc River, and the menu includes some delicious sandwiches at very reasonable prices. The sandwiches are very big, however, so the kids may want to split one (if you can get them to agree on one!). Freshly made soups and salads are also available. $

Polly's Pancake Parlor, Route 117, Sugar Hill, N.H.; (603) 823–5575. Here, as suggested in the name, you can get almost any kind of pancake you can dream up, with your choice of many luscious toppings. Whatever you choose, don't forget to drench it in New Hampshire maple syrup. In addition to a breakfast feast, you can also get lunches and light dinners here, with your choice of a great variety of homemade New England dishes. $–$$

Rosa Flamingo's, Main Street, Bethlehem, N.H.; (603) 869–3111. Rosa serves good pizza and casual cuisine, as well as some innovative entrees. The atmosphere is easy and friendly, perfect for kids. $

Where to Stay

Hilltop Inn, Main Street, Sugar Hill, N.H.; (603) 823–5695. This is one of our favorite places to stay in the mountains. Hosts Mike and Meri Hern not only treat you to a warm and comfortable atmosphere, but they also adore children and welcome babies and pets. This is a wonderful place for the family to come and relax. Rooms are not enormous, but everyone has the run of the house and Meri can always find room for the crib. Kids are treated royally. Breakfast is superb. $–$$

Sunset Hill House, Sunset Hill Road, Sugar Hill, N.H.; (603) 823–5522 or (800) SUNHILL. Another one of the grand hotels that has survived since its heyday, this place lives up to the word *grand*. Although at one time fallen into disrepair, the remaining building from the hotel that once crowned the entire hilltop has been restored well. From its windows you will see one of the most scenic views of the Presidential Range and other surrounding mountains, and the hilltop has some of the best sunset viewing in the state. Dining here is elegant, the food prepared and served with attention to every detail. In the spirit of the former resort, there is also plenty to do here, including golf, cross-country skiing, hiking, and even sleigh rides. $$–$$$

Camping

Lafayette Campground, Route 3, Franconia Notch, N.H.; (603) 823–9513. The sites here have plenty of space, and many of them are in the solitude of the woods. Many of the campground's activities are planned for children, and a convenient store is on site for campers who forgot something in town— especially for those s'mores emergencies! $

Lincoln, Woodstock, and Campton

Three towns lie alongside I–93 like points on a follow-the-dots game, and each leads to a clutch of nearby attractions. Weaving back and forth along the interstate highway is Route 3, and most of the sites listed below are either on that road or only a few miles from it. This is the heart of the most heavily visited part of New Hampshire, so don't expect to enjoy these places alone.

Clark's Trading Post (all ages)

Route 3, Lincoln, N.H.; (603) 745–8913; www.clarkstradingpost.com. Open weekends late May through June and September through mid-October, daily July and August 10:00 A.M. to 6:00 P.M. Admission: $–$$, under age 3 free. Tickets purchased after 4:00 P.M. are good for admission the next day.

This family-owned and -operated attraction, which has been entertaining White Mountains visitors for more than half a century, began with its performing bears. The purpose of this wholesome, spotless theme park is having a good time. Children love the ride on a shiny, bright steam train that hisses and toots along tracks from the little Victorian village through the woods. There's excitement and surprises as the cranky "hermit" tries to attack the train. The Victorian Main Street re-creates the era with brightly painted buildings, including some shops and museum-style displays. Parents will appreciate the fact that the shops are not filled with junk displayed at kid's-eye level. Whether or not you like performing animals, you will agree that the bears here are entertaining and obviously well-loved and treated like pets by the Clark family.

Scenic Drive

Kancamagus Highway (Route 112) climbs over the White Mountains, with much of the 35-mile stretch from Conway to Lincoln going uphill or downhill. The views from the top are great on both sides (you should make use of the parking pull-outs, since some of the best scenery cannot be seen from the road). While grand vistas usually don't impress kids too

Pay to **Use** Your Forests

It's true. You can no longer use the National Forest without paying to park your car, even if you plan only a five-minute stop. A permit is required, which costs $5.00 for seven days or $20.00 annually for each car. For $25 you can get an annual pass that covers two cars in the same family. Golden Age Cards, for those over age 62, cut the annual fee in half. Cars found without permits in parking lots for National Forest trails or alongside the roads within the forest will get a significant fine. The good news is that you can now buy the permits in several places, including the White Mountains Attractions office in Lincoln and other points close to most entrances.

much, some places to stop on the Conway side (east) will interest them more. Before the road begins to climb are Rocky Gorge and Lower Falls, both on the Swift River, popular for picnics and for splashing about on the rocks. Shortly after these, you will pass a covered bridge, and on the other side is a sloping ledge that kids love to climb and slide down. Our family's experience (our family has a camp near there, so we claim some expertise in this) is that one slide from the top will wear through the seat of an old pair of jeans. Opposite the ledge is the parking area for the Boulder Loop Trail.

Sabbaday Falls (ages 4 and up)
Kancamagus Highway, pull-off just past the covered bridge. Daylight hours. Free, with a National Forest Permit required for parking.

The falls are reached by a trail from the Kancamagus Highway, only a short distance west of the covered bridge. Here the stream flows through a gorge with 40-foot walls, and it has carved a big pothole in the rock at its feet. Unlike many waterfalls, this one has wooden stairs and railings that make it possible to look straight down at the waterfall and potholes. You will still want to hold the hand of a small child here, but you are not teetering on the brink with nothing but thin air separating you from the drop.

Hobo Railroad (all ages)
Route 112, Lincoln, N.H.; (603) 745–2135; www.hoborr.com. Rides daily late June through Labor Day, at 11:00 A.M., 1:00 P.M., and 3:00 P.M. Open through foliage season with 3:00 P.M. ride only on weekends. Fare: $$, under age 3 free. Hobo Picnic Lunch: $$.

The Hobo Railroad is a great ride along the Pemigewasset River in vintage cars. While on the eighty-minute ride, you can relax and enjoy the scenery while the kids feast on their own affordable Hobo Picnic Lunch (and pretend they sneaked on the train when no one was looking). Or, the whole family can enjoy ice-cream sundaes during the ride. The station has a gift shop.

Loon Mountain Ski Area (all ages)

Off I–93 exit 32 on the Kancamagus Highway, Lincoln, N.H.; (603) 745–8111; www.loonmtn.com. Open early November through early May for skiing. Rates vary.

Loon Mountain, which has a summit elevation of 3,050 feet, offers a full ski resort experience with a family feel and focus. There are eight lifts, including the Gondola, which is used for scenic tours in the summer (see description following). There are forty-four trails covering 19.4 miles—about 275 acres to ski. There is 99 percent snowmaking coverage, and snowboarding is allowed on all but one trail. About 20 percent of the trails are novice, 64 percent are intermediate, and 16 percent are expert. There are 35 kilometers of cross-country skiing trails, and rentals for snowshoes and all types of skis are available. The resort also offers ice-skating, day and night tubing even for tiny kids, and a climbing wall, with rentals available. There is a daycare center for little ones, and you can enroll youngsters in ski/daycare programs.

Several packages are available that can include lodgings on site, so it's easy to tailor one to your family's needs. The Snowsports School, which offers both group and private lessons for all age and skill levels, guarantees its instruction. If you are not able to ski on a beginner trail by the end of the day, you can come back at no charge until you catch on. Families will enjoy the Adventure Center, which holds special après-ski activities including magic shows and crafts. Don't miss storytime and chats with Loon Mountain's Wajoid, the Mountain Man. The resort's Web site offers daily conditions reports and a 360-degree virtual tour to help you get acquainted with the mountain before you even get there.

Loon Mountain is also a full summer resort, with a number of activities focusing on bike rides. You may rent a bike or bring your own, and there are many options, including a tour of Franconia Notch with shuttle service. Loon also offers in-line skating in their skate park, with rentals available. **Loon Mountain Park Equestrian Center** offers trail rides for every skill level and pony rides for youngsters. The **Archery Range** has lessons and equipment for children and adults. Lodging packages are available.

Loon Mountain Wildlife Theater is open year-round, with daily performances that teach about native animals and birds. The shows are interactive, so everyone gets to pet a snake or some other creature. (They may even get to meet a baby mountain lion!) Shows are lively and spontaneous, so kids will never notice the "E word" as they learn about the mammals, reptiles, and birds that share the mountains.

Loon Mountain Gondola (ages 6 and up)

Off I–93 exit 32 on the Kancamagus Highway, Lincoln, N.H.; (603) 745–8111; www.loonmtn. com. Open weekends 9:30 A.M. to 5:00 P.M. from late May to mid-June, and daily mid-June through mid-October. Gondola rates: $$, age 5 and under free, no extra fee to explore the caves.

The Loon Mountain Gondola is a great way to spend part of a clear day. The enclosed cars, which were the first used anywhere in North America, bring you on a relaxing ride to the top of the mountain. On the way up and down, you can see the spectacular views of the surrounding mountains. During fall foliage season, this is also a great way to see the spectacular palette of colors that nature paints over the landscape. This is New Hampshire's longest gondola ride. The gondola runs frequently, and they will remind you of the last departure time when you get to the top.

The **Summit Cafe** offers good food and great views while you eat, and a special all-you-can-eat Summit Pancake Breakfast on Sundays. A kiddie playground is right outside the cafe, and there are cut-out figures so you can take goofy family pictures. If you just want to relax and look out at the view, there is an observation tower. You may also visit the amphitheater, where Sunday services are held by Reverend Skip Schwartz at 11:00 A.M. from June 18 to October 15. Gondola rates for the service are $4.00.

Daily in the summer and on fall weekends, children will want to visit with the **Mountain Man,** who entertains with his stories about pioneer life in the mountains. You can find him at his log cabin, down the trail from the Summit Cafe.

Loon Mountain Glacial Caves (ages 6 and up)

Off I–93 exit 32 on the Kancamagus Highway; (603) 745–8111; www.loonmtn.com. Open weekends 9:30 A.M. to 5:00 P.M. from late May, and daily mid-June through mid-October. Accessed by the gondola (see earlier entry). No extra fee to explore the caves.

The top of Loon Mountain offers a great set of glacial caves to explore. A well-maintained walkway guides you through the caves, and signs will tell you all about them and indicate the level of difficulty if you want to pass through them. We recommend leaving at least forty-five minutes for your family to explore the caves. For families who would rather hike up the mountain to see the caves, there is a trail that can be accessed from the base lodge. (There is a small fee for use of the hiking trails if you are not riding the gondola, since all trails are well maintained for safe hiking.)

Agaziz Basin (ages 4 and up)

Less than ¼ mile east of the intersection of Routes 112 and 118 on Route 112, Woodstock, N.H., next to Gavoni Restaurant. No phone. Parking available until 4:00 P.M. Free.

This basin was carved by glaciers and continues to be sculpted by the water that flows through it. At this small, lesser-known spot, you can see bowls of rock that have been worn away by water and sediment, as well as a waterfall. This is a great place for a picnic. There are no facilities, but bridges are maintained to allow you to explore the basin. Stay on the trail and be especially careful during the fall, when wet leaves make the rocks slippery. Be sure to watch children carefully because there are lots of inviting rocks that can be dangerous.

Out Back Kayak (ages 11 and up)

Main Street, North Woodstock, N.H., just east of Route 112 on Route 3; (603) 745–2002 or (800) KAYAKKS.

Out Back Kayak offers not only kayak rentals but also guided river tours and kayaking lessons. They also offer llama hikes, paintball games, and even overnight camping along the

How the **River** Was Lost

Lost River began when a mile-deep layer of glacier covered the White Mountains. As the ice sheets moved, they broke loose big chunks of granite and carried them along. As the glacier melted, it formed streams that wore through the solid rock beneath, often finding cracks in the rock to run through.

One of these became Lost River. As water from the melting glacier wore away the rock and carved the bottom deeper, it was helped by stones and gravel that washed into the gorge and scoured out potholes and chutes as the debris and water swirled past. The largest pothole is 60 feet in diameter.

The severe winters that followed the Ice Age caused repeated freezing and thawing of water in the granite walls, tearing loose chunks the size of houses. They soon nearly filled the gorge, covering the river for about a quarter of a mile. Wind and water have continued to smooth and wear the caves and passageways.

river for the more adventurous families. Rentals start at $25 a day; guided tours start at $35. Call ahead for reservations.

Lost River (ages 4 and up)

Route 112, North Woodstock, N.H.; (603) 745–8031; www.Find LostRiver.com. Follow Route 118 west from exit 32 of I–93, turning north onto Route 112. Open daily from 9:00 A.M. to 5:00 P.M. mid-May to late October, and until 6:00 P.M. in July and August. Admission: $$, age 4 and under free.

The river isn't really lost; it just disappears for a while in a tumble of glacial boulders that have joined it in a steep ravine. Along with hiding the river, these boulders have created caves and passageways that merit names like "the lemon squeezer."

Kids aren't alone in scrambling through the narrow spaces between the boulders and inchworming along the tunnels. Lost River appeals to all ages, although we admit it's easier for little people to get through some of the passageways.

If you don't want to explore all the caves and wriggle through the tunnels, you can send the kids through and bypass them on boardwalks and stairs. But you don't have to worry about getting caught in the "lemon squeezer" because it has a measuring gate that makes sure you'll fit through.

Paradise Falls, the largest of several here, drops 35 feet. Lost River is a good activity for a hot day because the temperature in this rocky ravine is about six degrees cooler, and winter ice stays in the caves until mid-June.

Cafe Lafayette Dinner Train (all ages)

Lincoln, N.H., off I–93 exit 32, take Route 112 west about ¼ mile, on the left just after the I–93 overpass; (603) 745–3500 or (800) 699–3501 outside New Hampshire; www.cafe lafayette.com. Closed Monday and Friday during summer; call for spring and fall schedules. All aboard at 6:00 P.M. Call for reservations.

This is an elegant choice for a special night out. Prices (adults $55, children six to eleven $35, no one under six) include a five-course meal and the two-hour train ride, which travels over 20 miles of the Boston & Maine Railroad. You will be seated in one of the two Pullman dining cars. "Indian Waters" is a Victorian coach built in 1924, and "Granite Eagle" is a 1952 Pullman Planetarium car. The "Granite Eagle" features The Dome, which sits at a higher level and offers wonderful views. Floodlights shed light on the scenery outside the train as the sun sets, so you don't miss a thing as you tour the land surrounding the Pemigewasset River.

Parents **Night** Out

Kick up your heels in the new "Algon-quin," a coach on the Lafayette Dinner Train, which has been transformed into a piano bar with a dance floor. A full wine list and cocktail service are available to accompany the excellent food.

Pemi Valley Rock Gym (ages 6 and up)

Main Street, North Woodstock, N.H.; (603) 745–9800. Rock gym rates $$, full gear rental package (climbing shoes, harness, and chalk bag) $$.

The Pemi Valley Rock Gym offers a wide range of rock-climbing walls for all skill levels. Professional instruction is available to help your family learn how to climb the more than 2,500 square feet of climbing walls that reach up to 20 feet high. Rental services are inexpensive, and packages are available with lessons and rentals for families.

The Whale's Tale Water Park (ages 2 and up)

Route 3, North Lincoln, N.H., ½ mile from I–93 exit 33; (603) 745–8810; www.getsettoget wet.com. Open June through Labor Day, 10:00 A.M. to 6:00 P.M. All-day pass $$$$, under 3 and over 65 free.

Everything here is aimed at having fun on and in the water. Attractions include the new Harpoon Express, a waterslide for up to three at a time, and the Whale Winder Flume Slide. You can zip down high-speed Moby Dip slide, or take a tube down the Beluga Boggin and end up in Jonah's Escape, where you can float and relax. Admission to the park includes all activities, and you may come and go during the same day with no extra charge. Life-jacket and locker rentals are available, and there is a snack bar and surf shop that sells bathing suits, suntan lotion, and other stuff you may have forgotten. Special pools for young kids and toddlers provide them with their own mini-slides.

Waterville Valley Resort (all ages)

1 Ski Area Road, Waterville Valley, N.H.; (603) 236–8311 or (800) GO VALLEY (468–2553); www.waterville.com. Ski season is from mid-November through mid-April, weekdays 9:00 A.M. to 4:00 P.M., weekends and holidays 8:00 A.M. to 4:00 P.M., half-day starts at 12:30 P.M. Several special packages are available.

Waterville Valley is a full-scale resort that offers everything from fine dining and lodging to great skiing and other snow sports in the winter. Mount Tecumseh has 255 skiable acres, with fifty-two trails and 100 percent snowmaking. There are eleven lifts, which service both trails and special parks like Skittery Gulch tubing park and Exhibition Park. There is plenty of skiing terrain for beginners: 36 percent of trails are novice, 44 percent intermediate, and 20 percent advanced. Cross-country skiing, snowshoeing, and hiking trails begin around the Nordic Center, where equipment rentals are available. There is also an ice rink that offers rentals. Several packages are available for families, including the new Waterville Women's Wednesdays, which offers **free** child care and plenty of other freebies and discounts.

Winter visitors will not want to miss the sleigh rides across the frozen valley on a big sled pulled by a team of draft horses. But the resort is an all-season one, with bike rentals, canoeing in Cochrane Pond, plenty of hiking and biking trails, tennis courts, a sports center with Olympic-size pool, and a full schedule of activities for children. A shuttle bus connects the various activity centers, so older children can come and go safely on their own.

Where to Eat

Frannie's Place, Route 3 (½ mile south of I–93 exit 30), Woodstock/Thornton line; (603) 745–3868. Nothing fancy in this family-friendly setting, next to the Jack O'Lantern Resort, but the cooking is very good and the menu much more varied than you'd expect from the plain-Jane exterior. This is a chef who appreciates food and treats it with respect. $–$$

Wild Coyote Grill, White Mountain Athletic Club, Waterville Valley, N.H.; (603) 236–4919. Lunch on weekends only, dinner nightly. Creative dishes are served in a relaxed setting where kids will feel comfortable. $–$$

Woodstock Station, 80 Main Street, North Woodstock, N.H.; (603) 745–3951. This restaurant serves three meals a day and is adjacent to a brewpub. $–$$

Woodward's Open Hearth Steak House, Route 3, Lincoln, N.H.; (603) 745–8141. Closed November. Serves breakfast and dinner. A nice family atmosphere, with a children's menu and good grilled food. A good selection of healthy options, too. $–$$

Where to Stay

The Black Bear, Village Road, Waterville Valley, N.H.; (603) 236–4501 or (800) GO VALLEY (468–2553); www.waterville.com. Big family suites have Murphy beds in the sitting room and small kitchens so you can cook your own meals from groceries available at the little market nearby. The swimming pool features an indoor/outdoor swim-through, which kids like, and the staff is most accommodating. $–$$

Jack O'Lantern Resort, Route. 3 (south of exit 30 from I–93), Woodstock, N.H.; (603) 745–8121 or (800) 227–4454; www.jack olanternresort.com. A resort designed for everyone in the family, with golf, tennis, and swimming. The moderate rates at the inn, motel, and cottages can be chosen with or without meals at the resort's two dining rooms. $–$$

Mountain Club at Loon, Route 112, Lincoln, N.H.; (603) 745–3441 or (800) 229–STAY (7829). This is a modern hotel featuring balconies, swimming pools, cable TV, and other amenities. Packages here can include skiing or activities for other seasons. $–$$

The Snowy Owl, Village Square, Waterville Valley, N.H.; (603) 236–8383 or (800) GO VALLEY (468–2553); www.waterville.com. Mention Waterville to our kids and they immediately began asking if we can stay at the Snowy Owl. They love the rooms with balconies, where their beds are snuggled away far above the rest of the suite, and they can all fit into the big in-room Jacuzzi at once. (Be sure to ask about the configuration and facilities of each room, as they differ.) Downstairs, guests gather around the huge fireplaces to sing in the evening, and there are always plenty of other kids to play games with. The swimming pool is large and attractive, with spacious edges for parents to watch kids and yet remain out of the way of the splashing. $$–$$$

The Woodstock Inn, Main Street, Woodstock, N.H.; (603) 745–3951. This semi-formal inn maintains reasonable prices. It sits in two buildings that are centrally located in the town, and it offers wide dining options at its two restaurants. You can choose to be formal or have a less expensive, casual meal. Breakfasts included in rates. $–$$

For More Information

Franconia Notch Chamber of Commerce, Franconia, NH 03580; (800) 237–9007; www.franconianotch.org.

Waterville Valley Region Chamber of Commerce, Campton, NH 03223; (603) 726–3804 or (800) 237–2307 in New England.

White Mountain Attractions Association, Route 112 at exit 32 off I–93, North Woodstock, N.H.; (603) 645–9889 or (800) 346–3687 outside New Hampshire.

North Conway Area

Shopping has become synonymous with the stretch of Route 16 between Conway and North Conway, a gauntlet of outlet malls. Many families plan a part of their summer vacation here to outfit children for school at these shops. But there's much more to do in this valley, which has been a favorite of tourists since Victorian times, when city families came to spend their summers here.

Heritage New Hampshire (ages 4 and up)
Route 16, Glen, N.H.; (603) 383–4186; www.heritagenh.com. Open weekends Memorial Day weekend through Father's Day, then daily through Columbus Day 9:00 A.M. to 5:00 P.M. Allow at least ninety minutes for the tour. Admission: $–$$, age 3 and under free.

When you take the journey through Heritage New Hampshire, you watch all of New England's history unfold. You can't miss this museum's giant American flag, which proudly waves above the parking lot. This is the largest flag in the state—30 feet by 50 feet long. The front lawn is also decorated by the four largest whirligigs in the world (a fact recorded in the *Guinness Book of World Records*).

Your "journey" here begins in 1634, as you stand at the docks of Southampton, England, anticipating your long sea voyage to the promised land of the New World. After you sign the ship's register, your captain takes you to your "quarters" on the rocking boat, where he tells you what to expect from the long journey. After weathering a storm at sea (you can even feel the salt spray in the air), you finally sight land.

You step off the boat at Odiorne's Point (see the chapter "The Seacoast and Merrimack Valley") and follow the settlement from its early days through the American Revolution, the Industrial Revolution, and succeeding eras. Throughout the journey you will meet people of the times, both real and virtual, who will share their experiences with you. Stop in the town square to hear George Washington speak, or find out the fascinating workings of an 1850s farmhouse kitchen, where bread rises and pies bake.

Be sure to give a holler and listen to the echo at the replica of Profile Lake before hopping onto the trail through Crawford Notch and back into today. Adding to the historical experience are the unique and often very clever special effects. As you walk through, take time to answer the quiz questions on the walls, which contain interesting tidbits of history.

Story Land (ages 3–10) 🚂

Route 16, Glen, N.H.; (603) 383–4186. Open mid-June through Labor Day 9:00 A.M. to 6:00 P.M., September though Columbus Day 10:00 A.M. to 5:00 P.M. weekends only. If you arrive after 3:00 P.M., you receive a pass for another day that season. Admission $$$$ per person age 4 and up, which includes unlimited use of all rides and entertainment and use of available free strollers.

If this admission sounds steep (as was our first reaction), consider this: Story Land is chock-full of seventeen different theme rides, two shows that run every twenty minutes, and plenty of nooks and crannies to inspire the big imaginations of little people. To go through and do everything once would take about six hours. If this seems too long for your child's attention span or energy level, our suggestion is to go there early in your trip just past 3:00 P.M. and take advantage of their late arrivals free-pass policy. Then return later in your trip, earlier in the day to repeat favorite sites and see ones you missed the first time. This gives kids something to look forward to at the end of a trip and avoids overkill for young children by stretching the experience over two days.

The adventures in Story Land, as you might expect, revolve around favorite fairy tales, nursery rhymes, and classics of children's literature. A full description would take pages, so we'll stick to our favorites. Alice invites you though the rabbit hole into a wonderland that includes the mad tea party ride in colorful teacups. Peter Pumpkin-eater's house is just as every kid imagines it, with foot-thick orange walls, a pumpkin-faced clock and a separate "igloo-style" entrance for small fry. You can test the beds in the house of the Three Bears, meet Heidi's grandfather and her favorite goats, ride on a swan boat or a buccaneer ship, slide down the bamboo chute, or leave Cinderella's castle in style, riding in a pumpkin coach.

One grove includes animal-related stories, such as the Three Little Pigs with their houses (the pink piglets are a winner), Peter Rabbit, Little Bo Peep's sheep, and the Three Billy Goats Gruff with their bridge. Each of these includes a recording of the appropriate story.

Thoughtful touches abound. The well-distributed restrooms each include a separate quiet room for changing, nursing, and napping. Travelers with pets will find a **free** kennel, and there are **free** strollers available. Places for parents to sit are scattered throughout, and food at refreshment stands is priced well below what you would expect. Call ahead to learn the least crowded time to visit.

Conway Scenic Railway (all ages)

Main Street, North Conway, N.H.; (603) 356–5251 or (800) 232–5251; www.conwayscenic. com. Operates weekends mid-April through mid-May and November through mid-December, daily mid-May through late October. Notch train operates Tuesday through Sunday late June through August, and daily September through mid-October. Call ahead for current times. Fare: $$–$$$.

The ride begins from the North Conway Depot, which is in a classic Victorian building. Here, museum exhibits explain some of the railroad's history and that of the area, including displays of old brochures, conductors' uniforms, and photos. You can get a flier here that tells all about the depot buildings and the vintage train cars and engines on display outside. The train in operation will take you along the valley floor, where you can look up at the mountains. Alternatively, the Notch train will take you through Crawford Notch, where you can get up-close views of the formations of rocks. *NOTE:* The ride over the trestles is not for the faint of heart.

Mount Washington Observatory's Weather Discovery Center (ages 6 and up)

2936 Main Street, North Village Commons, North Conway, N.H.; (603) 356–2137 or (800) 706–0432; www.mountwashington.org. Open daily 10:00 A.M. to 5:00 P.M. Admission: $.

The Discovery Center is the world's only museum dedicated solely to the study of weather. Its interactive displays and presentations are well suited for children—so engaging that it's easy for the kids to get excited about the weather while learning about the science behind it. You will hear about the fascinating research being done at the Mount Washington Summit Observatory, which has been in operation since 1932 and has recorded the highest winds anywhere in the world. There is also a great gift shop that stocks scientific toys and books. You will find weather instruments that you can bring home to do experiments and make your own observations.

Northern Extremes Canoe and Kayak (ages 7 and up)

Two locations at Route 302 in Glen, N.H., and Main Street in North Conway, N.H.; (603) 383–8117 or (877) SACORIV (722–6748); www.northernextremes.com.

Here you can choose to rent canoes or kayaks and even go to the kayaking school. The family kayak package ($17 to $65) is for two adults and two kids ages seven to sixteen; it includes round-trip transportation, life vests, and paddles. Northern Extremes also offers white-water instruction clinics that start at $50 for kids and $80 for adults.

Cranmore Mountain Resort (all ages)

Skimobile Road, North Conway, N.H.; (603) 356–5543 or (800) SUN N SKI (786–6754); www. cranmore.com. Open daily November through May (weather permitting), 9:00 A.M. to 4:00 P.M. weekdays and 8:30 A.M. to 4:00 P.M. weekends and holidays.

Cranmore Mountain is dedicated to creating a place for the family to have fun in the snow. Day care is available, and special kids' lessons at Penguin Park with C-More the Penguin are a great way to get them involved. Snowmaking covers 100 percent of the thirty-nine trails, with nine lifts to bring you to the top. Beginners are well served: 36 percent of the trails are suited for novice skiers, 44 percent are for intermediates, and 19 percent are for advanced skiers. Several lesson packages are available, including the new Quick Tip Lessons, which are basically free-form private lessons spread throughout the day to help you progress and get the most out of the instruction. Lift tickets $19 to $35, age 5 and under **free.** Rental, lesson, and ticket packages also available from $35 to $75.

Cranmore Sports Center Summer Camps (ages 5–15)

Skimobile Road, North Conway, N.H.; (603) 356–6301; www.cranmore.com. Camps run for five days from June through August, 9:30 A.M. to 3:30 P.M. (tennis camp from noon to 3:00 P.M.).

These summer camps (prices range from $100 to $325 per day) are designed for daytime fun for the kids while parents go do "grown-up" stuff. There are plenty of programs to choose from, and various camps are appropriate for ages five to fifteen. The swim camp is designed for ages five to twelve; it includes not only plenty of swimming lessons but also games, crafts, art lessons, and other activities. The gymnastics camp is for the same age group and includes two-and-a-half hours of gymnastics plus other activities like swimming and crafts. The adventure camp is for slightly older kids, and includes biking, hiking, swimming, and field trips. The eight- to fifteen-year-olds can learn rock climbing on indoor climbing walls, then try climbing on natural rocks. There is also a kayak camp and an afternoon tennis camp for ages nine to fourteen.

Fun Yak Rentals (ages 6 and up)

Route 16, Conway, N.H.; (603) 447–5571. Kayak rentals $$$$, canoe rentals $$$$.

Yak Attack, their kids' program, offers rentals of special kayaks with "training wheels"— they are very hard to tip over, so they're ideal for beginners. A shuttle is available to bring you up the river, leaving three times a day.

Dahl Wildlife Sanctuary (ages 4 and up)

Route 16, just south of intersection with Route 302, North Conway, N.H.; (603) 224–9909; www.nhaudubon.org. Daylight hours. Donations accepted at trailhead.

The Dahl Sanctuary is operated by the Audubon Society of New Hampshire and includes fifty-four acres of land and 1,800 feet of Saco River shoreline. There are two trails, the half-mile Pine Trail and the 1-mile Woods

Road Trail. You should allow at least an hour for each mile to enjoy the sanctuary to its fullest. A pamphlet describing the trails and what you will see, as well as the sanctuary's history, is available at the trailhead. No bicycles, pets, camping, or fires are allowed.

Hartmann Model Railroad and Toy Museum (all ages)
Route 16, ¼ mile from the junction with Route 302, Town Hall Road, Intervale, N.H.; (603) 356–9922 or (603) 356–9933; www.hartmannrr.com. Open year-round 10:00 A.M. to 5:00 P.M. daily. Admission: $–$$, under age 5 free.

This is a museum, hobby shop, craft store, and cafe all in one. The museum features several model train sets in various scales, set up with full landscape and even miniature people. There is also a model of Crawford Notch as it looked in the 1950s. In addition, owners Roger and Nelly Hartmann display their own collection of model railroads from around the world, and they even have special displays that explain the differences in design of foreign models. All parts of the Hartmann buildings are wheelchair accessible, and photography is welcome.

Farm by the River (ages 3 and up)
2555 West Side Road, North Conway, N.H.; (603) 356–2694. Call ahead for reservations. Prices vary.

Pony rides on this valley farm delight small children, while older ones can ride or take riding lessons. Trail rides for all ages wind through the valley meadows and wooded trails of this multigeneration family farm.

Echo Lake State Park (all ages)
West Side Road, North Conway, N.H.; (603) 356–2672. Open 9:00 A.M. to 8:00 P.M. on weekends from Memorial Day through the last week of June and on the two weekends after Labor Day. During the rest of the summer, open every day during the same hours. Admission $; children under 12 and New Hampshire residents over 65 admitted free.

Set beneath the towering Cathedral Ledge, Echo Lake has a very nice swimming beach with picnic area, hiking trails, and changing facilities.

Where to Eat

Bellini's, 33 Seavey Street, North Conway, N.H.; (603) 356–7000. Closed Tuesday. Generous portions of Italian pasta and other classics like eggplant parmigiana and veal marsala. The children's menu has spaghetti and other kids' favorites. $–$$

Fandangles, Route 302 and Route 16, south of North Conway, N.H.; (603) 356–2741. Open all year. Informal atmosphere, with a large menu and children's menu. Carry out available. $–$$

The Ledges, White Mountain Hotel, West Side Road, Conway, N.H.; (603) 356–7100. Three meals daily, with a good variety and friendly up-scale atmosphere where children are welcome. $$

Tim's Chowder House, Route 16/302, North Conway, N.H. Open daily 10:30 A.M. to 3:30 P.M. In addition to the chowder (which is excellent) they serve ten specials, each under

$6.00, and a selection of sandwiches at even lower prices and what may well be New England's fattest lobster roll, with no fillers. Tables well-spaced, with cheery calico tablecloths, and the staff is a grandmotherly group that are as upbeat as the surroundings. $–$$

Where to Stay

Best Western Storybrook Resort, junction of Route 16 and Route 302, Glen, N.H.; (603) 383–6800. Motel-style rooms are spacious, with plenty of room for families. There are indoor and outdoor swimming pools, and the restaurant on site serves breakfast and dinner daily. $–$$

The Buttonwood Inn, Mount Surprise, North Conway, N.H.; (603) 356–2625 or (800) 258–2625; www.buttonwoodinn.com. Family suites are available at this secluded, comfortable inn just north of the town of North Conway. Rooms are very nicely decorated, each with a private bath and most with electric fireplaces. You will enjoy the well-kept gardens, and the kids will go crazy over their choice of breakfast made to order. The genial owners are enthusiastic about their region and can suggest the best hiking trails and swimming places. They have an outdoor swimming pool. $$–$$$, family rates available.

Farm by the River, 2555 West Side Road, North Conway, N.H.; (603) 356–2694 (information) or (888) 414–8353 (reservations). Standing in the flat valley surrounded by meadows yellow with goldenrod, and ringed by mountains, the setting of this venerable family farmhouse could hardly be better. Rooms are comfortable and attractive and spacious enough to accommodate an extra bed for a child. Some already have a twin bed in addition to the queen or double. All rooms have private baths, all but one en-suite. Each room is different and is named for a guest who once summered there when this was a guest farm run by the ancestors of the present owner. The atmosphere is homey and casual; breakfast is served in the cheery kitchen or on the terrace overlooking flower gardens. In the winter the farm has snowshoes for the guests. $$

Fox Ridge, Route 16, North Conway, N.H.; (603) 356–3151 or (800) 343–1804. Open May to November. Rooms in this hilltop motel are large and well-decorated, with balconies or terraces with views. Indoor and outdoor swimming pools, walking trails, tennis courts, **free** breakfast, and children's activities add to its attractions. $–$$

Green Granite Resort, Route 16, North Conway, N.H.; (603) 356–6901 or (800) 468–3666; www.greengranite.com. Don't picture your average motel here; the atmosphere and layout are far more like a fine inn, but with a decided family orientation. It's a modern hotel with pools, plenty of recreation space, and a sauna. Kids 15 and under stay **free.** $$

The Old Red Inn and Cottages, Route 16, North Conway, N.H.; (603) 356–2642 or (800) 338–1356. This is a beautiful, rustic farmhouse, built around 1810. Families will like the country cottages with gas fireplaces and color cable TV, as well as the large in-ground pool on the well-landscaped property. The inn is within walking distance of downtown and several outlet malls. $–$$

The Red Jacket, Route 16, North Conway, N.H.; (603) 356–5411 or (800) 752–2538. Although this inn is best known as a convention and meeting venue, during the summer it is a very popular resort for families. One reason is the attractive family loft rooms; another is their complimentary children's program. Indoor and outdoor pools, a playground, a game room, tennis courts, and fitness facility with spa. $–$$

Sunnyside Inn Bed and Breakfast,
Seavey Street, North Conway Village, N.H.; (603) 356–6239 (information) or (800) 600–6239 (reservations). In addition to regular rooms, there are cottages available for families; these include a full kitchen, television, fireplace, and other amenities. Cribs are available, and rates for children are reasonable. Babies under 6 months stay **free.** No pets are allowed, but there is a recommended kennel close by. Breakfast includes eggs, pancakes, and fresh-baked breads and muffins. $–$$

Camping

Passaconaway Campground, Route 112 (Kancamagus Highway), Albany, N.H. (west of Conway). A National Forest camping area with wooded, well-spaced campsites. $.

For More Information

Mount Washington Valley Chamber of Commerce, Route 16, North Conroy, N.H.; (603)–356–3171 or (800) 367–3364; www.mtwashingtonvalley.org.

White Mountains Attractions Association, Route 112 at exit 32 off I–93, North Woodstock, N.H.; (603) 645–9889 or (800) 346–3687; www.visitwhitemountains.com.

Annual Events

For a full calendar of events contact the Mt. Washington Valley Chamber of Commerce, Route 16, North Conway, N.H.; (603) 356–3171 or (800) 367–3364.

MAY

Kids Bike Festival, Waterville Valley, N.H., (603) 236–8311 or (800) GO VALLEY (468–2553); www.waterville.com, late May.

JULY

July Fourth Family Days, North Conway, N.H., (800) 367–3364, July 4.

Native American Cultural Weekend, Twin Mountain, N.H., mid-July.

AUGUST

North Country Moose Festival, Pittsburg, N.H., (603) 237–8216, late August.

SEPTEMBER

New Hampshire Highland Games, Loon Mountain, Lincoln, N.H., (603) 745–8111; www.loonmtn.com, mid-September.

Logging Competition and Fall Festival, at Northern Forest Heritage Park, Berlin, N.H., (603) 752–7202, mid-September. Lumberjack competitions, log building demonstrations, and other activities.

OCTOBER

Halloween Tradition, at The Rocks Estate, Bethlehem, N.H., (603) 444–6228, late October. Hay wagon rides, a haunted walk and barn, pumpkin carving, and spooky games.

NOVEMBER/DECEMBER

Christmas tree cutting at The Rocks Estate, Bethlehem, N.H., (603) 444–6228, late November through Christmas. **Free** rides in horse-drawn wagon with purchase of a tree.

Land of Lakes

The big, sprawling, blue patch near the center of the map of New Hampshire is Lake Winnipesaukee (pronounced "win-i-pe-SAW-kee"). It is a center for family tourism, with its beaches and the many child-oriented attractions that line its western shore. On that side, Meredith and Weirs Beach are the tourism centers, while Wolfeboro is the main town on the eastern side. A number of other lakes—Squam, Winnisquam, Wentworth, Newfound, and Ossipee, among others—surround Winnipesaukee, each with its own camps, beaches, and water sports opportunities.

Plymouth and Newfound Lake

(south to Tilton and Franklin)

Newfound Lake is a quiet and beautiful stretch of water with a state park on the south and two nature reserves on the northern shore. Close to I–93, Newfound's shores are lined by trees and bird-filled marshlands instead of cottages.

Wellington State Park (all ages)

Off Route 3A, Bristol, N.H.; (603) 744–2197. From Route 3A, about 1 mile north of Bristol, follow state park signs to the left at the foot of Newfound Lake. After about 1 mile, follow signs to the right. Open 9:00 A.M. to 8:00 P.M. on weekends from Memorial Day through the last week of June and on the two weekends after Labor Day. During the rest of the summer, open every day during the same hours. Admission $; children under 12 and New Hampshire residents over 65 are admitted free.

Along the shore of Newfound Lake, the half-mile of sandy beach is shaded by tall pine trees growing out of the sand right to the shoreline. This is an exceptionally fine beach, especially popular with families, since it is possible to sit in the comfortable shade and still be within a few feet of children playing in the water. A bathhouse provides changing facilities and a snack bar. Under the pines are plenty of picnic tables. A pleasant walking path circles a small peninsula, providing good views of the lake.

LAND OF LAKES

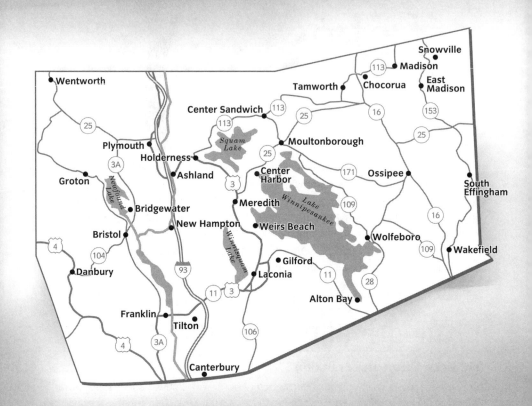

Wentworth

25

Plymouth
Holderness
Ashland

Groton

Newfound Lake

Bridgewater

Bristol

4

104

Danbury

3A

Center Sandwich
113

113

Squam Lake

25

25

Center Harbor

3

Meredith

New Hampton

Weirs Beach

Winnisquam Lake

Gilford

Laconia

11   3

Franklin

Tilton

3A

4

Canterbury

106

Moultonborough

171

Ossipee

109

Lake Winnipesaukee

Wolfeboro

Alton Bay

11

28

Tamworth

Chocorua

25

16

113   Madison

Snowville

East Madison

153

25

16

South Effingham

109   Wakefield

93

Newfound Audubon Center at Paradise Point (ages 5 and up)

North Shore Road, Groton, N.H.; (603) 744–3516; www.nhaudubon.org/sanctuaries/paradise. htm. Follow signs for Hebron and Groton west from Route 3A, between West Plymouth and Bristol. The center is open weekends 10:00 A.M. to 4:00 P.M. in spring and fall, and daily 9:00 A.M. to 5:00 P.M. from the last week in June to Labor Day. Free, but donations to the Audubon Society are welcomed. Trails open daylight hours year-round.

The small museum and interpretive center examines the life of the loon through hands-on and interactive exhibits. Here you can listen to the unusual and eerie cries of this reclusive bird and learn why loons are so scarce. Other local wildlife is featured as well. Pick up a descriptive pamphlet to help you identify the trees and plants along the trails that wind through the woods to the lake shore. A small shop sells nature guides, minerals, and nature games and activities. Naturalist programs explore the wildlife and environment on foot and by canoe.

Sculptured Rocks (ages 5 and up)

North Shore Road, Groton, N.H.; no phone. Follow signs for Hebron and Groton west from Route 3A, between West Plymouth and Bristol. Continue through the two villages and fol- low the sign to the left for Sculptured Rocks, which are about a mile from this turn-off. If you go in the summer or fall, a large State Park sign will tell you when you have arrived. At other times of year, look for an empty signpost and parking spaces beside the road. The rocks are on your right. Free.

Give running water enough time and it can wear away even New Hampshire's solid gran- ite, as it has done to form this gorge. In the process it has carved giant potholes, where the river has plummeted and swirled around with its cargo of rocks and sand. This scour- ing, in whirlpools formed by waterfalls, has carved holes that look as though they were formed by some giant drill press. They vary in size, with some as much as 10 feet in diameter.

The river has undercut the huge boulders that form the bank, creating fantastic shapes over and around which the water plays. A bridge crosses, and below it a trail leads to more waterfalls, pools, and moss-covered rocks, coming finally to a rock cliff with full-grown trees growing out of its side. Picnic tables overlook the chasm.

Polar Caves (ages 4 and up)

Exit 26 off I–93, Route 25 (Tenney Mountain Highway), Plymouth, N.H.; (603) 536–1888; www.polarcaves.com. Open daily mid-May through mid-October 9:00 A.M. to 5:00 P.M. Admission: $$, age 4 and under free.

The Polar Caves were made about 50,000 years ago by gla- ciers, which caused large boulders to break off from the side of Hawks Cliff. Throughout the park, you will learn about the glaciers from the informative plaques that explain the geology of the caves and offer facts about the local wildlife and plants. The caves themselves are quite remarkable and lots of fun to explore. Some are easily navigated

by anyone, but others require a bit of twisting and maneuvering to get through. Many of these caves were used by native Pemigewasset women and children as a hiding place during attacks by the Mohawk people. Some were even used as stops on the Underground Railroad, still others as hiding places for rumrunners during Prohibition. The extensive walkways and steps that lead you to all of the caves are kept in excellent condition.

You should come to the caves prepared by wearing comfortable, flat-soled walking shoes, because some spots inside the caves can be uneven, wet, or otherwise tricky. You will be given a map and guide to the caves, which are all numbered and named, that tell you about each cave and warn of any possible hazards or difficulties. Each cave is lighted, and some contain signs with information and stories about its history. Because this is a self-tour, you should stay with children at all times and be sure to stay on the trails. In addition to the caves, the park has several other attractions. The **Maple Sugar Museum** shows the sugaring process, and a **New Hampshire mineral display** offers more geology stories in an appealing and interesting way. One of our favorite things to do here is feeding the flock of personable ducks or letting the deer gently eat corn from our hands. There are also several resident pheasants and peacocks, as well as other birds. After your tour, you can relax at the **Polar Bar Ice Cream Shop,** or shop at one of the two gift shops.

Tenney Mountain (ages 3 and up)

151 Tenney Mountain Road, off Route 3A, Plymouth, N.H.; (603) 536–4125; www.tenney mtn.com.

A small, family-oriented ski area, Tenney has a ski and board school that welcomes children from the age of three. Facilities include daycare, rentals, and a sports shop. Tubing is offered most days and at least three evenings a week. Lines are short and the people friendly. It's a very comfortable place for children to ski.

Ragged Mountain (ages 3 and up)

Off Route 4, Danbury, N.H.; general information (603) 768–3475, snow conditions (603) 768–3971, lodging (800) 400–3911; www.ragged-mt.com.

Not as well known as nearby Mount Sunapee, Ragged Mountain's ski slopes are preferred by locals and others for the short lift lines. The area has thirty-two trails, at all skill levels, reached by six lifts. The longest trail is 1¾ miles. Lower rates than larger ski areas make it attractive to families.

Daniel Webster Birthplace Historic Site (ages 6 and up)

Off Route 127, Franklin, N.H.; (603) 934–5057 summer, (603) 271–3254 other times. Look for signs on Route 127 between Franklin and Salisbury. Open Saturday and Sunday 10:30 A.M. to 5:00 P.M., from mid-June to Labor Day. Admission (includes the house and museum displays): $, New Hampshire residents and age 18 and under free. Nature trail is free.

Daniel Webster was New Hampshire's most famous native son, a far greater name in American history than the state's only president (Franklin Pierce). The little cabin-like

Scenic **Drive**

The total distance of this loop through the Lakes District is about 160 miles. It takes you around Lake Winnipesaukee, through the attractive villages of Sandwich and Tamworth, and to the best view of Mount Chocorua across its lake. It also skirts Squam and Newfound Lakes, much less developed than the larger Winnipesaukee. Begin at New Hampton, exit 23 off I–93, following Route 104 east to Meredith. Go south on Route 3 through Weirs Beach and follow the shore of Lake Winnipesaukee on Route 11B to Gilford and Route 11 to Alton Bay.

Follow signs to Route 28, which drops into Wolfeboro, between Winnipesaukee and Lake Wentworth. Follow Route 109 along the shore to Moultonborough, then Route 25 to West Ossipee. Turn north (left) onto Route 16 to Chocorua. Continue north on Route 16 to see Mount Chocorua from the hilltop viewpoint and from the shores of the lake below, then return to Chocorua village. Follow Route 113 to Tamworth, taking Route 113A through the village of Wonalancet, and joining Route 113, which goes on to Center Sandwich. Route 113 continues along Squam Lake to Holderness, where it meets Route 3.

This leads to Ashland, crosses I–93, and turns north to Plymouth. Follow Route 25 to Rumney Depot, then an unnumbered road south (left) to Hebron (detour here for Groton and Sculptured Rocks). At Hebron, turn south (left) along Newfound Lake's west shore, bearing left along the lake to Route 3A in Bristol. Route 104 leads you back to New Hampton.

house in which Webster was born is typical of those homes built by the earliest settlers who cleared and farmed these wilderness lands. When Webster was born here in 1782, his father was serving in George Washington's army. Webster was secretary of state under three presidents, congressman from two states, and a man of great diplomacy who was able to find agreement between differing points of view. He was regarded as one of the greatest statesmen of his day.

His birthplace is more than a house, however, and his times are brought into modern perspective by a living-history project. Interpreters dressed in the clothes of Webster's day show visitors what life was like when he was a child here. Depending on the time of year and the weather, they might be spinning wool into yarn, sewing hems on the sheets for the bed in the next room, or preparing a meal over a fire in the large fireplace. They may invite you to try your hand at these activities or invite you to join in an early game that Webster might have played here.

Canterbury Shaker Village (ages 6 and up)

Exit 18 off I–93, Canterbury, N.H.; (603) 783–9511. The route to the village is well marked by brown signs from I–93. Open 10:00 A.M. to 5:00 P.M. daily May through October, same hours Friday through Sunday in April, November, and December. Tours begin every half-hour in July and August, on the hour the rest of the time. Admission: $$–$$$, under age 6 **free.**

Until just a few years ago, two remaining sisters of the Canterbury Shaker community lived in this village. No Shakers live here now—the sect is virtually extinct—but the Canterbury Shaker Village has been beautifully restored. The group of twenty-four buildings includes the former community's housing, farm, and workshops. The village has become a museum to show the art and life of these followers of Ann Lee, known as Mother Ann. Their celibate communal life centered around simplicity, a strong work ethic, and their fine craftsmanship. Shakers led in packaging and selling garden seeds and medicinal and culinary herbs, and they are still known for their practical inventions and improvements on simple tools, such as the flat broom and the clothespin. Designs and styles created by Shaker furniture craftsmen influence American design to this day. Tours show the buildings and explain the Shakers' philosophy and how they lived. The Shakers often took the responsibility of raising and educating orphaned children, and in Canterbury their schoolhouse was the village school for many years. The restaurant serves authentic Shaker meals (the chicken pie is delicious), and the Summer Kitchen sells more modern snacks.

Lakes Region Factory Stores (all ages)

Off I–93 at exit 20, Tilton, N.H.; (603) 286–7880 or (888) SHOP333 (746–7333). Open Monday through Saturday 10:00 A.M. to 8:00 P.M., Sunday 10:00 A.M. to 6:00 P.M.

This huge outlet complex has overstocked and out-of-season merchandise and "seconds" of name brands in fifty-four stores. In addition to the savings, prices are tax-free (New Hampshire has no sales tax). Back-to-School sales on children's clothing and accessories begin in early August.

Where to Eat

The Creamery Restaurant, Canterbury Shaker Village, N.H.; (603) 783–9511. Open for lunch May through October, Friday through Sunday. $

Frenchy Family Restaurant, Belknap Mall, Route 3, Tilton, N.H.; (603) 524–5299. Authentic French-Canadian dishes served in a no-alcohol family atmosphere, with a kids' menu.

American favorites, too, but our kids like the Quebecoise soul food, like their Memere used to make—especially the pork pie. Open daily from 10:00 A.M. until 10:00 P.M. $

The Italian Farmhouse, Route 3 south of Plymouth; (603) 536–4536. Open Monday through Saturday 5:00 to 9:00 P.M., Sunday 11:00 A.M. to 2:00 P.M. and 5:00 to 8:30 P.M. Italian food served in a cozy, casual New England farmhouse setting. $–$$

Thea's Restaurant, Route 104, 1/2 mile east of exit 23 from I–93, New Hampton, N.H.; (603) 744–2334. Open mid-May through mid-October, 11:00 A.M. to 9:00 P.M. Casual family restaurant with a children's menu. $–$$

Where to Stay

Cliff Lodge, off Route 3A, Bristol, N.H., just north of the West Shore Road intersection; (603) 744–8660. Rustic cottages for families overlook Newfound Lake from on high. $$

Comfort Inn, West Street, Ashland, N.H.; (603) 968–7668. No surprises here, but comfortable, dependable lodging close to I–93. $–$$

Hilltop Acres, Eastside and Buffalo Roads, Wentworth, N.H.; (603) 764–5896. Open May through October. Bed and breakfast with cottages, two with efficiency kitchens. Pets are allowed in the cottages. $$

The Inn on Newfound Lake, Route 3A, Bridgewater, N.H.; (603) 744–9111; www.newfoundlake.com. With its own private beach on one of the nation's clearest lakes and a location between two small family-friendly ski areas, this inn welcomes families year-round. $$–$$$

For More Information

Lakes Region Association, P.O. Box 439, New Hampton, NH 03256; (603) 744–8664; www.lakesregion.org.

Newfound Region Chamber of Commerce, P.O. Box 454, Bristol, NH 03222; (602) 744–2150; www.newfound chamber.com.

Plymouth Chamber of Commerce, 20 Highland Street, Plymouth, NH 03264; (603) 536–1001 or (800) 386–3678; www.plymouth nh.org.

Waterville Valley Chamber of Commerce, 12 Vintinner Road, Campton, NH 03223; (603) 726–3804 or (800) 237–2307; www.watervillevalleyregion.com. Information center off I–93 exit 28.

Eastern Winnipesaukee (Wolfeboro, Alton, Wakefield)

We've always thought that Wolfeboro ought to use the tourism motto: "On the Quiet Side of the Lake." The bustle and neon of the eastern lakeshore seem far away in this friendly, easygoing town and the area around it. Almost on the Maine border is the pretty village of Wakefield, once an important stagecoach stop but now bypassed by modern highways.

Wentworth State Park (all ages)

Route 109, Wolfeboro, N.H.; (603) 569–3699. Open Saturday and Sunday May and June, daily July and August. Admission $; children under 12 and New Hampshire residents over 65 admitted **free.**

Public swimming beaches are not as common as you might expect in this watery area. Although relatively small, the beach on Lake Wentworth, which is separated from Lake

Molly the Trolley

Located at 60 North Main Street, Wolfeboro, N.H. (603–569–1080), this handy trolley leaves from the Town Dock on the hour or from the Rail Station on the half hour all day. This means you can leave your car and travel throughout the lakefront area and to Carrie Beach. Hop on and off wherever you like, or take the entire forty-five-minute narrated tour to get a quick orientation to Wolfeboro. An all-day ticket will cost $.

Winnipesaukee by a narrow strip of land at Wolfeboro, is particularly attractive. Bath-houses and a picnic area along its sandy shore are about the only facilities, but that's all you really need.

Ellie's Woodland Walk at Ryefield Marsh (ages 4 and up)

Route 109, Wolfeboro, N.H.; no phone. Across Route 109 from Wentworth State Park (look for the stone marker at the trailhead). Open every day, year-round. Near the granite marker on Route 109, look for the black mailbox, which contains maps of the trail and explanations of the markers. Free.

The Wolfeboro Conservation Commission maintains this interesting path, an easy walk through a lowland along a marsh. Markers identify environmental sites along the way—a birch grove, a meadow, a beaver marsh—and the trail map tells about the animals and plants you'll see there. The best time to see beaver (you have to be very quiet) is in the early evening.

Doris E (ages 5 and up)

Board at the Town Dock, Meredith and Weirs; (603) 366-5531 or (888) THE MOUNT (843–6686); www.cruisenh.com. Cruises depart 10:30 A.M. to 6:30 P.M. on the ½ hour. Two-hour cruise $$–$$$; one-hour cruise $$. May split up round-trip ticket and reboard later in the day.

On the two-hour cruise of the islands on the east side of Lake Winnipesaukee, the captain tells local stories and explains the lake's history as he points out features on shore and on islands. Light refreshments are available.

Other Public Beaches in Wolfeboro

Allen A. Resort Beach entrance road is off the east side of Route 28/109, east of town, just after the Allen A. Motor Inn. This beach on Lake Wentworth has a long, sandy shoreline and places to picnic. Sandy Beach and Carrie Beach are also in Wolfeboro, on the shore of Lake Winnipesaukee.

E. Stanley Wright Museum (ages 8 and up)

77 Center Street (Routes 28/109), Wolfeboro, N.H.; (603) 569–1212. Open Saturday and Sunday in November and in February through April, daily May through mid-October, 10:00 A.M. to 4:00 P.M. Admission: $–$$, under age 9 free.

The kids are sure to spot this building, not because it's at all unusual in design but because it has a tank crashing through its brick wall. The homefront and military life during World War II is the theme of the exhibits here. It's a good introduction to America of the 1940s, with a barber shop, a soda fountain, and a dentist's office, along with a typical family parlor. An entire building of military hardware is filled with tanks and half-tracks. A Norden bombsight, one of the most secret of all devices used in the war, is here, too.

Klickety-Klack Model Railroad (ages 5 and up)

Elm Street, Wolfeboro, N.H.; (603) 569–5384. From Route 109 take Route 109A (Elm Street) a few hundred feet. Open July 1 to Labor Day, Monday through Saturday 10:00 A.M. to 5:30 P.M.; Memorial Day to July 1 and Labor Day through December, Thursday, Friday, and Saturday 10:00 A.M. to 5:00 P.M. A small admission fee is charged.

More than 1,000 feet of HO- and N-gauge track provide the landscape for twenty-two trains that whiz along, toot their whistles, chug through tunnels, and cross bridges. The Lilliputian locomotives go through idyllic New Hampshire villages with mountains overlooking them, passing a quarry and other local landmarks. The best thing about these trains is that you can operate half of them yourself, encouraged by signs explaining the tracks. All this is the work of one man, helped by his friends.

Nordic Skier Sports (ages 5 and up)

19 North Main Street, Wolfeboro, N.H.; (603) 569–3151. Open daylight hours, snow permitting. Rates are $$, children 12 and under ski free.

This all-season sports center rents bikes and maintains about 12 miles of well-groomed and -tracked cross-country trails overlooking the lake, with expansive views. The center also offers ski equipment rentals and lessons and is the unofficial headquarters for information on outdoor sports in the area.

Libby Museum (ages 6 and up)

North Main Street (Route 109), Wolfeboro, N.H.; (603) 569–1035. Open Tuesday through Saturday, June through mid-September, 10:00 A.M. to 4:00 P.M., Sunday noon to 4:00 P.M. Admission: $.

The natural history of the Lakes Region, as well as its human history, is the focus of this small museum. Abenaki artifacts are especially interesting, and the museum offers nature programs for children in July and August. You will also find items discovered during excavations at the nearby site of the summer home of New Hampshire's royal governor, Benning Wentworth.

Abenaki Tower (ages 4 and up)

Route 109, Wolfeboro, N.H. Follow Route 109 about 8 miles from the center of town; look for trailhead parking on your right. **Free.**

This twenty-minute gentle climb through the woods leads to an observation tower. Its steps may leave you puffing like the Little Engine That Could, but the views from the top are splendid, across the lake and mountains.

Museum of Childhood (ages 4 and up)

Mt. Laurel Road, Wakefield, N.H.; (603) 522–8073. Open May through early September, Monday and Wednesday through Saturday 11:00 A.M. to 4:00 P.M., Sunday 1:00 to 4:00 P.M. Admission: $.

No ordinary museum, this is the lifetime collection of two sisters who collected dolls and toys until their home could no longer hold their treasures. Now they enjoy showing visitors through an adjacent house and introducing them to more than 3,000 dolls and toys. From all parts of the world and from as far back as the mid-1800s, the collections include everything from clothespin dolls to priceless china-headed fashion dolls, teddy bears, and an 1890s schoolroom with all its furnishings intact. Children are enchanted with the stories that weave through the rooms as these collectors assure them that it's okay to go in the little girl's bedroom while she's "visiting her grandmother today." So many toy museums are designed for adults, but this one seems to reach all ages, as a well-crafted children's book does.

Where to Eat

Bittersweet, Route 28, Wolfeboro, N.H.; (603) 569–3636. Open Monday through Saturday, May through December, from 5:00 P.M., Saturday and Sunday also for brunch from 11:00 A.M. until 2:00 P.M. European dishes with a flair and American favorites. $$

Cafe Sweets and Treats, 11 Railroad Street, Wolfeboro, N.H.; (603) 569–4504; www.cafesweetsandtreats.com. For breakfast sandwiches and croissants, deli sandwiches at lunch, or between-meal stops for a good cup of coffee and a chance to check your e-mail (or let the kids play a couple of computer games), this friendly cafe is a

COOL Facts

The Winnipesaukee home of Royal Governor Benning Wentworth, which burned in 1820, is often called the first lakeside summer cottage in America.

place to know about. Open every day (but only until 2:00 P.M. on Sunday). $

Mast Landing Restaurant, Main Street, Wolfeboro, N.H. (in the middle of town); (603) 569–1789. Open daily until 3:00 P.M. for breakfast and lunch. Breakfast dishes are served all day, and if you call ahead they'll have take-out lunches waiting for you. Waitresses in this friendly eatery take time to describe the daily specials and joke with the children. The pie case is a pie-lover's paradise, almost always featuring apple, blueberry, chocolate custard, pumpkin, apricot, cherry, and lemon meringue. $

Where to Stay

Lakehurst Housekeeping Cottages, Route 11D, Alton Bay, N.H.; (603) 875–2492. Lakefront cottages that you can rent by the

night in May and June, or July through September by the week only. $$

Lin-Joy Cottages, Robert's Cove Road, Alton, N.H.; (603) 569–4973. Rustic, comfortable cabins with kitchenettes and a pool, in a setting that will remind you of summer camp. Weekly rates or by the night. $–$$

Tuc-Me-Inn B&B, 118 North Main Street, Wolfeboro, N.H.; (603) 569–5702. Warm and welcoming downtown B&B. Some rooms with private bath, some shared. Rates include full breakfast. $$

For More Information

Wolfeboro Chamber of Commerce, 32 Central Avenue, Wolfeboro, NH 03894; (603) 569–2200 or (800) 516–5324.

Western Winnipesaukee (Gilford, Laconia, Weirs Beach, Meredith, Center Harbor)

There's the unmistakable air of a beach town all along this western side of the lake all summer long. Traffic can keep you waiting, lines may be long, and reservations are a must, especially on weekends. But for all its air of honky-tonk, it's definitely a family zone. If the attractions are touristy, it's because so many tourists have delighted in this atmosphere over the many years since the first summer hotels were built overlooking the lake.

Even if you choose to stay elsewhere around the lake, you will find yourself coming here, especially if your vacation should include a rainy day or two. Here is the likeable bustle of people having fun, and it's contagious.

Sophie C (ages 4 and up)

Lakeside Avenue, Weirs Beach, N.H.; (603) 366–5531 or (888) THE MOUNT (843–6686); www. cruisenh.com. Departures at 11:00 A.M. and 2:00 P.M., Monday through Saturday mid-June through mid-September. Fare: $$–$$$, age 3 and under free.

The *Sophie C* is the only U.S. working mail boat on an inland waterway; it explores Winnipesaukee's harbors and secluded coves to deliver mail to people who live on the lake's five islands. You get a different view of life on the lake from this than from other boats. Mail delivery or sunset cruises are two to three hours long, and light refreshments are available at their onboard snack bar (which has ice cream!).

Mount Washington Cruises (ages 4 and up)

Mount Washington Dock, Weirs Beach, N.H.; (603) 366–5531 or (888) THE MOUNT (843–6686); www.cruisenh.com. Departs Weirs Beach daily, late May through October 10:00 A.M. and 12:30 P.M., with an added trip in July and August at 3:00 P.M. You can also begin trips in Wolfeboro, Center Harbor, Alton Bay, and Meredith.

This large boat has broad decks and inside seating areas, so you can see the scenery in comfort even if the weather doesn't cooperate. A narrator points out places along the shore and tells a bit of history about the lake but is not constantly in your ear. Breakfast and lunch are available on the boat. Family pass for two adults and two children $50 for 2½ hour cruise, $42 for two hours. Evening cruises offer a buffet dinner and dancing to live music ($29–$39).

Doris E (ages 4 and up)

Town Dock, Meredith, N.H.; See *Doris E* in section on Eastern Winnipesaukee.

Surf Coaster USA (ages 4 and up)

Route 11B at junction of Route 3, Weirs Beach, N.H.; (603) 366–4991; www.surfcoasterusa. com. Open daily late June through August 10:00 A.M. until 8:00 P.M. Admission: $$$–$$$$.

COOL Facts

Lake Winnipesaukee has 283 miles of shoreline and 274 islands. Many of these islands are inhabited in the summer, when residents come and go by their own motor boats or on the daily mail boat.

COOL Facts

Weirs Beach got its name from the fishing weirs that Native Americans used there to catch fish. A weir is a fenced area in the water where fish can swim in but cannot escape.

A number of water-soaked activities help beat the summer heat, including a wave pool, ten water slides, rafting, a lagoon, and a spray ground for small fry. Waterslides are graded for various ages and thrill levels, and the wave pool has a shallow end for younger children and realistic ocean-size breakers at the action end. The Crazy River simulates rapids, with turns and twists that kids navigate on tubes. All activities are covered in the admission fee. Changing rooms, showers, and lockers make this an easy place to go without getting car seats wet on the way home. Parents who prefer to remain dry have plenty of places to sit and watch the fun, including a cafe and a sundeck.

FunSpot (ages 4 and up)

Route 3, Weirs Beach, N.H.; (603) 366–4377; www.funspotnh.com. Open daily year-round. Summer hours Sunday through Thursday 9:00 A.M. to 10:00 P.M., Friday and Saturday 9:00 A.M. to 11:00 P.M. Fall opening at 10:00 A.M. Charges vary with activity; miniature golf is $$ for nineteen holes. Children under age 4 can play miniature golf free with adult admission.

FunSpot offers a nineteen-hole miniature golf course, bowling, kiddy rides, and a game arcade. The staff is super friendly and the variety of games and amusements is astounding. If you are not a New Englander, you may not be familiar with candlepin bowling, but ten-pins is also available.

Weirs Beach Water Slide (ages 6 and up)

Route 3, Weirs Beach, N.H.; (603) 366–5161; www.weirsbeach.net/waterslide. One mile north of the beach. Open daily mid-June through August 10:00 A.M. until 5:00 P.M. Admission: $$$–$$$$.

Another water-splashed park designed for cooling off in the summer. The waterslides vary in size and complexity, offering four different skill levels so they're suitable for all ages. The Super Slide is one of the longest in New England. Eighteen-hole minigolf is also available.

Winnipesaukee Scenic Railroad (ages 3 and up)

Board at Mill Street in Meredith or on Route 3 in Weirs Beach, N.H.; (603) 745–2135; www.hoborr.com. Operates weekends late May through mid-June, daily through Labor Day, and weekends through October. Summer departures from Meredith 10:30 A.M., 12:30 P.M., 2:30 P.M., 4:30 P.M., Wednesday and Saturday 6:30 P.M. Departs Weirs Beach on the hour, 11:00 A.M. to 5:00 P.M. Rides are $$.

Riding on part of the old Boston & Maine Railroad line, the train carries passengers along the scenic shore between the stations in Meredith and Weirs Beach and along Paugus Bay almost to Laconia. The longer rides depart from Meredith, picking up passengers for the shorter ride in Weirs Beach. An ice-cream parlor car serves sundaes, and you can reserve a hobo picnic lunch tied in a bundle on a stick. The $6.95 picnic contains a sub sandwich, chips, and a giant cookie. Evening rides twice a week include a turkey dinner in the dining car ($23.99 adults, $17.95 ages three to eleven, including train fare). Reservations are necessary for dinner trains. Special theme train rides take place from April to December.

Annalee Doll Museum (ages 9 and up)

44 Reservoir Road, Meredith, N.H.; (603) 279–3333; www.annalee.com. Museum open daily June through October 9:00 A.M. to 5:00 P.M. Free.

These flexible felt dolls have been prized by collectors since the first ones were created nearly sixty years ago. Each has a theme and is posed and dressed appropriately. Some seem ready for a favorite sport: fishing, golf, or tennis, Others are dressed for the holidays. Hand-painted faces, each with individual characteristics, are the hallmark of the line, which now includes animal characters. These are not playthings, however, and our experience is that even the cute animals leave small children cold. The shop, open all year, features hundreds of Annalee creations at factory prices. Special events for children are offered all year.

Gunstock Recreation Area (all ages)

Route 11A, Gilford, N.H.; (603) 293–4341 or (800) GUNSTOCK (486–7862); www.gunstock. com. Open year-round, skiing from December through March, weather permitting. Prices vary according to activity.

A county-operated facility, Gunstock adjoins the Belknap Mountain State Forest and offers year-round outdoor activities for families. In the winter, it is a well-established ski area— one of the earliest-opening in the state—with more than forty trails and slopes at all skill levels for skiers and snowboarders. It is known for its two ski jumps, which are often the site of championship contests. A cross-country center offers trails and equipment rentals. Snowmaking covers nearly all the trails and slopes. Ski rentals and childcare are available at the base lodge. Its low-key, friendly atmosphere makes it a favorite for skiing families. In the summer, the mountain is traversed by hiking and climbing trails, and you can take guided trail rides on horseback. Swimming, a campground, and children's nature programs are all here, and the park has a full schedule of special events that include an Oktoberfest and a woodsmen's festival.

Ice Cream, **You** Scream

- **Lakeview Creamery,** Route 3, Tilton (Winnisquam) (603–387–6469; lake viewcreamery@yahoo.com). One of the best ice-cream places we have ever been to, their motto is "any fresher it would moo." All of the milk for the ice cream is gathered weekly from their cows, whose pictures are on the shop's wall. All smoothies are made with real fruit, not syrup, and every ingredient used here is local. There is a unique selection of toppings for kids (including zoo animals!), and the sundaes are generous and loaded with toppings.

- **Kellerhaus,** on Route 3 in Weirs Beach (603–366–4466) is open all year. Ice-cream sundaes are the big draw here for kids. Make your own with their quality ice cream and a staggering array of toppings. The gift shop is equally staggering, and you can expect kids to go glassy-eyed there.

- **J.B. Scoops Homemade Ice Cream**, on Route 3 in Meredith (603–279–6703) and their Sundae Buffet offer fifty toppings.

- For ice cream in a less-hyper setting, stop at **Boardwalk Ice Cream** in the Mills Falls Marketplace (603–279–2200) on the lakefront in Meredith. This multistory complex of eighteen shops also has an excellent bookstore that features local books and has a large children's department.

- Or, if you are heading south along the lake, you'll pass a local institution, **Sawyer's Dairy Bar** (603–293–4422; see the section "Where to Eat").

Where to Eat

Boathouse Grille, at The Inn at Bay Point, Meredith, N.H.; (603) 279–2253. Open daily for lunch and dinner. $$–$$$

Giuseppe's Show Time Restaurant and Pizzeria, Mills Falls Marketplace, Meredith, N.H.; (603) 279–3313. Italian all the way, Giuseppe's loves kids and feeds everyone well, with pasta, pizza, steaks, and seafood. Takeout, too, and music nightly. $–$$

Mame's, 8 Plymouth Street, Meredith, N.H.; (603) 279–4631. Casual atmosphere in the historic setting of an 1825 home. It's a two-minute walk from the dock and Mills Falls

Marketplace in the center of town. Children's menu; lunch and dinner, Sunday brunch year-round. $–$$

Sawyer's Dairy Bar, Junction of Routes 11 and 11B, Gilford, N.H.; (603) 293–4422. Open in summer Sunday through Thursday 11:00 A.M. to 9:00 P.M., Friday and Saturday 11:00 A.M. to 10:00 P.M. Everyone comes here for their excellent ice cream, but they also serve burgers, sandwiches, and hot dogs. $

Victorian House, Route 11, Gilford, N.H.; (603) 293–8155. Open daily 5:00 to 9:00 P.M., in an elegant Victorian setting that welcomes children. Menu is outstanding and innovative, with good appetizers. $$–$$

Public Beaches

Public Beaches **Weirs Beach** and **Ellacoya State Park,** in Gilford, are the biggest beaches. Ellacoya's has 600 feet of sand, with a bathhouse and snack bar. Weirs Beach is close to the town's shops and eateries. **Leavitt Park,** on Route 25 between Meredith and Center Harbor, has a beach on Lake Winnipesaukee and **Waukewan Town Beach**, on Waukewan Street in Meredith, faces on the small lake of the same name. Bond Beach is in Laconia, and **Gunstock Recreation Area,** in Gilford, also has swimming.

Where to Stay

Clearwater Cottages, Neal Shore Road, Meredith, N.H.; (603) 279–6608. Each lakeside cottage has two bedrooms and a kitchen. There's a swimming dock and canoe access to the lake. $$

The Inn at Bay Point, Route 3, Meredith, N.H.; (603) 279–7006 or (800) 622–6455. Bright, modern rooms all overlook Lake Winnipesaukee. This is luxury all the way, with balconies, fireplaces, and whirlpool baths. $$$

The Inn at Mills Falls, Route 3, Meredith, N.H.; (603) 279–7006 or (800) 622–6455; www.millsfalls.com. This inn, featuring attractive rooms and hotel facilities that include a pool, could not be handier to the action. It is connected by a corridor to the Mills Falls Marketplace shops and restaurants. $$–$$$

The Margate on Winnipesaukee, 76 Lake Street, Laconia, N.H.; (603) 524–5210 or (800) THE MARGATE (843–6274). Attractive rooms, many facing the lake and the resort's private 300-foot beach. Indoor and outdoor pools and fitness center. $$

Camping

Clearwater Campground, Route 104, Meredith, N.H., 3 miles east of I-93 exit 23; (603) 279–7761; www.clearwatercampground.com. Wooded sites with a long, sandy beach, recreation facilities, and scheduled activities. Two rustic camping cabins are available. $

Gunstock Recreation Area, Route 11A, Gilford, N.H.; (603) 293–4341 or (800) GUNSTOCK (486–7862); www.gunstock.com. Of the 300 sites, more than a third have hookups. Laundry, small grocery store, recreation hall, pool, and pond with paddleboats. $

For More Information

Laconia Weirs Beach Chamber of Commerce, 11 Veterans Square, Laconia, NH 03246; (603) 524–5531; www.laconiaweirs.org.

Meredith Area Chamber of Commerce, 272 Route 3, Meredith, NH 03253; (603) 279–6121; www.meredithcc.org.

Web Sites

The site www.weirsbeach.com has information on the town and its many activities. It includes lodging and dining, history, location of public parking, and more.

The site www.lakesregion.org has details on the major local attractions.

Sandwich, Squam, Moultonborough, and Holderness

To many New Hampshire residents and visitors, Squam is the perfect lake. Smaller than its neighboring Winnipesaukee, and filled with scenic islands and islets, its irregular shores are not marred by cheek-by-jowl summer camps. Instead, the cottages are set back, most on large lots, and property owners are fierce in their determination to keep their lake pristine. It is a major loon habitat, and their nests are treasured and protected by everyone who lives on the lake. Not everyone was pleased by the burst of fame the lake received when it was the movie set for *On Golden Pond*.

Nearby Sandwich is a postcard town with a white-steepled church, tidy homes, and in the spring, lilacs blooming in dooryards along its quiet streets.

Golden Pond Boat Tours (ages 4 and up)

Route 3, Holderness, N.H.; (603) 279–4405. Departing from the docks in "downtown" Holderness next to Walter's Basin restaurant daily June through September, 10:30 A.M. and 1:30 P.M. Fare: $$$.

Two-hour tours meander at a genteel speed around the idyllic lake, passing loon nesting sites, discreet summer cottages hiding in the pines, and miles of wooded shoreline. The narration highlights both the natural and human history of this lake, which has been the hideaway of wealthy Boston families for generations.

Squam Lakes Natural Science Center (ages 4 and up)

Route 113, Holderness, N.H.; (603) 968–7194; www.nhnature.org. Summer hours are daily 9:30 A.M. to 4:30 P.M.; spring and fall hours are the same on weekdays but 1:00 to 4:00 P.M. on Saturday and Sunday. Admission during July and August is $–$$, lower in May, June, September, and October.

Daily programs in July and August encourage visitors to explore several different natural ecosystems along the center's trails and in a variety of exhibits. Placards and staff explain the complex interactions of plants and animal life in a marsh, stream, field, pond, and forest, and along the lakeshore. Questions are encouraged and are asked in signs, such as If the marsh were drained, who would suffer? The marsh community is the easy favorite of children, who can usually be found stretched out on the boardwalk, with their heads over the edge watching the endless variety of creatures below. Few places allow such up-close-and-personal encounters with painted turtles, leopard frogs, trout, and dragonflies. Birds perch on fences and keep up a constant chirping from the branches of surrounding shrubs.

In wildlife exhibits, you will meet a black bear, bobcat, river otter, deer, owls, and a bald eagle. Their enclosures are large and kept as

close as possible to the creatures' natural habitats. The **Gordon Children's Center** is abuzz with action, which most older kids find just as much fun as the younger set for which it is designed. Hands-on is the key, with plenty of activities always in progress. Children old enough to sit quietly for a moment will enjoy watching the birds and butterflies in a garden planted with flowers and herbs that attract them. The songbird exhibit has a large aviary.

Special weekend programs highlight some seasonal activity, such as snowshoeing or bird life. Occasional **free** concerts are also held here, featuring music for the whole family. Picnicking is encouraged at these concerts. For both you and your children, a visit here is a good introduction to understanding the natural world of the forests, fields, and waters that you'll travel through in both states.

Squam Lake Nature Cruises (ages 4 and up)

Squam Lake Natural Science Center, Route 113, Holderness, N.H.; (603) 968–7194; www.nhnature.org. Departures July through October, at varying times from 6:00 A.M. until 7:00 P.M. Fare: $$$.

Nature explorations on Squam Lake visit the habitat of the lake's colony of loons, led by a trained naturalist. The center's 28-foot pontoon boats, *Heron* and *Merganser,* leave at different times each day of the week, so it's best to check their schedule for the days you will be in the area. Each cruise focuses on some aspect of nature in the lake, which changes surprisingly with the time of day. For a lake few people see, go on one of the daybreak trips.

Rockywold–Deephaven Camps (all ages)

Route 113 (P.O. Box B), Holderness, NH 03245; (603) 968–3313; www.rdcsquam.com. $$.

We thought these wonderful places were long gone and were delighted to discover Rockywold several years ago. Since its origins in 1897 as a summer encampment, cabins have

Mountain Safety

Wherever you hike or climb, you are likely to find rocky areas and cliffs. The views are, after all, why most people climb or hike, and the best ones are usually from the tops of ledges or above a waterfall. It is important to discuss cliff-top behavior with children before the trip so they understand the dangers of standing near the edge. Even places that look quite safe can be dangerously undercut. Pine needles, moss, mud, and wet rocks are all slippery. Not every trail or waterfall is fenced off—in fact, few are. New Englanders don't like to ruin views with fences, so you are expected to judge for yourself whether your children are mature enough to stay away from dangerous overhangs and slippery ledges.

replaced the tents, but the cool, wooded compound on a peninsula of Squam Lake retains much of its aura of rusticity that was fashionable a century ago, when city families escaped to the lake. You won't see Rockywold advertised, because the same families have been returning for generations. Many cabins have fireplaces, and firewood and ice (cut from the pond in the winter and stored in an old-fashioned ice house) are delivered to each cabin daily. (Think of the fun your kids will have telling classmates that they stayed somewhere where people still use ice-boxes.) Family-style meals are served in two open wooden dining halls, and two libraries and lodges are rainy-day gathering places. This is not just a lodging, but a vacation of its own. The Squam Lake experience doesn't get more authentic than this genteel oasis free of modern conveniences, arugula, whirlpools, and speed boats. Leave your cell phone at home. Family packages include everything; you just arrive and settle in.

West Rattlesnake Mountain (ages 6 and up)

Route 113, about 5 miles east of Holderness, N.H. Park on the north (left) side of the road and walk back along Route 113 to the trailhead. Free.

What kid could resist climbing a mountain with a name like this (even though no one remembers ever having seen a rattlesnake here)?

A gentle climb and a wonderful view of the lake and mountains from a modest height above Squam Lake, the summit is reached by an old bridle path that leaves from the south side of the road. This is an easy climb for children, but be very careful at the top, where there are steep ledges. It's not a place for small children to be running around loose.

Red Hill (ages 4 and up)

Sibley Road, Center Harbor, N.H. From just west of the intersection of Routes 25 and 25B, follow Bean Road about 1½ miles to the fire tower sign, where you can park. Free.

The hike (more of a walk, really) to the overlook atop 2,000-foot Red Hill is pleasant and easy, and the view makes you feel as if you've climbed a real mountain. (Which is, of course, why they chose this easy-to-access spot for a fire tower.)

Meredith Children's Museum (ages 2 and up)

28 Lang Street, Meredith, N.H.; (603) 279–6307; www.thezeeum.com. Open Tuesday through Saturday 10:00 A.M. to 3:00 P.M. (shorter hours in winter). Admission: $$.

The blackboard sign in front and the schoolhouse-red paint on the building are as close as this place comes to seeming like a school. But kids will learn in spite of that as they explore the physical, natural, and creative world through the hands-on interactive exhibits and activities. Log building sets are inside a life-size log cabin. Small fry will like driving a fire truck or being captain of a lake police boat. Special programs and activities for families are scheduled frequently, as are workshops and other learning opportunities for all ages.

Pauline Glidden Toy Museum (ages 7 and up)

Entered from the Whipple House, 14 Pleasant Street, Ashland, N.H. For information, contact the Ashland Historical Society, P.O. Box 175, Ashland, NH 03217. Open July through Labor Day, Wednesday and Saturday 1:00 to 4:00 P.M. Admission: $.

Displayed in an 1810 house, this little-known museum contains thousands of antique toys. Although small tots will be frustrated at finding dolls and toys they cannot play with, the collections will fascinate older children. Along with the dolls are doll furniture, miniatures, games, model trains, and children's books.

Elisha Marston House (ages 6 and up)

Maple Street, Center Sandwich, N.H.; (603) 284–6269. Open Tuesday through Saturday June through September 11:00 A.M. to 5:00 P.M. Free.

Life in a small New Hampshire village in the mid-1800s is reflected in the home of the village shoemaker, which has been preserved by the Sandwich Historical Society. Old kitchen and household equipment shows the greatest contrast between life as our kids know it and the world of a century and a half ago.

Sandwich Home Industries

Main Street (Route 109), Center Sandwich, N.H.; (603) 284–6831. Open mid-May to mid-October Monday through Saturday 10:00 A.M. to 5:00 P.M., Sunday noon to 5:00 P.M.

One of the oldest craft cooperatives in New England, this shop sells handmade stuffed and wooden toys, as well as fine hand-sewn and embroidered children's clothing. Look also for quilts, handweaving, wooden ware, and pottery.

Beede's Falls (ages 5 and up)

Sandwich Notch Road, Center Sandwich, N.H. Follow Grove Street, bearing left at the road marked Sandwich Notch. This unpaved road is not maintained in the winter. Park in the small pull-out on the right before the road begins to climb into the notch.

A wooded trail leads to the river, which rushes through a miniature flume. Walk upstream to the 40-foot falls, where the river drops over a ledge into a sandy pool. Join the kids to explore the jumbles of glacial rocks to the left of the falls, where boulders create caves and passageways. Downstream from the trail is another area, a deep mysterious place of mossy boulders, which lean against and on top of each other to form caves and arches.

Pulpit Rock (ages 5 and up)

Sandwich Notch Road, Center Sandwich, N.H. Follow Grove Street, bearing left at road marked Sandwich Notch.

A short way beyond the trail to Beede's Falls (see previous entry), the road crosses two bridges over the Bearcamp River. Between these two crossings is a sheer rock face, almost overhanging the road, which is known as Pulpit Rock. Local history relates that it

COOL Facts

While it may seem odd that someone would choose a spot way out here in the woods to hold a religious service, these woods were once cleared fields and pastures. The narrow gravel road was the main route to the north country, and wagons loaded with supplies traveled it regularly.

was used as a pulpit by a Quaker pastor. Behind this rock are more rocks, all fun to explore. The adjacent level riverbank makes a fine place to picnic. If you decide to continue over the notch (the road is not very steep), you will come to Route 49, which continues to Waterville Valley if you turn right. A left turn will bring you to I–93.

The Old Country Store (ages 8 and up)
Routes 109 and 25, Moultonborough, N.H. Open daily year-round. Hours vary. Free.

The second floor of this working country store is a museum of local history, with a fascinating assemblage of old tools and household goods. You'll find saws, axes, a wooden snow shovel, farm implements, blacksmithing tools, maple sugaring equipment, advertising cards, sewing tools, yarn winders, and other things your kids will have fun trying to figure out the uses for. Cards label most of the collection, often in fascinating detail. Don't expect interactive modern museum exhibits here; they have the real things instead. Downstairs you can sample old-fashioned "common crackers" or some cheddar cheese from the wheel. This and other goods are sold from original country-store cabinets and cases, museum pieces themselves. Look outside, in the shed beside the front porch, to see an original Concord Coach. This one is thought to be the oldest remaining Concord stagecoach.

Castle in the Clouds (ages 5 and up)
Route 171, Moultonborough, N.H.; (603) 476–2352; www.castlesprings.com. From Route 25, just north of Moultonborough village, follow Route 171 east toward Tuftonboro and Ossipee. Look for the Castle Springs sign on the north side of the road. If you are coming from Wolfeboro, turn right onto Route 171 where Route 109 ends, 5 miles north of Melvin Village. Open weekends in May and early June, daily mid-June through late October, 9:00 A.M. to 4:30 P.M. Admission: $$–$$$, age 6 and under free.

The centerpiece here is the stone mansion of a former summer estate, built high on a hillside above Lake Winnipesaukee. A single admission, paid at the gatehouse before you drive up the long road to the castle, covers a house tour and a tram ride to the source of a spring, whose clear water is bottled for sale all over the state. You can feed the huge trout in the pool there or go for trail rides from their stable (extra charges apply). Access to walking trails along the hillside is free. Of course, there's a gift shop and snack bar.

COOL Facts

It took 1,000 stone cutters and three years to build Castle in the Clouds in 1914. The cost was about $1 million.

The Loon Center (ages 6 and up)

Lee's Mill Road, Moultonborough, N.H.; (603) 476–5666; www.loon.org. From Route 25, follow Blake Road about 1 mile, to Lee's Mill Road. Open daily 9:00 A.M. to 5:00 P.M. July through Columbus Day weekend. Closed weekends the rest of the year. Free (donations welcome).

Exhibits and videos tell about the life and habitat of the loon, whose nesting areas you can visit via the center's hiking trails. Other wetlands birds and waterfowl nest here, too.

Where to Eat

The Common Man, Main Street (Route 3), Ashland, N.H.; (603) 968–7030. Casual dining with a wide selection of main dishes and lighter fare. At their deli, you can purchase picnic makings or have them assemble sandwiches for your lunch. Lunch $, dinner $–$$

Hart's Turkey Farm, Route 3 at Route 104, Meredith, N.H.; (603) 279–6212; www.harts turkeyfarm.com. The Harts understand "family"—a generation of their own now runs the restaurant. Nearly everything on the menu, including the full turkey dinner, comes in "under-12" portions. A Tiny Tot Turkey Plate is designed for under-5 appetites. $–$$

The Woodshed, Lee's Mill Road (off Route 109), Moultonborough, N.H.; (603) 476–2311. Open Tuesday through Sunday from 5:00 P.M. Prime rib and steak are the specialties, but you'll find other favorites, including pork, lamb chops, and seafood, served in a rustic barn setting. $$

Where to Stay

See Rockywold–Deephaven, listed under the attractions.

Little Holland Court, Route 3, Ashland, N.H.; (603) 968–4434. Housekeeping cottages on Little Squam Lake, with boat rentals. Nightly or weekly rentals. $–$$.

Yankee Trail Motel, Route 3, 2 miles east of I–93 exit 24, Holderness, N.H.; (603) 968–3535. A small motel with a cafeteria where you can get breakfast. $–$$

For More Information

Squam Lake Association, Route 3 (Box 204), Holderness, NH 03245; (603) 968–7336. Holderness businesses publish a recreational routes map showing mountain bike and hiking trails as well as snowmobile and cross-country trails in town. You can get a copy from local shops or from the association.

Squam Lakes Area Chamber of Commerce, 31 Thompson Street, Ashland, NH 03217; (603) 968–4494.

Ossipee and Tamworth

Just east of the Lake Winnipesaukee region and just south of busy North Conway's shopping mall sprawl, these towns escape the frenzy of both. Several lesser-known lakes provide swimming and boating opportunities, and several natural attractions are located in Madison and Ossipee. The northern part of the area has the elegant backdrop of New Hampshire's most photographed mountain, Chocorua.

White Lake State Park (all ages)
Route 16, Tamworth, N.H.; (603) 323–7350. Open late May to mid-October. Admission $, children under 12 and New Hampshire residents over 65 admitted free.

Surrounding a beautiful clear lake, with views of Mt. Chocorua from its beach, this is one of our favorite state parks. Tall pine trees shelter its campground and picnic area and the swimming beach that stretches along one end of the lake. A 2-mile walking trail encircles its tree-lined perimeter. Wildlife is plentiful on the far side of the lake, where beavers munch away at trees and the woods are filled with the song of pine warblers.

Directly across the lake from the beach and picnic area is a seventy-two-acre pitch pine forest so unique that it has been declared a national natural landmark. The sandy soil here has created an environment in which these trees have thrived to a size and age unusual this far north, which is the northern limit of their range. This is a particularly fine example of a mature forest.

White Lake offers a boat launch and rowboat rentals and is also a popular spot for fishing.

Sumner Brook Fish Farm (ages 8 and up)
Route 16, Ossipee, N.H.; (603) 539–6073. Open Saturday and Sunday May and September, daily June through August.

Practice casting a fly rod with catch-and-release at the pools or keep your trout, paying by the inch. It's a good place for children to learn the art of fishing as lessons are available. Younger children will like watching baby fish swim in growing pools.

COOL Facts

Even tree experts can't tell how old the pitch pines at White Lake are. Pitch pine does not form annual growth rings, so this usual indicator isn't available, but their 2-foot diameter indicates a long life.

Madison Boulder (ages 5 and up)
Route 113, Madison, N.H. Free.

Thought to be the world's largest glacial erratic, this 83-foot-long solid piece of freestanding granite is the size of a large house. Even when you know this, it doesn't prepare you for such a big rock. It weighs 5,000 tons (we're not sure who weighed it), and some geologists believe it came from the cliffs of Mount Willard, in Crawford Notch, about 25 miles away.

Chebacco Ranch (ages 10 and up for riding)
Route 153, South Effingham, N.H.; (603) 522–3211; chebaccoduderanch.com. Fees vary by length of ride; most are part of lodging package.

As close as New Hampshire gets to a real dude ranch, Chebacco offers packages that include lodging (rooms in the nicely renovated barn are well suited to families), meals, and trail rides. Nonguests can go on the trail rides, too. Also in the barn are the game room, television, and a hot tub.

Remick Country Doctor Museum and Farm (ages 6 and up)
Tamworth, N.H.; (603) 323–7591 or (800) 686–6117; www.remickmuseum.org. Tamworth is less than 2 miles west of Route 16. Open Monday through Friday 10:00 A.M. to 4:00 P.M. year-round. July through October also open Saturday, and occasionally on Sunday of special event weekends. Free.

The role the country doctor once played in the life of a small upstate community is the theme of this museum complex. The complex was the family farm of a family with two doctors (father and son) who practiced here from the beginning of the 1900s. Two generations of medicine and the rhythms of farm life in rural New Hampshire are well shown through displays and the activities of docents.

Special weekends are the best time to go, when people are demonstrating such farm skills as butter-churning, blacksmithing, beekeeping, cheese-making, or shelling corn. The complex, in the center of the village opposite the Tamworth Inn, includes two homes,

COOL Facts

Glacial erratics are large boulders that were torn loose from ledges and mountaintops by moving glaciers. As the sheet of ice passed over solid bedrock faces, it tore loose large pieces and carried them in the ice. When the ice melted, these chunks of stone stayed where they had fallen. New Hampshire, all glacial terrain, has them scattered all over.

barns, and outbuildings. One of the homes, the Captain Enoch Remick House, is still occupied and is open for tours only on special occasions.

During special events, the kitchen buzzes with activity. Children dressed in period costumes are busy churning butter with the help of visitors, who can taste it fresh from the churn. Samples of fresh-made cheese, a demonstration of how sauerkraut is made, and a look at how bees make honey were on the agenda when we were there. Oxen, sledge rides behind a team of draft horses, barn tours, a chance to use a corn-sheller, and blacksmithing demonstrations might be among the activities during a special day. See the "Annual Events" section for details on weekend programs.

Chocorua Lake (all ages)
Route 16, Chocorua, N.H. Free.

Although "The Matterhorn of America," as it has been called, is certainly hyperbole, there is no mistaking the shapely silhouette of Mount Chocorua. The state's most photographed view is taken of its southern face, reflected in Chocorua Lake, either from the shore of the lake or from the hillside to its south, through a row of white birch trees that couldn't have been better placed if they had been planted by the state tourism office. The shore of the lake, where parking spaces and benches are conveniently placed under a stand of giant red pines, is a park. Although there are no picnic tables, you are welcome to spread your tablecloth on the soft blanket of pine needles or enjoy a tailgate picnic here. Few dining rooms can match the view.

Purity Spring Resort (all ages)
Route 153, East Madison, N.H.; in New Hampshire (603) 367–8896, out-of-state (800) 373–3754; www.purityspring.com. Follow Route 113 east from the village of Chocorua, turning south (right) in Madison. When the road comes to a T intersection, turn right; the resort is directly ahead. $$.

Everything is included at this old-fashioned family resort. Day care for children, tennis, canoes, rowboats, kayaks, and all activities are part of the rates. Each day brings a full schedule of things to do for all ages. You can share these with children, send them off with counselors while you read or kayak, or do what most families do—a little of each. The giant playground has comfortable chairs for parents, who can read while children frolic on the equipment.

A great part of the fun is conversing with the people you meet here. Grandparents will tell you that they first came here as children and have been returning ever since. Rooms and facilities are not fancy, but it's very comfortable, with a home-like atmosphere. Everyone seems to look out for the kids, including the chef, who creates such kid-pleasers as M&M pancakes. And remember Maypo? It's on the menu every morning. Thursday evening brings a lobster and steak cookout on their private island, and Monday breakfast is a cookout with everything cooked over the open fire. The American plan—all meals included—offers a choice of five entrees each evening, which include a vegetarian dish.

King Pine Ski Area (ages 5 and up)

Route 153, East Madison, N.H.; in New Hampshire (603) 367–8896, out-of-state (800) 367–8897; www.kingpine.com. Follow Route 113 east from the village of Chocorua, turning south (right) in Madison. When the road comes to a T intersection, turn left to the ski area. Rates vary.

A small, family-friendly ski resort, King Pine is the winter incarnation of Purity Springs. The same family-first ethic prevails, and American plan packages include the winter version of the resort's full complement of activities. The ski area's trails are at all skill levels, and four trails and the main slope are lighted for night skiing. The complete ski school has the same upbeat, you-can-do-it spirit as the resort itself.

Where to Eat

Snow Village Inn, Snowville, N.H.; (603) 477–2818 or (800) 447–4345. Turn east from Route 153 at Eaton, on the shore of Crystal Lake, following signs to Snowville. An outstanding menu promises great things, which the chef delivers expertly. Kids will love the special children's appetizer plate, with eye-appealing and quirky—but healthy—foods. $$

The Tamworth Inn, Main Street, Tamworth Village, N.H.; (603) 323–7721 or (800) 642–7352. Open Tuesday through Saturday for dinner, nightly mid-September through mid-October. Really creative dishes mix neatly with more traditional fare on the menu of this dining room in an 1833 inn. $$

The Yankee Smokehouse, Routes 16 and 25, West Ossipee, N.H.; (603) 539–7427. Open daily May to mid-November, mid-December through March. Our kids called this "The Pig-Out" because of the two jolly pink pigs pictured on the sign and because of the giant portions of moist, juicy barbecued pork, chicken, and beef they consumed there. Eat inside or at the picnic tables on the porch. Service is bright, bouncy, and upbeat.

If you can find room for them, order the baby back pork ribs and begin with the corn chowder. $–$$

Where to Stay

Snow Village Inn, Snowville, N.H.; (603) 477–2818 or (800) 447–4345. Turn east from Route 153 at Eaton, on the shore of Crystal Lake, following signs to Snowville. High on a hilltop, the inn has plenty of room to run, hike, or cross-country ski. Separate newer buildings have larger rooms perfect for families. The innkeeper's children keep this place kid-friendly. $$

The Tamworth Inn, Main Street, Tamworth Village, N.H.; (603) 323–7721 or (800) 642–7352. An 1833 inn, brought up to date without losing its warm, historic character. $–$$

Camping

White Lake State Park, Route 16, Tamworth, N.H.; (603) 323–7350. Open late May to mid-October. The campground has well-spaced sites under tall pine trees. Sites are large and open, and a sandy beach with a lifeguard is opposite the campground. $

For More Information

Greater Ossipee Chamber of Commerce, Routes 16 and 25W, West Ossipee, N.H.; (603) 539–6201 or (800) 516–5324.

Annual Events

FEBRUARY

Snowshoe Olympics, Squam Lake Science Center, Holderness, N.H., (603) 968–7194.

Winter Carnival, Gunstock Recreation Area, Gilford, N.H., (603) 293–4341 or (800) GUNSTOCK (486–7862); www.gunstock.com.

MARCH OR APRIL

Easter Bunny Trains, Winnipesaukee Scenic Railroad, boarding in Tilton or Laconia, N.H., (603) 745–2135.

SUMMER

Weekly fireworks displays at Weirs Beach.

SEPTEMBER

Tamworth History Day, Remick Country Doctor Museum, Tamworth, N.H., (603) 323–7591 or (800) 686–6117. Traditional crafts, including spinning, rug hooking, and wood-carving.

Grandparent's Day, Remick Country Doctor Museum, Tamworth, N.H., (603) 323–7591 or (800) 686–6117. Cattle barn tours, magic show, a petting zoo, and more.

OCTOBER

Pumpkin Fest, Remick Country Doctor Museum, Tamworth, N.H., (603) 323–7591 or (800) 686–6117. Bonfire, storytelling, pumpkin carving, and more.

Oktoberfest, Gunstock Recreation Area, Gilford; N.H., (603) 293–4341 or (800) GUNSTOCK (486–7862); www.gunstock.com.

Index

About the Authors

Both Lura Seavey and Barbara Rogers grew up in New Hampshire and had traveled through most of it and Vermont by the time they were teenagers. Now mothers themselves, they continue to travel with their own children, enjoying many of the same places. In addition to this book and portions of guidebooks to New England and the United States for Frommer's and Thomas Cook Publishing, Lura is the author of children's books on the Dominican Republic, Switzerland, and Spain. Barbara's previous books include *New Hampshire Off the Beaten Path, Adventure Guide to Canada's Atlantic Provinces, Adventure Guide to the Chesapeake Bay,* and *Signpost Portugal.* This is the second book that Lura and Barbara have written together.